# The House
# of Music

# The house of music

## ART
## IN AN ERA OF
## INSTITUTIONS

SAMUEL LIPMAN

David R. Godine, Publisher
BOSTON

First published in 1984 by
David R. Godine, Publisher, Inc.
306 Dartmouth Street
Boston, Massachusetts 02116

Library of Congress Cataloging in Publication Data

Lipman, Samuel.
   The house of music.
   1. Music—Addresses, essays, lectures. I. Title.
ML60.L467   1984      780'.07      83-49343
ISBN 0-87923-501-2
ISBN 0-87923-475-X (pbk.)

First edition
Printed in the United States of America

Acknowledgments

*Commentary:* Part I: 1,2,3,4. Part II: 1 (first section), 3. Part III: 1 (first section), 2,3,5. Part IV: 2,3. Part V: 1,2,4.
*The American Scholar:* Part IV: 1.
*The New Criterion:* Part I: 5. Part II: 1 (second section), 2,4. Part III: 1 (second section), 4. Part IV: 4. Part V: 3.

All these essays are reprinted with the kind permission of the periodicals in which they first appeared.

*Durch alle Töne tönet*
*Im bunten Erdentraum*
*Ein leiser Ton gezogen*
*Für den, der heimlich lauschet.*

(There sounds through all the tones
of this multicolored earthly dream
one gentle tone, drawn
for him who secretly listens.)

> Friedrich von Schlegel;
> used by Robert Schumann as
> the epigraph for his *Fantasia* (1836–38)

# TABLE OF CONTENTS

# Contents

# PROLOGUE

## *An Era of Institutions*

In *Music After Modernism* (1979), I attempted to describe the state of music as it seemed to me after the failure of contemporary music creation, in particular after the failure of that movement we call the avant-garde, to win a wide audience. As I continued to write after having finished the various pieces that made up *Music After Modernism,* I realized ever more clearly that the vacuum in new music which I had been chronicling was now being filled by institutions ranging from government to philanthropy, from orchestras to opera companies, from education to publishing, from broadcasting to public relations.

Though the focus of the present book is on these centers of musical power and authority, some of my older concerns can nonetheless be found in this work. I begin, for example, here as I had before, with Richard Wagner viewed as the last of a breed; while I still see him as a political presence, he now seems to me, in his immense success, to have lost his earlier artistic relevance. Dmitri Shostakovich seems unique in our time for his combination of the ability to write at least some deeply felt and lasting music and his suffering under the monstrous tyranny of a usurper state. Steve Reich and Philip Glass, still taken seriously by many who desire a pleasant modern music, demonstrate the fate of the avant-garde under the economic conditions of mass-marketing. The performance of such refined art as the *Lieder* of Hugo Wolf seems (at least for the moment) perceptibly distorted by successful attempts to take advantage of an ignorant audience for commercial purposes. The careers of Walter Legge and John Culshaw demonstrate both how performing careers and images have been made in serious music after World War II, and how even this partially unsatisfactory state of affairs seems, in retrospect, to be better than what is going on today.

Perhaps because I was trained as a performer, I retain (despite several attempts to abandon my past) a strong interest in those star personalities who make music live for audiences. The ability of the magically successful Herbert von Karajan to summon up an entire tradition of past musical glories, no less than the personal tragedy of Glenn Gould as a public figure, seems to me to speak volumes about the attenuated state of our present musical life. In a similar vein, it seems necessary to point out that the new wave of Russian émigrés is not bringing us any strong musical potions to cure our afflictions. Even an older Russian émigré, the legendary Igor Stravinsky, now seems to be worshipped more through historical misperception and sentimentality than through insight and authentic commitment.

The chapters on performing institutions themselves document four sad stories, three of present troubles and one of a better time, which in the case of the Hollywood String Quartet was sadly short-lived. But the New York Philharmonic, the Metropolitan Opera, and the New York City Opera are very much with us; their problems, in differing degrees, are inadequate leadership, insufficient intellectual courage, and failing imagination.

Writing about music still seems largely an individual activity; indeed, given the small size of the critic's readership, things are all too private. But even here George Bernard Shaw—widely viewed as the best music critic ever to have written in English—now appears a quaintly outmoded freebooter. More typical by far are such diverse phenomena as Harold Schonberg of the mighty *New York Times* and the massive new edition of *Grove's Dictionary*. And somehow belonging very much to our time is a scandal-mongering biography of Vladimir Horowitz, dependent as it is on unnamed sources for widely known gossip.

I have chosen to end this book with a consideration of three wider institutions central to our musical life. I start with music education, and the pressures under which it is so inadequately done today. I go on to discuss the role of radio and television broadcasting of fine music, beginning with how things seemed to me several years ago and how they look now on our broadcasting flagship, the television component of the Public Broadcasting Service. And finally, I try to describe the National Endowment for the Arts, that fountainhead of state support and blessing in cultural matters, as it appeared to me on the threshold of its greatest activity during the Carter Administration.

Here, then, is a description of the pieces that make up this book. I cannot pretend that I found very much to celebrate. As a critic, it seems insufficient to me to write about music in the old-fashioned manner of celebrating beauty and lamenting its absence. The critic who now finds musical power increasingly shifting from music makers to those who are either not musicians or who are not acting for solely musical purposes has little choice, it seems to me, but to confront the process openly, even when he thus must write more about commerce than about art. Throughout this book I have attempted such a confrontation.

Reprinting essays written under the pressure and inspiration of disparate and hardly coeval events may perhaps disappoint those who hold strict cohesion and integration as essential values in a book. I hope that the many loose ends readers may find herein will be balanced by the immediacy which only timely journalism can provide. Therefore, save for an occasional correction of detail or a minor improvement (I hope) in style, I have not altered these pieces from the form in which they originally appeared. I have, in particular, resisted the temptation to update articles from as long ago as 1979 and 1980. Despite such developments as the arbitrary decision by the New York Philharmonic to renew the contract of the poorly regarded Zubin Mehta, little of basic importance seems to me to have changed in the matters I have written about, and, more important, I feel comfortable with the judgments I have expressed.

In these pages, I am aware, I have often been negative. I would indeed be sad if my pessimistic analysis of musical life today were to be taken by some readers as a sign of an essential hostility to music and musicians. To such readers I can only say that it is always unwise to confuse the state of an art with the fortunes of its salesmen and retainers. And to all my readers, I can only state what I believe to be a fundamental tenet of criticism: The business of a critic is to criticize.

# The House
of Music

# I

# REPUTATIONS

# Greatness and Decline
## of Richard Wagner

Exactly one-half century ago Thomas Mann stepped to a podium at the University of Munich, and delivered an address on the fiftieth anniversary of the death of Richard Wagner. The next morning Mann left Germany for exile.

Mann's lecture on that celebratory occasion was the now famous "Sufferings and Greatness of Richard Wagner." Since its initial delivery, which was almost immediately followed by repetition in Amsterdam, Brussels, and Paris, it has become firmly established as the brightest jewel in the Mann nonfiction canon. It appeared in April 1933 in the prestigious *Neue Rundschau;* it was published in German, alongside essays on Goethe and *Don Quixote,* in his 1935 *Leiden und Grösse der Meister* ("Sufferings and Greatness of the Masters"); in English translation, it has become a central part of both the hardback *Essays of Three Decades* and the softcover *Essays.*

Like all milestones in the writing of cultural history, Mann's creation was Janus-faced. It looked backward to an epoch of Wagner's hegemony, and it also looked forward to a future in which the workings of the *Zeitgeist,* at once aesthetic and political, would destroy that hegemony forever.

It is not difficult to justify the use of the word hegemony here. The first performances of the *Ring* in Bayreuth in 1876 and of *Parsifal* in 1882 were world events in a way that we today can scarcely comprehend. For royalty no less than for musicians, for millionaires as for intellectuals, Bayreuth was (*mutatis mutandis,* like Woodstock) the central manifestation of an entire cultural epoch. The most talented composers and musicians of Europe were happy to sit at the Master's feet; among their number was even to be found Wagner's father-in-law, Franz Liszt. To such a young aspirant as Gustav Mahler, a visit to Bayreuth to hear *Parsifal* just five months after Wagner's death in 1883 was an event of life-consecrating magnitude: "When I came out of the *Festspielhaus,* completely spellbound," he said, "I understood that the greatest and most painful revelation had just been made to me, and that I would carry it with me unspoiled all my life."

Wagner had been wreaking similar carnage on the French. Baudelaire's declaration of loyalty even before the Paris *Tannhäuser* of 1861 was to be renewed by many subsequent enthusiasts—despite the humiliation (so welcomed by Wagner himself) suffered by the French in the Franco-Prussian War of 1870. Mallarmé was a worshipper at the shrine; the very name of a publication that had little to do with music but everything to do with symbolist aesthetics, the *Revue wagnérienne* (1885–88), showed in the plainest way the commanding position of Wagner in cultural life.

As for French musicians, Saint-Saëns, Gounod, and Chabrier were supporters. Saint-Saëns even managed to range himself on the side of the Wagnerians without giving up his Gallic objectivity: "*La Wagneromanie est un ridicule excusable; la Wagnerophobie est une maladie*" ("Wagnermania is an excusable absurdity; Wagnerphobia is a disease"). And according to a fellow composer, Vincent d'Indy, when Chabrier heard the first note of *Tristan* at Bayreuth, he began sobbing: "The person sitting next to him turned around to inquire whether he was feeling well, and our good Chabrier replied between two sobs: 'I know it's stupid, but I can't help it. . . . I've been waiting for ten years of my life for that A on the cellos. . . .' "

But Wagner's power in the last two decades of the nineteenth century transcended art—even an expanded definition of art. He had already played an important role during the 1860s in the politics of King Ludwig's Bavaria. He wrote voluminously—and was read widely—on subjects ranging from Germanness to Jewry, from the proper understanding of women to the proper treatment of animals. Wagner Societies were springing up all over Europe, started originally to help pay for Bayreuth; for their members the sacred texts were more Wagner's ideas than his musical notes.

Wagner had been a major influence on the young Nietzsche; this brilliant but unstable philosopher had written in eminently Wagnerian accents (in *The Birth of Tragedy*) of the "renovation and purification of the German spirit through the fire magic of music." For Wagner, of course, Nietzsche was a boy angel who soon fell. After they broke, his place in the pantheon of Wagnerian thinkers was to be taken, only a few years after the composer's death, by the more assiduous and dutiful Houston Stewart Chamberlain. That this sincerely German thinker was actually English only demonstrates the true scope of Wagner's cultural influence.

As we know from the recent study by Geoffrey Field,[1] Chamberlain (no relative to the famous Neville) was a convert before he had seen a single Wagner opera. When he finally did see one—*Rheingold* in the 1878 Munich *Ring* premiere—Chamberlain struck the proper note of transport ("truly an ocean in which man may blissfully immerse himself to gain learning"). And whatever reserve Chamberlain may initially have maintained on the seductive doctrines of Wagner vanished for good when he saw *Parsifal*—six times —in its first performances at Bayreuth:

> Hitherto, my life had been so artistically barren, but now I had reached the font of the purest Art. Schiller speaks of an "aesthetic culture which should combine the dignity and bliss of humanity": I have discovered the place of this culture.

Had Chamberlain done no more than live the rest of his life—he was to die in 1927—as a combination of fan and publicist, he would merely have been another melancholy example of a weak mind meeting its master. But Chamberlain's magnum opus, the infamous *Foundations of the Nineteenth Century* (1889), with its echoes of Wagner's equally infamous pamphlet of 1850, *Das Judentum in der Musik* ("The Jews in Music"), became the principal inspiration of the anti-Semitic cultural doctrines of Nazism as expounded by Alfred Rosenberg.

At the same time as Wagner was a major political force, his literary influence remained strong. For example, there was Thomas Mann's use in short stories of *Tristan* and *Die Walküre* to suggest doomed and illicit passion. But Mann did more than appropriate the story lines and characteristic sounds of Wagner's operas; he actually used Wagner's *Leitmotiv* technique to achieve unity of tone and style over the long stretches of his great novels.

Marcel Proust too knew and felt his Wagner. It is difficult to miss a similarity between the remarkable use of the madeleine at the beginning of *Remembrance of Things Past* as the key to the narrator's world, and the famous E-flat-major chord at the opening of

---

1. *Evangelist of Race: The Germanic Vision of Houston Stewart Chamberlain,* Columbia University Press, 1981.

*Rheingold* as the very stuff out of which the world is made. And for Proust, as for so many other artists, *Tristan* was central ("And as the friend then examines a photograph which enables him to fix the likeness, so over Vinteuil's Sonata, I set up on the music-rack the score of *Tristan,* a selection which was being given that afternoon, as it happened, at the Lamoureux concert").

Meanwhile, of course, Wagner's sway continued to have its base among musicians. Certainly we would never have had Strauss's *Salome* (1904–05) and *Elektra* (1906–08)—not to mention the earlier tone poems *Tod und Verklärung* (1889) and *Ein Heldenleben* (1898)—without Wagner; indeed, Strauss could be called, to emphasize his descent from Wagner, "Richard the Second." Yet the compositional career even of such an avowed anti-Wagnerian as Claude Debussy is inconceivable without Wagner, not just as something to react against but even more as a model.

In this respect it is instructive to examine what may be considered Debussy's masterpiece, *Pelléas et Mélisande* (1893–1902). Reserved, restrained, implicit rather than explicit, making its points by elision and ellipsis rather than iterative demonstration, Debussy's opera self-consciously opposed itself in every way to the Wagnerian afflatus. But in running away from the cosmic tub-thumping of the *Ring,* Debussy only seemed to fall into the emotional stasis of *Parsifal.* As the English composer Robin Holloway has convincingly shown,[2] the frequent parallels between *Pelléas* and *Parsifal* could only have been produced by Debussy's total immersion in the Wagnerian ethos, an immersion so complete, it seems, as to explain and even demand its denial by Debussy.

While Debussy's debt to Wagner may still strike some as surprising, the same can hardly be said of the relation of the Second Viennese School—in particular Arnold Schoenberg and Alban Berg —to the master of Bayreuth. Schoenberg's string sextet *Verklärte Nacht* (1899) is Wagner's *Tristan* with the words absorbed into the music. The *Gurrelieder* (1900–11) is also an unabashed Wagnerian epic in harmony, mood, ambition, and, one must also add, sentimentality.

Berg too nailed his colors to the Wagnerian mast, in his case by quoting *Tristan* in the *Largo desolato* of the *Lyric Suite* (1926), his

2. *Debussy and Wagner,* Eulenberg Books (London), 1979.

first large work to make use of Schoenberg's twelve-tone procedure. But what, after all, was twelve-tone music in its inception but a codification, with diabolically strict rules, of the beginning of the *Tristan* prelude, the very same music that, as we have seen, reduced Chabrier to sobs?

As with all fructifying movements in art, Wagnerism showed its strength not just by the fervor and creativity of its adherents, but also by the distinction and enmity of its opponents. Like the adherents, the opponents came both from within and without music itself. Thus, in one of the great intellectual best-sellers of the 1890s, *Degeneration,* Max Nordau wrote:

> Richard Wagner is in himself alone charged with a greater abundance of degeneration than all the degenerates with whom we have hitherto become acquainted. The stigmata of this morbid condition are united in him in the most complete and most luxuriant development. He displays in the general constitution of his mind the persecution mania, megalomania, and mysticism; in his instincts vague philanthropy, anarchism, a craving for revolt and contradiction; in his writings all the signs of graphomania, namely, incoherence, fugitive ideation, and a tendency to idiotic punning, and, as the groundwork of his being, the characteristic emotionalism of a color at once erotic and religiously enthusiastic.

Nor was Wagner universally accepted as a musician. Even during the composer's lifetime, Eduard Hanslick had made much of his reputation as a major critic by setting the Viennese favorite Brahms against Wagner. By the 1920s the very up-to-date Stravinsky, still fresh from his scandalous triumph in 1913 with *The Rite of Spring,* felt free to leer at the sainted Wagner. In 1924, for example, a Belgian interviewer quoted Stravinsky as saying:

> Wagner . . . is certainly not a real musician. He has had recourse to the theater at every moment in his career, and this remains an obstacle to his musical ideas, whose progress is hindered by his philosophy. Every time Wagner was tempted by pure music, he was hit on the nose. . . .

Indeed, the course of musical composition during the period after World War I was not determined by just one school. To the lead-

ership of Schoenberg was counterposed the school not just of Stravinsky but also of the French *Les Six*. Darius Milhaud, one of the
leaders of this group, was particularly anti-Wagner in his critical
writings as well as in his iconoclastic music:

> When the Concerts Pasdeloup announced yet another Wagner
> Festival, I headed my article simply: "Down with Wagner!"
> which provoked a veritable scandal. I received protesting let-
> ters, insults, and even anonymous letters. Wagner was wor-
> shiped like the golden calf. And I hated his music with
> every day that passed, for it represented a type of art that I
> detested. . . .[3]

But such controversy, of course, is the very stuff of which artistic
viability is made. If proof is needed of the vital and commanding
presence of Wagner's works in the 1920s, it can be found in the
high and flourishing condition of the performances he received in
this period. To mention such singers as Lauritz Melchior, Lotte
Lehmann, Frida Leider, and Friedrich Schorr, and such conductors
as Karl Muck, Arturo Toscanini, Wilhelm Furtwängler, and Bruno
Walter, is to evoke a golden age of which the phonograph remains
today a poignant, if incomplete, witness.

Perhaps the stage is now set for Thomas Mann's historic intervention on Wagner. Despite the massive political currents then
swirling about Germany, Mann's presentation was ostensibly not
about current politics at all; it was rather about Wagner's achievement and how it seemed to a German and European writer fifty
years after the composer's death.

From the outset, Mann is at pains to separate Wagner from his
political admirers of the Hitler period. He begins by linking the
composer indissolubly to a past, and, for some, a despised epoch—
the nineteenth century "whose complete expression he is." Here is
the hidden agenda of Mann's position: Wagner belongs to someone
other than the Germans of 1933.

Accordingly, Mann stresses Wagner's parallels in nineteenth-
century Europe: French Impressionism in painting, the English and

3. When I was studying with Darius Milhaud in California during the early
1950s, he told me (in connection with this story, which appears in his fascinat-
ing memoirs as I have quoted it above) that whenever he heard by mischance the
music of Wagner in a concert, he always put on a recording of Mozart when he
returned home, to "clean my ears."

French novel in literature. He finds a kinship in "spirit, aims, and methods" between Wagner and Zola. He notes in Wagner and Tolstoy a "common possession of social and ethical elements." He remarks on a likeness between Wagner and Ibsen, both "social-revolutionary in youth, in age paling into the ritual and the mythical."

If, for Mann, Wagner rises so high above all his operatic predecessors, it is because of his use of psychology and myth. Psychology, for Mann in 1933 as for us today, means (the Jewish) Freud—and Mann is quick to point out how Wagner's stress on physical love has "an unmistakable psychoanalytical character." And Wagner's use of myth, though Mann does not go so far as to mention it, is another link to Freud. For is not Siegfried's cruel treatment of his (grand)father Wotan in Act III of *Siegfried* neatly explained along the lines of the Oedipus complex?

Mann, however, has little use for Wagner as an aesthetic philosopher: "What left me cold was—Wagner's theory. It is hard for me to believe that anyone ever took it seriously." Having rejected Wagner's view that a synthesis of all the arts (exemplified in his own operas) is superior to the component arts standing by themselves, Mann then casts doubt on Wagner's attitude toward these individual arts. He says Wagner was uninterested in the Italian plastic and graphic arts; though he revered poetry, his own was "not really written verse but, as it were, exhalations from the music. . . . in the nature of directions for a theatrical performance."

Even as a musician, Wagner is to Mann an incomplete creator. He sees the "ever-craving chromatics" of Isolde's so-called *Liebestod* as a "literary idea"; the opening of *Rheingold* with its famous 136-measure E-flat-major triad Mann calls an "acoustic idea." So curiously reserved is Mann toward Wagner even as a composer that it hardly seems a compliment when Mann calls him "a musician who can persuade even the unmusical to be musical."

Mann continues his attack on Wagner as a universal genius. Wagner, for some the very idea of the world seer, is for Mann only a special case of the artist, who "is not an absolutely serious man . . . effects and enjoyment are his stock-in-trade." In fact, says Mann, "Wagner's art *is* dilettantism, monumentalized and lifted into the sphere of genius by intelligence and his enormous willpower."

Though Wagner is not for Mann a bourgeois—that loathsome creature hated by both far Right and far Left—he still has "the atmosphere of the bourgeoisie, the atmosphere of his century about him, as has Schopenhauer, the capitalist philosopher: the moral pessimism, the mood of decline set to music." As if tarring Wagner with the bourgeois brush were not enough in itself, Mann goes on to accuse him of carrying bourgeois taste to the point of degeneracy. At first he exculpates Wagner from the charge that in order to work he needed the stimulus of creature comforts; had not, Mann wonders, even the noble Schiller needed questionable stimuli in order to create? But Schiller was different: "in all Schiller's work there is no trace of the odor of decay which stimulated his brain, but who would deny that there is a suggestion of satin dressing gowns in Wagner's art?"

Moreover, Wagner is really more of a socialist—a dangerous charge indeed in the Germany of 1933—than a patriot, for, after all, there is no real folk music in Wagner, not even in *Die Meistersinger*. Indeed, Mann characterizes Wagner's Germanism as cosmopolitan at heart. And before he ends by discussing the true relevance of Wagner's work, Mann cannot resist one final dig at Wagner the Nazi hero: ". . . this bold musical pioneer, who in *Tristan* stands with one foot already upon atonal ground—today he would probably be called a cultural Bolshevist!"

What then is Wagner's true relevance? Simply, "Let us be content to reverence Wagner's works as a mighty and manifold phenomenon of German and Western culture, which will always act as the profoundest stimulus to art and knowledge."

Here, truly, we have witnessed Mann at his most subtle and complex. In the course of some 25,000 words he manages the not inconsiderable feat of being a totally committed Wagnerite while at the same time leaving not a stone of Wagner's reputation unturned.

To be sure, the great enemy of Wagner's reputation was not Mann but Hitler; Wagner's reign was ended not in the libraries and bookstores but on the battlefield. This having been said, it still would seem that Mann's intellectual labor of detaching Wagner from his reputation as a prophet and seer, and representing him as a "mere" artist, is the turning point in our perception of this master. For if the first fifty years after Wagner's death marked the summit of his aesthetic and sociopolitical centrality, the next fifty have marked Wagner's admission into the category of accepted—and safe—classics.

Not surprisingly, this full acceptance waited on the conclusion of World War II. As late as 1943, Virgil Thomson questioned Wagner's status at the highest level of musical masters. According to Thomson: "Unless there is unanimous acceptance of a man's work, which is rare, it is the people who don't like it that have the last word in its evaluation." In this category of the un-unanimously accepted, Thomson puts Wagner, along with other composers from Berlioz and Gluck to Milhaud and Copland. All these artists have detractors and thus, despite their fans, they continue to be special tastes in a way that marks them off from the universally approved Bach, Mozart, and Beethoven.

But even in 1943 Thomson was on weak ground in refusing to allow Wagner into the musical pantheon. For the remarkable aspect of Wagner's fate during World War II—at least in America—was that he continued, despite the hatred of things German, to be performed. His operas remained staples at the Metropolitan in particular and in symphony concerts in general; new careers—like that of the great St. Louis dramatic soprano Helen Traubel—continued to be made in this music.

Once the war was over, in 1945, all barriers to Wagner were quickly lifted. The pent-up demand for great music performed by authentic European artists exploded both in concerts and on recordings. Austria and Germany again became places of musical pilgrimage. Chief among these holy spots was Bayreuth, where in 1951, still under the control of the Wagner family, his operas once more played to ecstatic audiences from all over the world.

No longer, however, were these works seen as being the particular property of a people, nation, party, or even philosophical and aesthetic school. In the eyes of Wagner's grandchildren, Wieland and Wolfgang, the operas were ecumenical, part of the common inheritance of mankind. Toward this end the *Ring*—surely the most influential production of the 1951 season—was presented as a nonspecific myth, owing much to cultural anthropology and Jungian psychology, but nothing to any special race or culture. Much too was later accomplished for the wider acceptance of Wagner by the simple expedient of turning almost all the stage lights out, thereby

rendering both the music's action and its ideas open to any interpretation the spectators wished to supply.

As to these interpretations, in general there have been two
schools of thought since the war as to what Wagner means.
Roughly put, they have been the Marxist-economic and the psychoanalytic.

The economic interpretation of Wagner has found its happiest
employment in the *Ring*. Building on Shaw's *The Perfect Wagnerite*
(1898), producers have used the story of the theft of the gold, and
the subsequent attempts of various gods and monsters to control
the destiny of the world through possession of the gold, as an
allegory of capitalism in victory and defeat. On the stage this
approach reached its apogee in the 1976 centennial production by
Patrice Chéreau at Bayreuth. Here, in a stage conception which is
finally being vouchsafed to the American public on PBS this season,
one can find capitalists, factories, machines, and Wall Street. One
can also see an extraordinary mélange of styles and costumes, from
baroque to mercantile. Sometimes the dominant atmosphere seems
not that of a political allegory but of an artist's ball gone haywire.

Off the operatic stage, the economic approach to Wagner has
been rather more inventive, if hardly as clear. Pride of place in this
regard must be given to the work of Theodor Adorno, the renais-
sance man of socio-Marxist criticism. It is not easy to summarize
someone whose unclarities extend to both factual statements and
logical connections. But the following quotation gives the flavor of
Adorno's point of view. For him, Wagner's operas

> provide eloquent evidence of the earlier phase of bourgeois
> decadence. . . . Wagner is not only the willing prophet and
> diligent lackey of imperialism and late-bourgeois terrorism.
> He also possesses the neurotic's ability to contemplate his own
> decadence and to transcend it in an image that can withstand
> that all-consuming gaze.

The psychoanalytic interpretation of Wagner, subspecies Jung,
has been classically formulated by Robert Donington in his *Wagner's
Ring and Its Symbols* (1963). On this view, the *Ring* is not about
capitalism but about creation, birth and rebirth, the self, ritual
marriage, destiny, and redemption.

It may appear churlish to pass summary judgment on such intelligent—and even overintelligent—attempts at explanation. Yet while past efforts in this line, ranging from the fevered reactions of Chabrier and the French to the poisonous politics of Chamberlain, have at least seemed to begin in an authentic response to Wagner's operas themselves, these more recent approaches strike one as artificial. For they seem to proceed from the author's own world view to the material provided by Wagner, instead of the other way around.

There is one crucial piece of evidence for this harsh verdict. Whatever the actual content of Wagner is now seen to be, his work is everywhere beloved and cherished. Not only does this mood of good feeling extend to the composer's work; it even seems to inform the relationships among contending schools of interpretation. Let a hundred flowers bloom; let a hundred schools of Wagnerian exegesis abound. Where everyone's right, no one's right. Or should it really be vice versa?

And so, in this spirit, we have arrived at the hundredth anniversary of Richard Wagner's death. The continuing flood of publications in both German and English is astounding. Picture books, learned studies of the composer's sketches, numerous new biographies cautiously and minutely going over the same material, all the detailed projects born of musico-literary minds—all these deserve mention, if only for their sublime pointlessness.

But what remains the simplest and most important point about Wagner today is just how badly he is being performed. The worldwide shortage of competent Wagnerian singers is public knowledge; in the case of male singers above the range of bass, the word shortage must be replaced by drought. The lack of conductors capable of bringing broad culture, sensitive musicality, and the requisite technical competence to this music is an open secret, only concealed from unsophisticated listeners by the sloth of music critics.

Last season, for example, America's greatest opera house was only capable of doing two operas, *Rheingold* and *Siegfried,* out of the four of the *Ring.* The Met must have known how poor the performances would be, for they were scheduled for the fall, well out of range of radio broadcast. But these performances were not just poor; they were embarrassing. Weak singing, lackluster conducting, shaky orchestral playing: the only question was why all this had been put on the stage in the first place.

Other Wagner operas fared almost as badly at the Met. *Tannhäuser* seemed to this listener unredeemed even by the signs Leonie Rysanek displayed of sympathy for the role of Elisabeth; once again the tenor lead was pitiable. *Parsifal,* although well received in the press, nevertheless provoked one critic to wonder whether the plush atmosphere of the Metropolitan Opera House was really congenial to this work.

We can, of course, always look to Bayreuth. Not only do we have its 1976 Chéreau production of the *Ring* to see on PBS; in addition, the musical segment of this production, conducted by Pierre Boulez, is separately available on Philips Records. Glossily packaged in a red, white, and black tote box, the records are accompanied by an equally glossy booklet carrying a long essay by Boulez. This essay, at once intelligent and revealing, may fairly be taken as Boulez's testament on Wagner, a description of why an avant-garde and deeply French musician has chosen to spend a decade and more in the closest association with what might have been thought an uncongenial métier.

Boulez begins with the assumption that Wagner's stage works can be separated from the historical currents that accompanied their birth. It is music, not history, which Boulez finds at the heart of the *Ring:*

> . . . it is the music which is in fact entrusted with the structure of these mythological persons; it is the music which lends articulation to characters, gestures, and actions. The dramatic myth becomes effective by means of, through, and within the musical structure.

Wagner's themes, furthermore, "lead a life independent of the dramatic action"; finally "the musical structure becomes so rich and proliferous that it unites, indeed literally absorbs the stage characters. . . ."

Precisely because Boulez properly puts so much weight on Wagner's music, it comes as a particular disappointment to find on his records of the *Ring* so little of musical distinction. To begin with the vocal roles: conductors other than Boulez have a high opinion of Gwyneth Jones as Brünnhilde that seems impervious to her poor singing. A vocally pale Wotan, a callow Siegmund, an overextended Sieglinde, a barking Siegfried, shrieking Valkyries—it all makes one rather regret that opera must, alas, be sung.

But opera—especially opera of this musical greatness—can survive a good deal of bad singing. The poorer the singers, the better must be the conductor. Although one is not happy to say this about such an intellectual and direct musician, Boulez conclusively demonstrates in these records that what seemed in 1976 (when he first led the *Ring* at Bayreuth) an absence of personal expression in the music is in fact a lack of any deeply rooted conception of how the music ought to go.

This is most obvious in the paucity, across the whole expanse of the four operas, of firmly held and firmly integrated tempos. It is well known that Wagner himself preached (not just for his own works) a doctrine of tempo flexibility, and indeed such flexibility is necessary for any idiomatic performance of his music. But Boulez carries this cautionary principle rather further:

> Wagner's motives, if they are presented at first in a definite tempo, at a definite speed, are never, or at least very seldom, bound to this specific tempo or speed. . . . It is just there that the novelty of his motives is to be found: not only are they not tied to any particular tempo, but they are also unattached to any preceding formal hierarchy.

The baleful results of this extended doctrine are everywhere on the Boulez records. The orchestra isn't together within itself; chords lack a discernible attack; and the articulation of basic rhythmic motives—as in the difficult dotted rhythm of the "Ride of the Valkyries"—is often indistinct where it is not actually incorrect. Time and again the singers and conductor are not together, and at important points of cadential arrival Boulez is so consistently ahead that the singers are reduced to a kind of involuntary *parlando*.

These faults are at their worst in the great set pieces of the *Ring,* the famous "bleeding chunks" that still figure in the orchestral concerts. The closing scene of *Rheingold,* with its troubled hymn of Wotan to the as yet unlived-in Valhalla; Wotan's farewell to Brünnhilde, girt by flame to wait for Siegfried, at the end of *Walküre;* the Siegfried–Brünnhilde duet at the end of *Siegfried;* the great stretch of music running from Siegfried's funeral march through Brünnhilde's immolation, which closes *Götterdämmerung:* all these, in Boulez's performance, fail to be either moving or memorable.

Here, then, is the paradox. Everywhere there is worship of Wagner: publications personal, commemorative, and scholarly; recordings, television programs for the masses, all the panoply of contemporary musical sainthood. Ideological friends and enemies meet in admiration of his greatness; musicians from ultramodern to hidebound conservative vie to play his music. That classic status which so long eluded him is now his. At last, a century after his death, Wagner has finally come home to musical heaven.

Would he have thought the fruits of his elevation worth the battle? Would Richard Wagner, so fanatically desirous of being central to life on earth, have been satisfied with a permanent residence in the world everlasting? I haven't his answer, but I have my own, though perhaps it is the answer to a different question. With Wagner's canonization, we mark the final laying to rest of the nineteenth century in music, of the heroic age of music as we know it today. The best sign that we have done this is that even Wagner is no longer controversial.

And yet, like the glance of Freia which gleams through the Nibelung treasure and requires Wotan to give up the ring itself in order to cover it up, Wagner, in at least one spot on this earth, is still controversial. In the state of Israel there still are people who care about Wagner; indeed, they care so much that they won't let his music be played. Because for the Israelis, Wagner the man, Wagner the anti-Semite, is still alive, they take him seriously. Perhaps in so doing they pay him a compliment which we, with our easy acceptance (and forgiveness) of genius, no longer can. Thomas Mann might well have appreciated the irony. One can, as always, only wonder about Wagner.

[1983]

# Shostakovich in Four Parts

When Dmitri Shostakovich died in Moscow in August of 1975, he was mourned in his homeland as a great Soviet composer. Behind all the obligatory declarations of faith in the present and future of socialist art lay the unspoken acknowledgment that with Shostakovich's death had passed away the last great Russian musician worthy of standing with such immortals as Mussorgsky, Tchaikowsky, Scriabin, Rachmaninoff, and Prokofiev.

The reaction to Shostakovich abroad, both in death and in life, has hardly been so wholehearted. Indeed, it could be said that over a period of nearly sixty years the musical reputation of this prolific writer has functioned as an accurate barometer of wider Western opinion concerning the Soviet Union as an economic, social, political, and military power.

In the 1920s, for example, the bold, brash, and biting works of Shostakovich the student were seen as manifestations of the *élan vital* of the triumphant Bolshevik revolution and its scornful rejection of convention. The energetic First Symphony (1924–25), written before the composer was twenty, and *The Nose* (1927–28), an opera based on a short story by Gogol, satirizing the old Russia of Czar Nicholas I, strengthened the perception of Shostakovich as a new broom sweeping music clean. While bourgeois society in the West was the target of Shostakovich's witty attacks in a ballet, *The Age of Gold* (1927–30), prerevolutionary Russian society again provided the butt for the composer's attacks in *Lady Macbeth of the Mtsensk District* (1930–32), a four-act operatic setting—strongly influenced by Alban Berg's *Wozzeck* (1914–21)—of Leskov's tale of rural lust and murder. Successful on their appearance in the USSR, these works quickly became caviar for the enlightened in the West, and Shostakovich's status as one of the leading modernist composers of the day seemed secure.

But what the revolution had given, it could take away, not just at home but also abroad. The same iconoclastic vitality that had won admirers for Shostakovich all over the musical world won him the enmity of the leading Soviet music critic—the polymath Josef Stalin. Under direct orders from Stalin (and perhaps incorporating his own words of wisdom as well), an article appeared in *Pravda* in 1936 titled "Muddle Instead of Music"; the target was *Lady Macbeth,* which Stalin had just seen and hated. The result was predictable. The opera was withdrawn, as was Shostakovich's Fourth Symphony (1935–36). All of the composer's work now lay under a cloud, and in the gathering fury of the Great Purge, his life itself, and the lives of his family too, must have seemed in peril.

For a time Shostakovich lapsed into a relative musical silence. His answer to the fury, when it came, turned out to be yet another symphony, this time his Fifth, inscribed "A Soviet Artist's Practical, Creative Reply to Just Criticism." Gone was the bitterness of tone, expressed in harsh dissonance and mocking instrumental timbre, which had marked the early Shostakovich. In its place, in consonance with the new aesthetic policy of socialist realism, was an expansive symphony with a happy ending; here was a work portraying the life cycle of Soviet man and, so we are told, appealing to him en masse. At home Shostakovich became the crowned composer laureate, in demand for works and performances as well as for pronouncements on all manner of musical subjects. Film music by the carload came from his facile pen, as did a Sixth Symphony (1939). The film music is now forgotten, and the symphony, true to the demands of Soviet power, is blessed with a last movement described by the American critic David Hall as "straight 'public square' Shostakovich, trivial but enjoyable for all that, winding up with a marching tune that might well accompany a Komsomol parade down Red Square."

However edifying this spectacle of an artist writing music to political order in return for his continued physical safety may have seemed to Stalinists outside Russia, the effect of Shostakovich's musical demarche was an immediate loss of respect among many musical intellectuals. Not only did his capitulation lose Shostakovich all claim to a place in the modernist world of Stravinsky, Schoenberg, and Bartók; those of more traditional tastes, who had been repelled by the stridency of his offenses against "good taste," refused to go along with what they saw as yet another example of the composer's bending to extramusical criteria. Thus, in the 1940

Supplementary Volume of *Grove's Dictionary of Music and Musicians,* the great champion of Russian music, M. D. Calvocoressi, moved from a castigation of Shostakovich's now-reviled older music to a laconic rejection of the new: for Calvocoressi, in his earlier works Shostakovich was

> misled by his eagerness to conform to Soviet requirements [and] overshot the mark. . . . [The] Union of Soviet Composers took up the matter and blamed the composer for his "formalistic and insincere" methods. He accepted the verdict. . . . He then composed a fifth symphony [which] was described in the Russian press as profoundly significant and free from the errors for which the composer had been censured. In Paris it was found disappointing and commonplace.

As it happened, however, Shostakovich's positive orientation to Soviet reality was to prove in tune both with domestic political and artistic pressures and in a wider sense with the altered state of world affairs brought about by the German attack on the Soviet Union in June 1941. What Stalin had lost in world opinion by his pact with Hitler and his overrunning of small neighboring states was more than recouped when a Russian defeat at the hands of the Nazis seemed imminent.

Into the new climate of patriotism at home and sympathy for the Soviet partner abroad stepped Shostakovich with another new symphony, this time the Seventh, subtitled "Leningrad." Written in part from inside that city while it was under siege, the composition presented a panorama from peace to war, from attack to defense, and from defeat to final victory in C Major. A huge success at home, the work—shipped on microfilm by military plane, passing through Iran, North Africa, and South America on its way—was played in the United States for the first time by Arturo Toscanini and the NBC Symphony on a radio broadcast. Here it was attacked by such highbrow critics as Virgil Thomson and B. H. Haggin, who found the work thin and pretentious. But for a middlebrow critic like Winthrop Sargeant, writing in the *New Yorker,* it was "the closest thing to a great work of art that has appeared in music during the past generation." The symphony received more than sixty performances in the 1942–43 season, by the greatest conductors of the day.

As the military crisis on the eastern front passed, so too did the widespread enthusiasm for Shostakovich. The Eighth Symphony (1943), though in the eyes of serious critics a better work, was a success neither domestically nor internationally. At home the work seemed a departure from the optimism incumbent on Soviet artists; in the United States, as strains between the wartime allies began ominously to gather, it remained little known. The jaunty, almost neoclassical Ninth Symphony (1945), received at home as a stinging rebuke by those who had wanted a victory ode along the lines of the Beethoven Ninth, fared hardly better abroad.

Having shown once that he could be turned around by a political drubbing, Shostakovich faced Stalin and his henchman Andrei Zhdanov again in 1948. Yet despite the violence of the crackdown on such putatively formalist composers as Prokofiev and Khachaturian, in addition to himself, Shostakovich this time had little left to give. It seemed the arbiters of Russian culture liked his songful style no better than they had liked his ventures into patriotic pastiche, such as his *Poems of the Motherland* (1947), a set of arrangements of other—and lesser—composers' tunes.

It might be said that he did indeed have something to give—his voice as a propagandist for Soviet foreign policy in the Cold War. A year after being denounced in 1948, he was sent to New York to the notorious Waldorf Peace Conference, organized as it was by well-known Soviet sympathizers. There, bitingly critical of Western countries and their foreign policies, he attacked Stravinsky, delivered a warning to Prokofiev, and admitted to all the "crimes" he had so recently been charged with at home. Though he received a standing ovation in Madison Square Garden from the massed fellow-travelers, he found himself now deeply unpopular in the United States. Upon his return home he responded—or was ordered to respond—by delivering further insults to the Americans.

For Shostakovich, the next few years were a time of dissimulation. Publicly he behaved as a loyal Soviet cultural worker; privately he was humiliated and fearful. He was now, it seems, unable to write the blockbuster symphonies that were the mainstay of his position in the official Stalinist musical hierarchy. Instead he maintained and increased his output of essentially trivial film music; to this he added such easily forgotten works as *The Song of the Forests* (1949)—a tribute to Stalin's forestation campaigns—and the very drab and cool Twenty-four Preludes and Fugues (1950–51) for piano.

Since his 1936 beating over *Lady Macbeth,* Shostakovich had become practiced at writing two kinds of music, one large in scale and overbearing in emotion to please his masters, and the other intimate in aim and economical in means to express his personal feelings. To the public Shostakovich, we owe his Soviet symphonies and his film music; to the private man, we owe the chamber music he had been writing since the First String Quartet (1938). So massive were the pressures now operating on Shostakovich in the late 1940s, that to these two categories he now added a third: music written "for the drawer," i.e., not to be performed under prevailing conditions. Three works so composed—the First Violin Concerto (1947–48), the song cycle *From Jewish Folk Poetry* (1948), and the Fourth String Quartet (1949)—now are widely and rightly considered among the most valuable of Shostakovich's entire output.

Stalin's death, in March 1953, initiated a thaw in Soviet policy at home as well as in foreign affairs. For Shostakovich, this relaxation meant a chance to write a public music that lay closer to his heart. He worked on his Tenth Symphony during the summer of 1953; it was first performed in December of the same year. The symphony, which for the first three movements is tragic in mood, seems concerned with the suffering under Stalin—until the last movement, where the optimism so dear to Soviet ideologists once again takes over. At home the symphony became a beacon for liberals, and in the United States its warm reception, at a time of Western hopes for accommodation with Russia's new rulers, made possible a resuscitation of Shostakovich's tarnished reputation.

As if to prove that despite his musical transgressions and personal doubts he remained a Soviet composer, Shostakovich's next symphonies, the Eleventh (1957) and the Twelfth (1961), returned to the grand revolutionary programs: the former was written to the subtitle "The Year 1905," and the latter was simply dubbed "1917." Predictably, this blatantly political music was vastly more successful at home than it was abroad.

But however comfortable the accommodation between Shostakovich and the Soviet state now seemed, the composer was holding a surprise in store for those in power. His Thirteenth Symphony (1962), written to texts by the then semi-dissident poet Yevgeni

Yevtushenko, occasioned official rejection not for its music, but for the poet's verses, the now famous "Babi Yar." This impassioned protest by a non-Jewish Russian poet against a Nazi massacre of Jewish victims, uncommemorated by Soviet authorities, seemed doubly offensive when set by a non-Jewish Russian composer. Because Yevtushenko had singled out Jews as objects of Nazi murder, changes were demanded before the work could be performed a second time; the most significant of these changes required an emphasis on the sufferings of all Soviet citizens at Nazi hands, thereby obscuring Yevtushenko's protest against continuing *Soviet* anti-Semitism.

Shostakovich had never possessed a strong constitution, and ill health now began to take an increasing toll of his strength. In the years before his death in 1975 he managed to write two more symphonies. The Fourteenth Symphony (1969), like the Thirteenth, was a setting of poetry, this time by Lorca, Apollinaire, Rilke, and a Russian contemporary of Pushkin named Küchelbecker. Calling for a much smaller orchestra than all his other symphonies, this work emphasized gloom and death. The Fifteenth Symphony (1971), by contrast, used a normal large orchestra, and contained quotations ranging from the *William Tell* Overture to *Tristan und Isolde,* and, surprisingly for a Soviet composer, *Götterdämmerung.* Speaking for official opinion, Tass found the work optimistic; the quotations from Wagner alone would seem to argue against such an interpretation.

Fittingly, Shostakovich's last works returned to the smaller forms in which he had so often taken refuge during his life: two more quartets, bringing the total to fifteen; three sets of songs, including one to texts by Michelangelo; finally, a lengthy sonata for viola and piano, absolute music culminating in an adagio in memory of Beethoven.

Through their music, composers have the opportunity to speak from beyond the grave in a way given to few mortals. In Shostakovich's case, however, a posthumous salvo at his own government came in the form of a set of published monologues covering his entire life.[1] The response to these recollections, smuggled as they

1. *Testimony: The Memoirs of Dmitri Shostakovich,* as related to and edited by Solomon Volkov, translated from the Russian by Antonina W. Bouis, Harper & Row, 1979.

were out of the USSR, was both volcanic and predictable. For the Soviet government, the whole project was a fabrication and a provocation, designed to heat up the arms race.[2] In the West, the evidence the book provided of the overwhelming tragedy of Shostakovich's public life and his bitter consciousness of his own suffering guaranteed a sympathetic hearing even from those not hitherto distinguished by their dedication to anti-Communism. Indeed, the contemptuous rejection of the entire Soviet system contained in the Shostakovich account seemed all the more damning in the light of the composer's unblemished record of publicized activity on official missions.

To be sure, it was immediately noticed that the provenance of *Testimony* was something less than unimpeachable. As editor, Solomon Volkov—an émigré new to the West—had written up his memory of conversations with the composer, to whom he had undoubtedly been close. Each chapter of the result bore, in the manuscript, the handwritten inscription "Read. D. Shostakovich." Experts have testified that the signature was that of Shostakovich; the real question was whether the same could be said of *all* the words ascribed to him. Further doubt about the material arose when it became known, through an article in the *Russian Review,* a publication of the Hoover Institution, that some of the supposedly contraband material Volkov used had been legally printed in Russian musical literature. And serious factual discrepancies were found in Volkov's work as well.

Beyond the question of historiographical authenticity, important as it is, lie questions concerning the political and personal tone of the Volkov effort. Politically, it seems surprising to find Shostakovich's spleen vented not only on Stalin and his lackeys, but also on such heroes of the Russian opposition (each in his own way) as Andrei Sakharov and Aleksandr Solzhenitsyn. Surprising, too, is the contempt shown not just for Shostakovich's tormentor in 1948 and thereafter, the composer-bureaucrat Tikhon Khrennikov, but also for Shostakovich's colleagues and fellow political sufferers Ser-

2. The Soviet musical establishment, in fact, wasted no time in circulating its own version of Shostakovich's life. This attempt, *Pages from the Life of Dmitri Shostakovich,* by Dmitri and Ludmilla Sollertinsky (Harcourt Brace Jovanovich, 1980), was patently puerile and sanitized; it passed almost unnoticed in this country.

gei Prokofiev and Aram Khachaturian. So much loathing unavoidably makes Shostakovich seem as much a misanthrope as an opponent of injustice. Yet this perception would not seem to square with that of people in the West who were able to observe him at close range.

Still, despite all the doubts the Volkov book has raised, the verdict on it for the time being must be that it presents a fair picture, in broad outline, of how Shostakovich felt at the end of his life. His quoted words on the first page of these recollections— "Looking back, I see nothing but ruins, only mountains of corpses. And I do not wish to build new Potemkin villages on these ruins" —ring true, both about Russia and about Shostakovich.

The fact that his words may not all have originated in quite the way presented, or that some details do not quite tally, suggests a resemblance with other well-known examples of the Russian musical memoir. After all, similar questions have been raised about the *Recollections* of Sergei Rachmaninoff (as told to Oskar von Riesemann) and the several volumes of Stravinsky's Robert Craft-inspired memoirs. In the area of politics, such questions have also been raised concerning the Edward Crankshaw-Strobe Talbott *Khrushchev Remembers*. In the case of Shostakovich no less than that of Khrushchev, we are probably lucky, given the political context, to have found out so much.

Whatever the undoubted interest of the posthumous controversy over Shostakovich, it cannot but have the effect of placing his music second to the political storms which have swirled around him as a Soviet composer. While the excitement has surely guaranteed that his name would be well known, it has also rendered more difficult a judicious consideration of his artistic achievement.

Any such consideration must begin with the fact that there is not, as the Soviet party line would have it, one musical Shostakovich, writing music for the appreciation of the broad masses of Soviet society. Nor, for that matter, are there two Shostakoviches, as the more enlightened Soviet critics would hold—a public orator speaking to great occasions and a private bard speaking to musicians and cognoscenti. There were rather, it now seems, four separate creative personalities operating at various times and to various degrees during the career of Dmitri Shostakovich. Each of these personalities produced a body of musical composition which suffered one distinct fate at home and another, equally distinct, fate abroad.

The earliest of the personalities was that of the youthful scourge. The iconoclasm was at first tentative and even sometimes parodistically lyrical, as in the successful First Symphony. Soon, however, the sarcasm went beyond the bounds of spoofing, and the element of parody began to feed on itself. The *Age of Gold* ballet, meant as a ridiculing of bourgeois culture abroad, now seems like hurdy-gurdy music, brittle and nastily shallow. *The Nose,* with its mean and thin-sounding orchestration and its talky vocal lines unsupported by either orchestra or melody, conjures up—as Shostakovich no doubt meant it to do—a good-for-nothing, pointless society. *Lady Macbeth* suggests not only a rotten social order, but the less appetizing idea that all human beings are animal creatures, driven entirely by instincts of sex and brutality.

This aspect of Shostakovich's creative work was destructive, and intended as such. In the Soviet Union of the 1920s such destructiveness could be seen as directed against a prerevolutionary social structure, and thus a continuation of political upheaval by other, i.e., artistic means. And hostility to the past also fit into the modernist disillusion so rampant in the West in post-World War I artistic circles.

At home, however, Shostakovich was to discover the precious political truth that in every revolutionary calendar there is a Thermidor, a time when the revolution, in ending, turns on its own protagonists. Though it was Stalin's evil genius to replace the terror of Lenin with a greater terror, any regime holding power in Russia would have attempted to promulgate policies of construction, order, and personal discipline. In such a climate, the artistic attitude exemplified by *Lady Macbeth* could hardly have been supported. And in a society based upon state monopoly of power, what cannot be supported must be violently rejected. Such a rejection had in fact begun with the reaction of some critics to *The Nose* on its appearance in 1930; the mess over *Lady Macbeth* six years later only capped a developing cultural policy.[3]

Unfortunately for Shostakovich, in our century youthful iconoclasm has not proved sufficient to make an entire career. In the case of Stravinsky, the iconoclasm of *The Rite of Spring* and *The Soldier's Tale* was replaced, in *The Wedding,* by a return to a sympathetic

3. While it has often been thought in the West that the cause of Stalin's anger at Shostakovich was the dissonant *musical* texture of *Lady Macbeth,* it seems now that the root of his displeasure lay in the licentiousness of the libretto.

consideration of his Russian origin and, in *Oedipus Rex* and *Symphony of Psalms,* to veneration of the past and of religion. For Shostakovich, the replacement of deconstruction by construction meant the writing of Soviet symphonies, the first of these being the Fifth. The times—as pictured by Stalin—demanded sincerity, melody, largeness of gesture, and optimism; all these Shostakovich seemed to supply in abundance. But there was one flaw. The reality of life in the USSR was not one of joy and creation, but one of fear and murder. No musician could sing authentically of the happiness of the present and the future, and no one, including Shostakovich, did.

That Shostakovich came fairly close to making a success of the required aesthetic lie is a tribute to his own immense talent and facility, and also to his appropriation of something of Gustav Mahler's technique of mocking romanticism while reveling in it. But ultimately, as with all lies in art, Shostakovich's attempt failed. Not only do the slow movements of the Fifth and Sixth symphonies now seem forced, bloated, and windy, but the jaunty ending movements seem almost pathetically incapable of finishing with conviction what began at such length in lyricism. Much of the same must be said of the Seventh and Eighth, or wartime, symphonies; the inability of Shostakovich even to attempt a triumphal Ninth Symphony is telling proof that he himself knew the hollowness of the efforts he had been making for almost a decade.

Nevertheless, to the end of his life Shostakovich continued to essay the grand rhetorical statement. When he could use his weighty manner to express his thoughts outside of the official aesthetic, the results were more convincing. The Tenth Symphony, written in the wake of Stalin's death and amid hopes for a thaw, is in large part a success—thanks, one suspects, to the new freedom he felt; the terrifying scherzo (which according to Shostakovich's account in *Testimony* was meant as a picture of Stalin) seems particularly true. The *"Babi Yar"* Symphony, too, though not especially memorable as a piece of musical creation in itself, lacks the pretentiousness which came so easily to Shostakovich in treating great subjects.

Another aspect of Shostakovich's music can be passed over quickly. His film music now seems totally undistinguished, the product of an easy pen and no inspiration at all. The same goes for his openly party-oriented music, such as the *Song of the Forests* and the 1970 *Loyalty,* eight ballads for unaccompanied male chorus. The text of the latter work is a particularly maudlin example of "positive" Soviet music; the first ballad, for example, goes:

> I shall walk on toward Lenin in spite of life's limitation, just as in that immemorial year people walked all across Russia. I shall seek his advice, I shall keep nothing from him, and in the enlightened quietude I shall find an answer. I shall understand; I shall achieve; I shall become invincible.

The music to this evocation of Lenin as Jesus is old Russian polyphony, reminiscent equally of church and court. But Shostakovich, by all testimony, was an atheist, and he suffered for the last forty years of his life from a tyranny of which Lenin was the father. Is it then surprising that the music seems both unrooted in time and empty of personality? As so often happens in such art, what begins in enforced patriotism ends in forgery.

If these three modes of Shostakovich's works—the brittle, the grandiloquent, and the trivial and false—were all that comprised the composer's claim to greatness, he would retain little of permanent interest for music lovers. But there is a fourth Shostakovich, smaller in scope, much more refined in taste and execution, and direct and honest in feeling. This Shostakovich is not simply someone who wrote for a small audience rather than for the great Soviet public (composed equally of the masses and the bureaucrats); it is a Shostakovich who, at his best, did not care whether his music was performed in the foreseeable future at all.

So it is hardly surprising that the greatest music of Shostakovich is precisely that music he composed for himself at the darkest period of Stalin's rule, the period of renewed terror during the postwar years. Most important of this music is the First Violin Concerto, written in 1947–48 but not performed until 1955. In the work's four movements the composer managed to use (in a way he did in no other of his large-scale works) an integrated musical fabric to express a consistent and authentic mood. Gone is the omnipresent urge to juxtapose bathetic melody and circus tunes; nowhere is vulgar material invoked to convey high emotion. No program seems necessary to explain the work, for the attention it compels is drawn by the worth of the music in itself. Altogether this is the best concerto for violin since those of Berg and Bartók.[4]

Not quite such high praise can be given to all the eleven songs of the cycle *From Jewish Folk Poetry.* Unperformable when it was written in 1948, it too was first heard in 1955. Eight songs, sung variously by a soprano, an alto, and a tenor, depict in moving terms the whole range of Jewish suffering in pre-1917 Russia, running the gamut from the death of a child to the terrible winters endured in poverty. So powerful was the sway of Stalinist power that even music composed in secret had to take it into account: thus Shostakovich ended this cycle with three songs based, as a summary of one of them puts it, on the need to "Forget the bygone grief and rejoice in the present." The first two of the three invoke the blessings of collective farms. The last describes the good fortune of Jews under the new dispensation. The summary runs:

> An elderly couple go to the theater. And later that evening they speak of how fortunate they are. She was only a shoemaker's wife but their sons would be doctors! What a bright star shines over their heads!

The star in question is, of course, not the Star of David but the Star of Stalin. The music for these celebrations is, not surprisingly, glib, catchy, and childishly gay. Had the cycle ended after the eighth song, it would have come close to the greatness of Schubert's *Die Winterreise;* as written, it is a standing rebuke to the influence of politics on art.

No stricture of this kind applies to the Fourth String Quartet, written in 1949 and played first in 1953, eight months after Stalin's death. Shostakovich's chamber music had always been attractive, reflecting a formal economy and discipline absent from his larger works. But the Fourth Quartet shows a new sophistication of musical conception, contemporary and spare. The lyricism is unforced and affecting, and the rapid movements are both necessary and serious.

It is plain, indeed, that Shostakovich's consistently best music lies in the fifteen string quartets he wrote over a period of almost

4. It is a pleasure to report, given the record companies' present rapid deletions of important contemporary works, that a great performance of this concerto, by David Oistrakh with Dimitri Mitropoulos conducting the New York Philharmonic, is still available on Columbia MG-33328.

forty years. Even the least of them are solid and interesting, and the best are highly eloquent. The last four quartets, beginning with the Twelfth in 1968, use such modernist devices as tone-rows and unconventional instrumental effects; the result seems never to attack the idea of traditional music but rather to reinforce a prevailing tragic mood.

Proof of the quality of Shostakovich's quartets lies in their present repertory status, at least in the West. This status does not reflect a mass popularity; nor have famous instrumental ensembles been intent on bringing them to public notice. Indeed Shostakovich's music has been selected by young groups (among them several English quartets) searching for music with which to establish their own claims to artistic distinction. Recent complete performances of the quartets in New York by the Fitzwilliam Quartet have been successful and publicized; record catalogues will undoubtedly soon begin to reflect this musical fact of life.

Given Shostakovich's success in the smaller genre of chamber music, it would be tempting to blame his failure in larger forms entirely on Stalin & Co. But to do this without making the proper distinctions would be to overlook the fact that much of the best music of the last fifty years throughout the entire European musical world has been written in just those smaller forms in which Shostakovich excelled. One thinks immediately of the last two quartets of Bartók, the last quartet of Schoenberg, the chamber music of Prokofiev. Here in the United States, there is a special distinction to the quartets of Walter Piston, Roger Sessions, and William Schuman; the First Quartet (1940) of Harold Shapero remains an extraordinary work.[5]

While the Soviet Union is a special case because of the enormous discrepancy there between the phony grandeur of public life and the alienation of the individual, it does seem that nowhere in recent years has there been the kind of easy correspondence between society and individuals which might make authentic large-scale work possible. The special crime of the Soviet dictators has not been simply the demand that works be written which glorify the state; it has rather been the ruthless elimination of every other open artistic tendency that has dared to arise. It cannot be repeated too often that while the state has a right to wish to support only "construc-

5. This work was available until recently on Columbia CMS 6176. It is worth searching for.

tive" art, this does not mean that it has a right to bar art of any other kind.

What is at issue in Soviet Russia (one does not speak here of the terror and the slaughter) is not the aesthetic taste of the rulers and bureaucrats. Such taste, it seems at least from the data of our century, is a constant. What is at issue is totalitarianism itself, the horrid idea that the state or party can determine the course of all of life in society. Here, not in the realm of taste and aesthetics, is the reason for the destruction of the flourishing world of Russian art, literature, and music accomplished after the 1917 revolution by the Communists.

The lesson of Shostakovich's life and music is, therefore, an old but unfamiliar one. Art and life both do best under freedom. Had Shostakovich possessed more of that precious good, he might well not have written so many artificially forced compositions, and he might have written even more of the smaller works for which he had such a great gift. That he wrote so many of these intimate masterpieces is to our musical good fortune; it is also a sign that creation survives even in the shadow of death. Because Shostakovich has once again taught us this needed lesson, his music—and he— will live.

[1982]

# From Avant-Garde to Pop

In music composition at the present time, anything goes. Vanished are the days of the enforced styles associated with post–World War II modernism—serialism, neo-Dadaism, and indeterminacy among them. The erstwhile avant-garde has retreated to the academy in two senses: not only has it exchanged the living present for historical status, but in many cases its remaining younger practitioners are contentedly giving up any dream of liberation for the reality of college tenure.

In the place of the dogmatic styles of Stockhausen and Boulez, of Babbitt and even Cage, we now find—especially in the United States—the aesthetics of the cafeteria. Suddenly everything from both the present and the past has become available for a composer's use. Going far beyond the immersion in antique idioms associated with Stravinsky and Hindemith, even a single piece—as in works of the American George Rochberg (born 1918)—can contain a medley of several composers' musical styles and even contents. And increasingly, musical elements both basic and simple, and dating back hundreds of years, can once again be presented proudly as the latest discovery.

It is plain that this lack of a single, unified aesthetic is itself an aesthetic. In the same way as Stravinsky's very impersonality constituted his musical personality, the multiplicity of available choices marks the character of today's new music, both in what composers are searching for and in what they have found.

No artistic movement, no matter how unprecedented it may seem, arises out of nothing. The roots of the present post-avant-garde compositions lie, not surprisingly, in the avant-garde itself. Notwithstanding the evident failure of the modernist movement of the past generation to achieve its twin goals of destroying and replacing the past, that movement did—from 1945 to the end of the 1960s—train a generation of students, critics, and intellectual hangers-on; indeed, from its current commanding position in musical education, it continues to do so.

So it is only to be expected that many of its leading ideas—in such attenuated form as befits the survival of a failed ideology—should exist in the present to inform contemporary activity. This is the case with the central preoccupations of musical modernism: freedom—expressed internally as experimentation and externally as social provocation—and order—advocated as a means of extracting an aesthetic product from an originally anarchic insight. What once bound these two conflicting aesthetic principles together was the artist's inarticulate major premise, that somewhere, somehow, an audience existed for his compositions. Whether the avant-garde would have declined and died eventually from intrinsic musical causes alone is perhaps inherently unknowable; in any case, it can hardly be doubted that the avant-garde in music carried no audience with it, and that the internal disabilities of the new were more than matched by the apathy and outright hostility of a sophisticated music-loving public.

This hankering after an audience—a dirty little secret, which so many avant-gardists always denied and continue to minimize—came out into the open with the rise of the youth culture more than a decade ago. The social sex appeal of the educated young masses, so seductive when exhibited in front of the Pentagon, seemed to provide both an irresistible inspiration and a tempting market for the artist. What was true for the painter and the writer was true for the composer as well; an honorable way had to be found to seek out this pleasurable destiny, which had for so long eluded the musical avant-garde.

It can now be seen that the way which was found involved the putting into effect of avant-garde ideas stemming exactly from the notions of freedom and order—but without making any attempt to combine them. And still more important, whatever the value of these notions as jumping-off points, no attempt was made to carry them out rigorously, to pursue their logical implications to the absurd conclusion of popular failure. In this combination—the splitting up of hitherto yoked conceptions and the avoidance of their logical (and ideological) denouement—may be found the key to understanding today's new music.

This new music would seem to be made up of three major strains. Purely for the sake of descriptive convenience I have chosen to call them the aurally-sensuous, the revolutionary-political, and the pop-hopeful. Not only are they brought together by their common descent from the avant-garde, and their obvious interest in finding an audience; as a corollary of their efforts to implement this interest, they have been successful, in a way quite foreign to the products of the real avant-garde, in reaping favorable comments from critics and publications hostile in the past as well as from those friendly to musical modernism.

Beauty of sound, of course, has always been one of the features and attractions of music. A sweet voice, a rich-toned violin, a noble concert-grand piano, a symphony orchestra of varied colors and wide dynamic range—all these have served to carry melody, harmony, and structure, thus enabling music to make its obviously powerful effect. At various moments in the history of music, and especially in the hands of a few distinctively gifted performers, sound per se has assumed dominant interest; the careers of vocal and instrumental virtuosos (and more recently conductors) have been often based on their own "special" sound. And regardless of who might be playing it, the rise of the piano, for example, in the nineteenth century, was particularly marked by the appeal of its basic acoustical character. Similarly, the continuing development of new orchestral instruments and their featured use in romantic music served as a means of exciting the rapidly growing audience.

But essentially, as virtuosos came and went and orchestral colors became familiar to the public, more purely musical considerations —*which* notes were written and played, rather than just how they sounded—became once again the basis for judgment. Such a process operated, for example, with the music of Liszt, initially so successful because of its brilliant use of the characteristic sound of the piano. As time passed, however, the critical verdict has tended to find musical substance lacking in Liszt, and thus to relegate him as a composer to the second rank. This process has had a rather different outcome in the case of Debussy, whose initial impact was owed largely to the vague "impressionist" sound he drew from the orchestra and the piano alike; but here critical judgment has increasingly stressed rich, profound harmonic and structural features.

For the avant-garde after 1945 (basing itself solidly upon pre–World War II developments) new aural possibilities—pursued in the name of the liberation of sound from the tyranny of music—became, to a historically unparalleled extent, an end in themselves.

Not only was magnetic tape established as a means of bringing the "concrete" noises of everyday life into this new kind of music, but electronics itself was seen as a means of generating hitherto unheard and even unimagined sounds. In the nonelectronically generated field, so-called acoustic instruments were explored in three areas: nonconventional methods of playing conventional instruments (including new techniques of vocal production); use of non-European instruments drawn from Oriental cultures as well as from nonwhite peoples previously considered primitive; and sounds produced by everyday objects mostly used percussively but sometimes in ways producing perceptible pitches. And as part of the spillover from the general fascination with electronics, all these sound sources, new and old alike, were subject to often massive electrical amplification.

In the hands of avant-garde composers, these sounds only seemed to repel rather than attract audiences, a consequence that at least fit well into the modernists' public mission of social provocation. But as the avant-garde weakened in the 1960s under the impact of the revolution of the young, it began to appear possible that sounds which had been used so often to offend could also be used to charm. It is precisely this search for pleasure rather than pain that has marked the compositional career of the most widely successful of the aural sensualists, George Crumb.

Born in West Virginia in 1929, Crumb studied with Ross Lee Finney, an American composer who was himself a student of such earlier avant-garde musicians as Nadia Boulanger, Alban Berg, and Roger Sessions. It is already possible to find in Crumb's *Five Pieces for Piano* (1962), one of the earliest of his works still played today, the composer's interest in varied instrumental usages—in this case playing on the strings as well as on the keys. His *Night Music I* and *II* (*Four Nocturnes*), written in 1963 and 1964, share a title derived (one assumes consciously) from the most atmospherically colorful music of Bartók; the second work in particular seems a kind of Webern without tears, as if the composer had deliberately set out to be a sheep in wolf's clothing.

This impression is reinforced by the two sets of *Madrigals* of 1965. Here the use of avant-garde writing techniques, including a singer employing glissando and flutter-tongue in addition to conventionally sung notes and the nonclassical sound of a vibraphone, creates the unsettling paradox of modern means being used for sensual and even sentimental aesthetic purposes. Nor is this paradox anything but heightened by the fact that the *Madrigals* are settings of fragments from the poems of the Spanish writer Federico García Lorca; the fragments include such lines as "To see you naked is to remember the earth" and "Drink the tranquil water of the antique songs."

Crumb's next works, *Echoes I* ("Of Autumn") and *Echoes II* ("Of Time and the River") were written in 1966 and 1967 and are nostalgically concerned with the passage of time. *Echoes I* is again based on words by Lorca: ". . . and the broken arches where time suffers." *Echoes II* (winner of a Pulitzer Prize for 1968), in addition to quoting again the preceding Lorca phrase, also quotes the West Virginia state motto *Montani semper liberi* ("Mountaineers are always free") with a question mark added by the composer; one of the movements ends with the strings using the eerie-sounding harmonics so beloved of the avant-garde to muse on "Were You There When They Crucified the Lord?" Additional instrumental effects in these works include a xylophone tapping out the name of the composer in Morse code and the equipping of the strings with antique cymbals and glockenspiel plates.

More Lorca-inspired pieces followed, including the *Songs, Drones and Refrains of Death* (1968), two further sets of *Madrigals* (1969), and *Night of the Four Moons* (1969), a work (according to the composer) expressing an ambivalent attitude toward the Apollo lunar landing. In the last work, the earlier marked resemblance to Webern disappears, for thinness of sound is replaced by lushness, and increasingly the music becomes intermittently more tonal and more reflective of great works and styles of the past.

All this can be seen to best advantage in Crumb's most highly publicized and best-known work, *Ancient Voices of Children* (1970), a cycle of songs on texts by Lorca, for mezzo-soprano, boy soprano, oboe, mandolin, harp, electric piano, and percussion. Ranked by hopeful critics soon after its appearance with such pillars of modernism as Schoenberg's *Pierrot Lunaire* (1912), Boulez's *Le Marteau sans maître* (1954, revised 1957), and Stockhausen's *Gesang der Jünglinge* (1955–56), it suggests in its text the mood of Mahler's *Kindertotenlieder;* as for the music, it veers in style from flamenco Spain to the spooky Orient and the Casbah, and along the way employs a fragment (played on a child's toy piano) from the *Anna Magdalena Bach*

*Notebook* and a gentle reminiscence (again from Mahler) of *Das Lied von der Erde*. The instruments, in addition to those listed above, include Tibetan prayer stones, Japanese temple bells, tuned tom-toms, a harmonica, and a musical saw (to be played "hauntingly"). The sounds are not so much combined as alternated, and the general effect is of a tuneful, albeit melancholy, radio trip to the exotic lands and peoples far from our provincial shores.

This impression of tunefulness is increased in *Black Angels* (1970), written for electrified string quartet, and by *Vox Balenae* (voice of the whale), in which whale sounds are imitated by a masked flutist singing into his flute. Still more tuneful is *Lux Aeterna* (1971), a setting of the Latin requiem text; in this work, the performers are requested to wear black masks and robes, and a single candle is to be seen burning at the center of an otherwise dark stage.

Just how Crumb's music sounds when deprived of the sentimental associations of Lorca's poetry, the washes of color provided by unfamiliar instruments and vocal techniques, and the theatrical effect of costumes and stage lighting, may be gathered from his most recent sets of solo piano pieces, *Makrokosmos I* (1972) and *Makrokosmos II* (1973). These works are each subtitled "Twelve Fantasy-Pieces after the Zodiac for Amplified Piano," and come, as is typical of Crumb's music, with extended directions in the score for producing the requisite sound effects. Each individual piece is assigned to an astrological sign, and further associated with someone of the composer's acquaintance born under that sign. In some of the pieces, the musical notation is contained (as is often the case with post-1945 music) on staves running in directions other than the customary left to right. This eye-catching layout, not required in Crumb's case for reasons of performer convenience, is employed to reinforce the programmatic mood of the pieces' titles; thus in *Crucifixus* (associated with Capricorn) a cruciform arrangement of the staves is used, with the left arm of the cross played first, followed by the right arm, and only then the notes on the upright staff.

But purged of all these extramusical elements, the music—given the piano's characteristic timbre, which is much more easily degraded than varied—sounds at its best like warmed-over Debussy, as comparison, for example, with the piano prelude "What the

West Wind Has Seen" will quickly show. Indeed, it is plain that to a large extent the music of Crumb represents an advance backward from avant-gardism to impressionism. It is this impressionism which has been responsible for Crumb's work being seen, as by Donal Henahan in the *New York Times,* as "ritual music for a religion of pure sound, a religion without dogma or guilt." But at the same time it is impressionism with a difference: for this new emphasis on sheer sound is not rooted, as was the music of Debussy, in a still creative nineteenth-century musical culture and a coeval intellectual and social culture capable of informing both private creation and public loyalty.

Crumb is hardly to be blamed for not having been born in another time and another place. Still, however praiseworthy his interest in other cultures and the popular symbols of our time may be, more is required for authentic art than sensitivity to outside stimulus. Shorn of the necessary internal foundation, Crumb's music seems all too solidly based on the sacred icons of the fashionable liberal culture, from the work of a Spanish poet killed by the Franco regime to astrology and concern about the humpback whale, all expressed by an arbitrary choice of instruments chosen from the world over.

The attempt to interest and please an audience through the essentially passive contemplation of sound is clearly one way to write new music. Another seemingly viable way is to concentrate on a different element of the avant-garde inheritance—its concern with the artist's revolutionary social and political position and mission.

The idea of the artist as vanguard element in society is hardly new; in the popular mind it goes back at least to the rise of the artist as bohemian in nineteenth-century France. Even earlier, Beethoven saw his work as the carrier of a revolutionary message of freedom and brotherhood. Chopin, writing from France, expressed in his piano pieces the stirrings of Polish nationalism. Wagner actually went so far as to draft lengthy schemes for the far-reaching reconstruction of the individual and the state.

In our own century, the relations between politics and the arts have been tangled, perhaps ultimately to the severe disadvantage of the artist. Nowhere has this been more true than in the Soviet Union, where music carrying a governmentally approved revolutionary message has been regularly produced by and required from

Russian composers. But in the West it is significant that, whatever the political alignments of such aesthetic movements as Dadaism and Surrealism, and whatever the politics of such writers as the Mann brothers, among leading composers of the period between the wars the provocations offered were musical, not political; the politics of Bartók and Hindemith, of Schoenberg and Berg, of Stravinsky and Poulenc, hardly seem determining of or relevant to (even where known) their music. And in the few cases where politics were important—as with the German Communist Hanns Eisler— the result has been to relegate the music to the status of propaganda.

After World War II, however, a new edge of churlishness and polemics appeared in the way modernist musicians saw their artistic role. The fight for new music seemed a part of the general struggle against the "system." Less than a decade ago, John Cage was speaking admiringly of Mao; Pierre Boulez, almost at the same time as he was becoming music director of the New York Philharmonic, was saying:

> Our Western civilization would need Red Guards to get rid of a good number of statues or even decapitate them. The French revolution decapitated statues in churches; one may regret this now, but it was proof of civilization on the march.

And while Boulez's compositions have seemed apolitical, those of the Italian avant-garde composer Luigi Nono (an avowed Communist) have in several cases been based on Third World liberation movements.[1]

Though by the end of the 1960s a large number of avant-garde works were informed by explicit political inspiration, the same questions could be raised about them as were asked about avant-garde music in general: for whom were these productions meant, and who, in fact, was listening to them? These questions were the subject of a savage polemic entitled *Stockhausen Serves Imperialism* (1974),[2] by the sometime British avant-gardist Cornelius Cardew. For Cardew, now a Maoist, avant-gardism, under the conditions of what Herbert Marcuse called "repressive tolerance," meant writing

1. For a description of one such work, see the chapter "Yesterday's New Music," in my *Music After Modernism*, Basic Books, 1979.
2. For my review of this book, see *Commentary*, December 1975.

for coterie audiences and capitulation to the ruling class. Even those of his colleagues who agreed with him politically were found guilty of obscuring the clarity and ease of communication of their revolutionary message to a wide, musically unsophisticated working-class audience.

One of Cardew's colleagues so criticized was the American composer Frederic Rzewski, born in Massachusetts in 1938 and educated at Phillips Academy, Harvard College, and Princeton University. His early interest in avant-garde music led to an acquaintance with the work of Boulez, Stockhausen, Cage, and the composer-pianist David Tudor (the first performer of Cage's "silent" piece, 4'33"). In 1966 Rzewski became a cofounder of the Musica Elettronica Viva (MEV) group in Rome, a pioneer in experimental electronic improvisation.

The earliest of Rzewski's pieces available on records, *Les Moutons de Panurge* (1969), plainly emerges from his avant-garde interest in improvisation. In this work, a single melody is played in ever lengthening and then diminishing segments by "any number of instruments of any kind" in unison; when the players lose their place and are no longer playing with each other in unison, they are directed to continue to play without reuniting. The monotonous nature of the composition is thus enlivened by a whiff of anarchy, in which the worst (i.e., the most disorganized) performance is the best one.

While the social message of *Les Moutons* is implicit rather than explicit, in the composer's next work, *Coming Together* (1972), it is quite obvious. The music is a setting of eight sentences out of a letter written from prison by Sam Melville—a radical terrorist of the 1960s who was later killed in the Attica rebellion—describing his feelings in confinement. The sentences begin

> I think the combination of age and a greater coming together
> is responsible for the speed of the passing time. . . .

and end

> I read much, exercise, talk to guards and inmates, feeling for
> the inevitable direction of my life.

The eight sentences are each broken into seven parts; each sentence is declaimed seven times by an actor (on the record, a longtime member of the Living Theater). The music consists of a single seventh chord on G with one note added, a C. All the musicians play essentially similar material, and are encouraged to improvise as long as they do not get lost. The result is jazzy, and by the end monotonous, for in the last section the performers are all playing in unison or in octaves—a reference to the "coming together" mentioned in Melville's letter and the work's title. Unfortunately, both the text, in its concern with self, and the music, with its emphasis on unity, suggest that the fulfillment so broadly hinted at in the phrase "coming together" is rather more solitary than reciprocal.

A 1973 work for piano, *Variations on "No Place To Go But Around"* (originally conceived for the Living Theater), is chiefly interesting for its demonstration, in the composer's own recording, of his colorful, warm-toned, and altogether extraordinary piano playing, and also of the use of revolutionary songs as melodic material. For Rzewski this technique came to fruition in the 1975 *Variations on "The People United Will Never Be Defeated."* This gigantic work—it lasts more than forty-nine minutes—is based on a radical song dating from the Allende period in Chile. It is simple, singable, catchy, and written in a multiplicity of styles, from Beethoven to jazz; Rzewski's treatment of it uses every conceivable kind of variation writing, classical and modern, to clothe the tune, but nonetheless the theme is usually recognizable and almost always close to the music being played. For all its occasional use of avant-garde devices, the work too rarely covers territory any more interesting than the Horowitz version of the Liszt variations on Mendelssohn's "Wedding March." As a result, Rzewski's piece resembles at bottom nineteenth-century paraphrases of contemporary operatic or orchestral hits, and gives pleasure for the same reason these chestnuts do—melodic appeal and virtuoso display.

A recent New York performance of the work by a pianist closely associated with the avant-garde occasioned the following praise from the *New York Times*'s musically conservative senior critic, Harold Schonberg:

It is an ingenious, heartfelt piece.
. . . It is of course not necessary to consider Mr. Rzewski's politics or the message he was clearly trying to convey. The set of variations stands by itself as one of the few piano works of our time with real substance.

One may wonder whether a similarly ingenious and heartfelt piece based on an Afrikaner marching song would be granted a similar exemption from consideration of its politics. But in any case, Schonberg is right: so unrelated is the style of the music to Rzewski's revolutionary ideology that here, at least, politics can safely be ignored.

Whereas Rzewski's music now seems more conventional than innovative, another contemporary trend features what has variously been called solid state, minimalist, or trance music. There can be little question that this music depends heavily on transistor technology (frequently for tone generation and always for audibility) and that it resembles 1960s conceptual art in its emphasis on repetitive elements and its stripping down of both content and style. But there can also be little doubt that, as in other areas of the youth culture, it is the drug experience that has somehow provided the formative inspiration.

Whether the experience of this music is meant to substitute for or enhance drug usage, the first impression a listener gains is boredom. The music goes on at great length, changes little, and achieves no noticeable climax. Drugs aside, such music, at least in a superficial way, was not unknown in the past. Though it is impossible to know how listeners of the time heard the less distinguished music of the eighteenth century, it now seems to many music lovers attractive precisely because of its availability in large quantities, its moment-to-moment predictability, its relative lack of contrast and of specific memorability. All this, of course, changed in the nineteenth century; here the emphasis for composer as well as listener was on the assertion of the individual composer's personality as against the personalities of his colleagues. As a result, part of the early twentieth-century reaction against the immediate past took the form of denigrating the composer's pretensions and relegating music from the foreground of listener attention to the background.

Much of this change can be seen mirrored in the work of an avant-garde cult figure, the French composer Erik Satie (1866–1925). His music, though sometimes deeply moving, was heavy on charm and wit but light in traditional weight and "significance." Two of his works are often cited as prophetic of later modernist developments: the *Musique d'ameublement* (furniture music) was conceived with Darius Milhaud in 1920 as something to be performed but not listened to while people went about their business, and the earlier *Vexations* (*ca.* 1892–93) simply directed the performance of a half-page of music 840 times slowly and quietly.

But however provocatively this music was meant, Satie could not have hoped it would be taken seriously. It was quite otherwise with the avant-garde productions of the 1950s and '60s, which owe so much to Satie's example; these composers conceived of their work as an unlocking and a new definition of the very nature of the musical experience. No more typical representative of this new ambition, so different from the devil-may-care attitude of Satie and his followers, may be found than La Monte Young (born 1935), a reclusive and hermetic figure on today's new music scene. Trained as an avant-garde musician, Young was a pioneer in the writing of works in which (as in the case of Cage's *4′33″*) a few words replaced all the notes. In his *Composition 1960 #9,* even words disappear. In Young's own description, the work "consists of a straight line drawn on a piece of paper. It is to be performed and comes with no instructions." What remains to be explained is how this trifling content quickly became transmuted by Young and his followers into a music of enormous dimensions in time, frequent sound levels of barely tolerable loudness, and grandiose philosophical and artistic claims.

The answer is that this minimum of music now was to be clothed in a maximum of technology. In the work of Young, the process may be seen in *Dream House 78′17″,* the only recording (made in 1973) of his music now available. One side of this record consists of chants and drones, particularly influenced by Indian music, performed by two voices—the composer's and his wife's—a trumpet and trombone, and electronically generated sine waves controlled by the composer. This music is a subsection of *Map of 49's Dream: The Two Systems of Eleven Sets of Galactic Intervals Ornaments Lightyears Tracery,* a section of the even longer work *The Tortoise, His Dreams and Journeys* (1964–   ), the tortoise in question being a pet turtle named 49, now roaming the Pennsylvania woods. The entire composition is, in the composer's words, meant to be "perpetuated through the establishment of . . . long-term Dream Houses designed especially for its continuous performance." The second side of the record contains three sine waves (again controlled by the composer) all coming from the bass end of the audio spectrum.

The pitches sung and sounded are in a complicated system of tuning based upon a just intonation rather than the tempered scale used in Western music since the eighteenth century. The outstanding characteristic of this tuning system is the extent to which pitches so derived form pure intervals with each other, thus providing a sense of harmonic resonance and reinforcement rather than the frequent semi-clashings of our established even temperament. But whatever the theoretical complexities—and despite the composer's subtitling the recording "The Theater of Eternal Music"—the musical effect is one of interminable repetition of uninteresting fragments, extreme monotony when produced by voices, and total nullity when produced by electronic means alone.

At this point, Young's work seems the focus of a narrow, if dedicated, cult; he has, however, influenced several figures whose primary orientation has been toward an altogether wider, less committed, and quite unrigorously selected audience. The first of these more popular successes was Terry Riley (born 1935). He burst on the scene with *In C* (1964), called (by the respected new music critic Alfred Frankenstein in *High Fidelity*) on its recorded appearance in 1968, "one of the definitive masterpieces of the twentieth century . . . conceivably the most important since the *Sacre [du Printemps]*" and "the global village's first ritual symphonic piece" (by Janet Rotter in *Glamour*). This composition, its complete score reprinted on the record jacket, is in C major and consists of fifty-three separate motifs played against a steady background of a repeated C octave on the piano. The motifs are played in order, each one as many times as each individual performer wishes; when all the performers arrive at motif fifty-three, the performance is over.

Later recorded works by Riley, *Poppy Nogood and the Phantom Band* (1968) and *A Rainbow in Curved Air* (1969), both more dependent on electronics and more pop-oriented in sound and jacket copy, lack the earlier work's obsession and discipline. Something of the accommodation of the later works to the then prevailing youth culture may be gathered from the poem quoted on the jacket to accompany *Rainbow;* it describes the ending of all wars, the Pentagon "painted purple, yellow and green," "the energy from dismantled nuclear weapons" providing "free heat and light," and the "concept of work . . . forgotten."

In turning from these juvenile banalities to another practitioner of minimalist music, Steve Reich (born 1936), one finds early work based upon the use of tape, and particularly the use of loops (short pieces of tape of prerecorded material) as a means of infinite repetition. In *Come Out* (1966), Reich combined this technical device with the principle of phase shifting, in which identical material, recorded on different tape tracks, is allowed to grow slightly but increasingly apart, and then is just as gradually rejoined in perfect unison. The text of *Come Out,* again showing the heavy influence of avant-garde political ideas in some post-avant-garde music, comes from the words of a member of the "Harlem Six," a group arrested for murder during the Harlem riots of 1964. The passage describing how one of the prisoners got hospital treatment for his police-inflicted wounds—"I had to, like, open the bruise up and let some of the bruise blood come out to show them"—is endlessly repeated and divided, first into two voices, and then into four and eight. Not surprisingly, the resultant unexpected dislocations of sense and timing do little to relieve the ponderous didacticism; the work, however, only lasts thirteen minutes.

From these weighty beginnings, Reich has moved on to a more widely appealing music. Significantly, he has dropped the use of tape, though hardly of amplification. *Four Organs* (1970) is twenty-four minutes of a repeated, gradually augmented and lengthened chord, played by electric organs against a steady maracas beat. After listening to the piece awhile, the listener becomes conscious of many tiny changes, all adding up to a set of distinctions without any real difference, of change without development, of process without direction. More ambitious still is *Drumming* (1971), influenced by the composer's trip to Africa to study native percussion performance techniques. While the work uses some African instruments, its sound is more that of a rhythm band substituting busyness for exoticism and mystery. Though the whole piece, which lasts ninety minutes, uses voices (and also whistling) and piccolo in addition to drums, glockenspiels, and marimbas, the total effect, because of the slow rate of change and the lack of perceptible growth, remains lackluster.

The same can be said of *Six Pianos* (1973), a cut-down version of Reich's idea to write a piece using all the pianos in a piano store. Strikingly different, however, is Reich's most recent work,

*Music for Eighteen Musicians* (1974–76). Now available in a recording by the composer's own ensemble, it presents the familiar combination of repetition and length in an overall pop sound, justifying its release on a popular label rather than the classical labels of the previous Reich records. Totally gone are the telltale avant-garde characteristics of simultaneous thinness and stridency, of dryness and provocation. In place of these adversary elements is a sound that is soft-edged no matter how loud, harmonically lush, and altogether perfect for a family Christmas. The release was met with universal applause: the *New York Times*'s John Rockwell called it one of the ten best pop records of 1978, and the *New Yorker*'s Andrew Porter thought it "well described as 'an unbroken hour-long stretch of scintillating sounds in joyous patterns.' "

Even more successful than Reich in achieving public recognition for his music has been another American, Philip Glass (born 1937). A student of the traditionalist composers William Bergsma and Vincent Persichetti at Juilliard, and of Milhaud at Aspen and Boulanger in France, Glass became interested in non-Western music through writing for the Indian sitarist Ravi Shankar in 1966; soon thereafter he studied the tabla with Alla Rakha. By 1968 he had founded his own ensemble (Steve Reich was a member for two years) of amplified keyboard and wind instruments, which is to this day associated with his music.

An early work for amplified solo violin, *Strung Out* (1967), in most ways stakes out Glass's harmonic, structural, and rhythmic territory: simple modal and diatonic harmonies, simple melodic fragments augmented and diminished but always repeated and recognizable, and an insistent rhythmic pulse. These features—rhythmic and structural especially—may be assigned to the influence of non-Western music; still present in *Strung Out* is a pervasive aridity of texture, no doubt a legacy of the avant-garde propensity for transforming music into a lecture.

But from that point on, Glass's music was to lose this debilitating quality. Subsequent works, beginning with *Music in Similar Motion* and *Music in Fifths* (both 1969), explored rudimentary musical procedures aptly described by the titles; the violin used earlier was replaced by an ensemble including electric organs and saxophones. What had previously seemed at least partially non-Western now seemed, due to the triumph of rock music's heavy, electrified beat and repetitive chord structures, thoroughly domesticated.

In *Music with Changing Parts* (undated on the record jacket but presumably 1972 or before), Glass's sonic mix was augmented by the addition of amplified voices contributing quasi-instrumental sonorities; the result faintly suggests the then pandemic sound of long-haired girl folksingers crooning into microphones about the villainy of technology. This work, and its immediate successors—*Music in Twelve Parts* (1971–74) and *Contrary Motion* and *Two Pages* (both apparently *ca.* 1974)—might, in their incessant iteration and underlining of patterns and progressions, strike a hostile observer as what Bach would sound like to a tone-deaf listener.

After this period of striving for a means of converting the basic elements of music into a personal language, Glass was able, in 1974, to produce his most successful work. *Einstein on the Beach,* a five-hour opera written in collaboration with the post-avant-garde scenic designer and quasi-dramatist Robert Wilson, was performed numerous times across Europe, and twice in New York at the Metropolitan Opera House in 1976. It is not clear that this static and massive work is an opera in any conventional vocal or dramatic sense; still less clear is any real association with Einstein, though the use of *On the Beach* in the title (referring to Nevil Shute's novel about the fate of mankind after a nuclear holocaust) seems to see the great scientist as symbolic of our contemporary plight. Viewers of *Einstein* in performance were enthusiastic in their appreciation of the striking stage images, and of the cumulative effect of the music as well.

Condensed in its just-issued recording to under three hours, the music is divided into four acts containing nine scenes and five connecting interludes (called, for no explained reason, "knee plays"). All this is performed by four actors with speaking roles, a solo violin (a further suggestion of Einstein), a small and a large chorus, and the usual Philip Glass ensemble. The music was written to accompany—and perhaps to intensify—such stage images as a train, a trial, a prison, a building, a bed, and a spaceship. Also heard, sometimes in the background and often in the foreground, are six speeches, three of them surrealistically evoking, among other pictures, a child's sailboat, the problems of eyeglass wearers, and an earthquake. Three apparently straightforward passages include a long sentence about a supermarket, a purposely clumsy tribute to

Paris, and a sentimental story about two lovers on a park bench with which the opera closes.

To those who have listened to Glass's earlier music, what he has written here is almost entirely familiar. But the total effect is vastly greater and indeed moving. No longer is Glass writing pure music, expressive of the technical concerns so perfectly encapsulated in his simple titles. Now there are powerful symbols, informing both the composer in his writing and the listener (through the extensive text and illustrations that come with the recording).[3]

The images Glass and Wilson have chosen to include, beginning with the genius and the devastation of the work's title and including the train, the trial, the prison, the bed, and the spaceship, are central to our modern mass sensibility. This is imagery that the pop-musical sound authentically reflects, and that deeply moves creators and audiences alike. And not content with these powerful pictures, the opera ends with the thrice-familiar harmonic cadences providing background for the following tremulously spoken romantic sentiments:

"How much do you love me, John?" she asked. He answered "How much do I love you? Count the stars in the sky. Measure the waters of the oceans with a teaspoon. Number the grains of sand on the seashore. . . ."

The return from the avant-garde is thus complete. What began as musical revolution and social provocation has ended with hymn-tune harmonies and a homily to true love that every teenager in the throes of puppy love will find immediately convincing. In the context of a historical triumph so massive and unexpected as this one, it is hardly possible to begrudge Glass the commercial success for which he is striving and which the applause of the *New York Times*'s John Rockwell and Robert Palmer would seem to augur.

Much has been made of the extent to which Reich and Glass represent a crossover phenomenon—the replacement of the traditional narrow audience for serious music by the masses who attend popular culture. This proposed convergence of elite and mass art, which assumes the possibility of a wide audience for this new music,

3. In this connection, it is significant that the recording of Glass's latest (1979) work, *North Star* (written for a film about the sculptor Mark Di Suvero), seems to the listener, because it lacks any accompanying descriptive material, an altogether less affecting experience than *Einstein*.

founders on two observations. The music is not casually danceable and it lacks lyrics. It thus requires for its appreciation a kind of sophistication no broad group possesses. So it is not surprising that when a recent Carnegie Hall benefit, sponsored by the Columbia University student radio station WKCR, featured personal appearances by both Reich and Glass (among others less well known), it attracted only an overwhelmingly white, educated, and affluent audience. The conclusion is inescapable: Reich and Glass have lately written what is no more than a pop music for intellectuals, an easy-to-listen-to music free of the rage so marked in black-oriented music and the pop culture of the 1960s.

But, as far as serious music itself is concerned, the musical and ideological implications of the rise of this new music seem hardly comforting, save on the principle that any enemy of an enemy is a friend. No matter how much music in general will profit when shorn of the anger and bitterness of the avant-garde, the consequences of these new developments are hardly positive. While the avant-garde has indeed lost, no one has won. Wherever one looks, whether at Crumb's sensuous sounds, or at Rzewski's return to the writing of nineteenth-century entertainments, or at Glass's employment of an idiom taught at the beginning of first-year harmony, one finds little on which serious musicians can grow. However attractive a return to simplicity may seem in moments of complex failure, recapture of a discarded innocence is as impossible in art as it is in life.

Unless a way can be found to use the past as foundation rather than shelter, the defeat of the avant-garde will have been in vain. And no matter how much the ideological opponents of modernism in general may rejoice to see it replaced by the eternal verities, it is difficult to escape the feeling that the wider culture will be impoverished by the loss of a leading edge, even if that edge has all too often arrayed itself with the forces of social dissolution. What price we shall pay for the end of a two-party system in culture is unclear; it does not seem too much to say that, in being deprived of a force against which it might define itself, conservatism has lost as much as our rejected modernism.

[1979]

# Singing Wolf

Like so many other forms of serious music, the German *Lied*—a musical setting of a short poem, often about love or suffering and their various combinations—can now be seen as having a completed history. Originating in the tentative, if touching, efforts of Mozart and Beethoven, the *Lied* as we know it found its first full artistic expression and its greatest fame in Schubert's unsurpassed outpouring of pure melody. The works of Schumann and Brahms, though distinguished and beautiful, neither rivaled Schubert's lyricism nor occupied as central a place in each composer's oeuvre, and by the time of even such a master as Richard Strauss, the *Lied* seemed to display retrospection and nostalgia rather than its original freshness.

For all these composers the beginning was not the word, but the melody. The greatness of their songs was in the music and was often unrelated, for better or worse, to the value of the words being set. There was, however, one nineteenth-century composer of whom this was not the case. For Hugo Wolf, in the beginning was the poem, and the poem dictated its own treatment. The result was a music different for each poet and for each song. The transcendence that was achieved—as it must be in all successful works of art of mixed origins—was not of the poetry but of the music. At their greatest Wolf's songs are poems enriched and writ large.

The gods who are thought to grant happiness scattered as little of it on Hugo Wolf as they did on any other major musical figure of the romantic era. He was born in 1860 in Windischgräz—a small bastion of German culture then part of Austria but now in Yugoslavia—the son of an impecunious petit-bourgeois family. His leather-merchant father was something of an amateur musician, and he saw to it that his son received music lessons. The boy, though obviously gifted, was hardly a prodigy, and nothing suggested that he possessed preternatural ability. Indeed, the young Wolf was expelled from the Vienna Conservatory on a (presumably unfounded) charge that he had threatened the life of its director.

He did contrive a personal contact with Richard Wagner, who was at the time taking Viennese musical life—or at least that part of it not committed to his great rival and antagonist Brahms—by storm. But Wagner put Wolf off with personal kindness and an evident lack of musical interest.

The elder Wolf was clearly in no position to do more than send his son the barest minimum of financial support; even this insufficiency was accompanied by doleful letters which, a century later, still seem heartrending. Yet during this period of poverty and ignominy, a peculiar combination of musical talent, nervous intensity, heightened enthusiasm, and self-absorption brought the budding composer a small but devoted circle of friends and patrons. Together they found him a few piano pupils, in whom Wolf took only a desultory interest. More helpful to his income was the interest of the Köchert family, court jewelers in Vienna and important advertisers in a prominent local society weekly.

That paper, needing a music critic, was induced to try Wolf. For three years he joined the ranks of such composer-critics as Berlioz and Debussy. What his criticism lacked in breadth and objectivity —he was by now a confirmed member of the anti-Brahms faction —it made up in Wagnerian fire and brimstone. Not surprisingly, the enemies he made in his writing continued to oppose him and his music for the rest of his life.

Wolf's career as a composer was starting to assume its lifelong character of small successes and large failures. He had a burning desire to write for a large orchestra, and his main effort along this line was a symphonic poem (1883–85), titled after Heinrich von Kleist's *Penthesilea*. Its preliminary reading by the Vienna Philharmonic, which Wolf had reason to hope would end in a performance, instead resulted in public embarrassment and rejection. His incidental music to Ibsen's *The Feast at Solhaug* (1890–91), performed under unsatisfactory circumstances, fizzled. And his lifelong search for a viable opera libretto, though it produced *Der Corregidor* (1895), a setting of Alarcón's *The Three-Cornered Hat,* brought him neither the fame nor the profit of which he had dreamed.

The fate of his songs was, on the whole, happier. Thanks to the efforts of his friends and also two powerful Wagner clubs, then flourishing in Austria and Germany, the songs began to be performed even during his short lifetime. He wrote them in spurts, long fallow periods being followed by intense creative activity. By the time he died, in 1903, he had composed close to three hundred songs, almost all of them to good poetry and some, indeed, to the greatest masterpieces of German literature.

In 1888 Wolf set fifty-three poems of the then little-known Eduard Mörike; these appeared the next year, along with settings of twenty poems by Joseph von Eichendorff. Fifty-one Goethe settings were published in 1890, followed by the forty-four songs of the *Spanisches Liederbuch,* written to poems and folksongs translated from the Spanish by Emanuel Geibel and Paul Heyse. The same year he started the *Italienisches Liederbuch,* settings of Heyse's translations of short Italian lyrics. He finished twenty-two of these by 1891 and another twenty-four in 1896. His last three works were written in 1897 to poems by Michelangelo. The title of the second of these, *Alles endet, was entstehet* ("All Things Created Come to Dust"), serves fittingly to express not only the despair that marked so much of Wolf's life but also the wisdom he was able to extract from his suffering.

This suffering was at once physical and mental. What could only be hinted at in Ernest Newman's 1907 biography was made clear in Frank Walker's 1951 extended study: Wolf's death was due to syphilis marked, in its final form, by six years of insanity and progressive paralysis.

The circumstances of venereal infection are hardly the ordinary stuff of music criticism. Yet Wolf's case is of great interest to students of both music and *fin-de-siècle* culture. Such evidence as we have about how Wolf contracted syphilis comes from the writings of Alma Mahler, the composer's widow. Alma Mahler is not always reliable, but what she says about the matter in the 1940 edition of her reminiscences has special force because Mahler had been a fellow student of Wolf at the conservatory, shared an apartment with him, disagreed with him on an abortive opera project, and then became a major character in his psychotic fantasies. According to Alma:

Hugo Wolf as a very young man was taken by Adalbert von Goldschmidt into the so-called *Lehmgrube* (a brothel) where Goldschmidt played dance music, for which he received each time a young woman without charge. He presented his honorarium once to his friend Wolf, and Wolf took away with him "the wound that will never heal."

Whether or not this lurid anecdote is literally true, it has the ring of symbolic truth. The dark side of the romantic era was an obsessive concern with disease and death, and in particular with tuberculosis and syphilis, both of which were believed to have some connection with creativity. Among musicians Chopin, with his pallor and evident physical weakness, was the very model of the consumptive artist. Schubert and Schumann—and even Beethoven —were widely thought to belong to the ranks of the syphilitic.

The idea that sensual indulgence brings both the punishment of insanity and demonic insight survived into the twentieth century with Brunold Springer's *Die genialen Syphilitiker* ("The Inspired Syphilitics," among whom he of course includes Nietzsche, but also Woodrow Wilson and Mussolini). Indeed, Thomas Mann's great novel *Doctor Faustus* is about just such a diseased composer; significantly, Mann uses material from the life and letters of Wolf to flesh out the figure of his own fictional Leverkühn.

The relationship between an artist's life and his work is never easy to understand. In Wolf's case the facts of his biography have had a strong influence on how his art has been perceived and performed. The morbid psychological pathology and physical disease from which he suffered have served both as a key to the understanding of his art and as a bar to a surer appreciation of his achievement.

To see why, we must first examine the breadth and depth of Wolf's musical output. At an initial glance, these hundreds of short vocal compositions, all save one performed with piano rather than orchestral accompaniment, express a wide range of human emotions and make significantly varied demands on both performers and listeners. There are, in Wolf, simple songs and charming ones, light pieces and witty conceits. Some songs take an Olympian view of the universe and some indulge in a kind of publicly proclaimed emotion verging on what can only be called bathos.

As pure music—melody, harmony, and rhythm considered without any reference to the text—Wolf's songs seem highly competent without possessing immortal distinction. The overall musical impression is of melodic shortwindedness, of tunes which begin promisingly and lack either continuation or conclusion, of brief motives reiterated countless times. Thus unlike the great songs of Schubert—among them the *Erlkönig, Gretchen am Spinnrade,* and *Ungeduld*—which have been widely played in beloved piano transcriptions, the songs of Wolf are unknown in any other than their original, vocal form.

But to treat Wolf's songs as pure music is to miss the core of his achievement. That achievement—based technically on the careful and felicitous matching of word to note—was the projection of text and music as a unity, a unity in which the text, not the music, was *primus inter pares.* Had his music been, by itself, more memorable, that unity would have suffered; had his melodies, carried by a consistent and distinctive style, been able to survive in our collective musical consciousness, his name would have been vastly more famous, and his achievement less remarkable. For it is the very plainness of his music that enables the words to be heard not just as the vowels and consonants necessary to clothe the vocal line, but as the bearers of detailed and connected meaning.

According to current received opinion, whatever emotion Wolf expressed he caught deep and whole. Such an attribution of universality seems unfounded. A coy note of preciosity is often present in the smaller songs; Wolf's treatment of love and passion seems all too stylized, all too dependent upon the artificial elements of jealousy and scorn associated in the popular mind with Mediterranean forms of courtship. Where Wolf's greatness cannot be questioned, however, is in his many settings of poems that deal with human suffering, the urge for deliverance, and man's drive to be as a god himself.

At the head of these stand the *Harfenspieler-Lieder,* settings of the verse in Goethe's *Wilhelm Meister* given to the pathetic old harp player. The three songs—*Wer sich der Einsamkeit ergibt* ("He Who Gives Himself to Solitude"), *An die Thüren will ich schleichen* ("To the Doors Will I Creep"), and *Wer nie sein Brot mit Tränen ass* ("He Who Has Never Eaten His Bread with Tears") are adequately summed up in Carlyle's free rendering of the final poem:

Who never ate his bread in sorrow,
   Who never spent the darksome hours
Weeping and watching for the morrow,
   He knows ye not, ye gloomy powers.

To earth, this weary earth, ye bring us,
  To guilt ye let us heedless go,
Then leave repentance fierce to wring us;
  A moment's guilt, an age of woe!

Wolf's music to these gloomy words serves as frame and background, support and wrapping. Though the content is the poet's, the total effect is heightened and made permanent as much by the music's restraint as by its presence.

Wolf's directly religious songs are concerned with the figure of Christ as evoked by the two powerful images of birth and crucifixion. The songs describing the infant Jesus are immensely appealing, whether the words being set are from the Spanish Songbook or from Mörike. Here the simplicity of the music evokes something of the simplicity of childhood, and the attitude of the composer is one of rapt wonder.

Gripping indeed is his larger-scale treatment of verse describing Christ as the comforter. In *Herr, was trägt der Boden hier* ("Lord, What Will the Soil Bring Forth"), one of Wolf's most harshly powerful songs, the poem from the Spanish asks whether the fate of the sinner is thorns; it ends with Christ taking the thorns and giving the sinner flowers in their place. Here the music is stark and sometimes brutal; the same simplicity that for Wolf enhances a childlike religiosity now emphasizes human nakedness before God.

Perhaps the two greatest songs Wolf ever wrote—settings of Goethe's masterpieces *Ganymed* and *Prometheus*—are both about man's arrogance in thinking himself divine, and the punishment for such hubris. In *Ganymed,* Goethe describes the unashamed love of a beautiful youth for Zeus, and Wolf's repetitious, almost monotonous, chromaticism achieves an ineffable ecstasy by its very incessance.

*Ganymed* is, of course, about a quasi-human love. By contrast, *Prometheus* deals with a Titan's defiance of Zeus himself. Goethe's poem describes in symbolic terms man's grudge against heaven and ends with a pledge of eternal defiance regardless of the penalty. To clothe these words Wolf has written a dramatic scene resembling in all ways but one Wagner's similar treatment of Wotan in the *Ring*. In Wolf's song—brilliantly orchestrated by the composer and thus capable of even greater impact than in the original piano version—

all Wagner's gestures of fist-shaking and thunderclaps are present; only lacking is the independent power of the music, which incorporated Wagner's metaphysical flights, profound and windy alike. As he consistently does, Wolf finds motives, which he states in the piano (or the orchestra), and arrays these short groups of notes against the declamatory line in the voice. The total result is again the triumph of the poetry, a triumph the music supports and perhaps even makes possible, but hardly shares. Here as elsewhere in Wolf there is a kind of denial, extended both to the audience and to himself. It is as if the composer, in his greatest songs, were reminding his listeners that they had not come to him for pleasure.

The ability to sing Wolf has always been a great specialty, a gift possessed by few. In Schubert, the demands are simple, albeit difficult to satisfy: a beautiful voice, musical phrasing, and a talent on the part of the singer for ingratiating himself with the audience. In Wolf, on the other hand, the problems to be solved and the talents needed belong to the domain of the speaker—and possibly to that of the sage.

While a few of Wolf's songs have always found their way into *Lieder* recitals, they have mainly been heard through phonograph recordings made by those dedicated to this recherché art. Indeed, Wolf's reputation today is largely due to the pioneering efforts, extending throughout the 1930s, of the late Walter Legge, the English record producer who was responsible for getting His Master's Voice to record large chunks of the then unrecorded musical repertory. Legge also developed the concept of selling records through subscriptions pledged in advance, rather than through the more normal method of over-the-counter purchase.

By 1931 Legge had already put forward the idea of a Hugo Wolf Society, to record (on 78 RPM discs) large numbers of the songs, most of them still unknown and certainly unrecorded. He received powerful public help from Ernest Newman, not only a Wolf biographer but also one of the most prestigious English music critics of the day. (To make his scheme commercially viable, Legge needed only 500 subscribers; though they were slow coming in, he was able to go ahead with a scant 470—a vital 111 of them coming from Japan.)

The singers Legge garnered for his records were among the leading—and also the most intelligent—*Lieder* interpreters of the period. Almost all were either German or German-speaking. They included the historic figure Elena Gerhardt, who had recorded some *Lieder* as early as the first decade of the century with the great conductor Arthur Nikisch at the piano. Gerhardt did the first album of the six that ultimately appeared. She was followed by such important singers as Herbert Janssen (a Wagnerian baritone with a distinguished career at Bayreuth and later, after Hitler, at the Metropolitan), and the tenor Karl Erb. Another historic figure included in the project by Legge was Elisabeth Rethberg, the creator of the title role in Strauss's *Die ägyptische Helena* (1928). Still another was the Russian-Jewish bass Alexander Kipnis, an artist with a rock-solid voice and a radiant musical intelligence. Legge also arranged the participation, for one song only—*Prometheus*—of the great Wagnerian bass Friedrich Schorr (famous for his portrayals of Hans Sachs and Wotan). An equally important catch for two songs—including *Ganymed*—was the celebrated Irish tenor John McCormack.

While the other artists participating in the Wolf Society records may not be on quite this distinguished level, the whole set has stood up amazingly well, and fully deserves the honor of its recent LP transfer and reissue in England.[1] In this reissue, the original six 78 RPM albums, each now with an LP record to itself, have been joined by a seventh LP composed mostly of performances unissued upon the outbreak of war in 1939.

The importance of Walter Legge in establishing the songs of Hugo Wolf hardly ends here. He continued his work for EMI, the parent company of HMV, after the war, now producing records also for Columbia (England), another branch of the conglomerate. Here, in addition to sponsoring the international career of the conductor Herbert von Karajan, he oversaw the work on records of the then young soprano Elisabeth Schwarzkopf, whom he later married. In his capacity first as record producer and finally as husband, he not only supervised her career but also formed her vocal and musical personality.

Just how he went about being a musical Svengali (the term is Schwarzkopf's own) is clear from an article he wrote about his wife:

> First I set out to widen by recorded examples her imaginative concept of the possibilities of vocal sound. Rosa Ponselle's

1. His Master's Voice (England) RLS 759.

vintage port and thick cream timbre and noble line; the Slavic brilliance of Nina Koshetz; a few phrases from Farrar's Carmen . . . one word only from Melba . . . some Rethberg and large doses of Meta Seinemeyer to show how essentially Teutonic voices can produce brilliant Italianate sound. Then Lehmann's all-embracing generosity, Schumann's charm and lightness, McCormack's incredible octave leap in *"Care Selve,"* Frida Leider's dramatic tension. . . . From the analysis of what we found most admirable in these diverse models we made our own synthesis. . . .[2]

The result of all this picking and choosing in the cafeteria of vocal success was Schwarzkopf's career, fabled not only in opera and recorded operetta, but also in *Lieder.*

Of the work of Hugo Wolf in particular she has made numerous recordings, including a two-record set of the Goethe songs with pianist Gerald Moore, and one record, from the 1953 Salzburg Festival, with Wilhelm Furtwängler as keyboard partner. A famous vocal colleague on her Wolf records has been the German baritone Dietrich Fischer-Dieskau; with him she has recorded the complete Italian and Spanish Songbooks, dividing the individual songs according to their appropriateness for a specific vocal gender. Together, they have Legge's imprimatur: they are, for him, "Wolf's greatest living interpreters."

Fischer-Dieskau is himself the most-recorded singer of Wolf— and for that matter of almost everything else—to emerge since 1945. His discs are numberless, and it appears to be his conscious ambition to record every serious work, whether classical, romantic, or contemporary, that can be sung by the male voice. Of Wolf alone he has recorded (in addition to those with Schwarzkopf) three sets of three records each with Daniel Barenboim at the piano for Deutsche Grammophon; on HMV there is a seven-LP set with Gerald Moore.

If Schwarzkopf and Fischer-Dieskau may be taken as the new wave of Wolf singing, and the Wolf Society recordings as the older tradition, what can be said about the character of each approach? And just as important, what can the answer to this question tell us

2. *Opera* (England), April 1976.

about the course of vocal and musical performance in this refined part of the repertory during the last half-century?

In listening to all these records, it immediately becomes evident that the older and newer styles, despite their being linked by the figure of Walter Legge, are quite different.

The best of the older performances give an impression of simplicity combined with grandeur, of sensitivity to each poem's mood combined with a clear, unforced, and restrained projection of the individual words. Among countless examples must be mentioned Gerhardt's searing cry on the first word of *Herr, was trägt der Boden hier*, a cry all the more terrifying for the self-control guarding its expression. Similarly, Schorr's performance of *Prometheus* manages always to be sung rather than barked—even during the moments of the poem's greatest stress. John McCormack's *Ganymed* is neither effeminate nor sentimental, neither cloying nor piteous; even the final astounding falsetto slide upward on the word *Vater* never loses either the integrity of the character or the detachment with which Goethe could view the extremities of feeling. In Herbert Janssen's singing of the overtly Christological *Schlafendes Jesuskind* and *Auf ein altes Bild*, the straightforward character of both poetry and music is never sacrificed for momentary effects of dramatic virtuosity. And the same holds true in the *Harfenspieler-Lieder*, where Janssen expresses utter desolation without any show of special pleading.

To go from this to Schwarzkopf and Fischer-Dieskau is to leave an atmosphere of what now seem like classical limits and to enter a world of blossoming details, of an infinite series of dramatic takes dwarfing their wider contexts, of feeling chosen over understanding, of turns of phrase emphasized at the expense of the orderly progression of the poetic idea. Here, it seems fair to say, is a vulgar rather than a refined art.

In the case of Schwarzkopf, it is difficult not to feel that, in this repertory, she is simply overmatched as an artist. However magnetic her stage personality may have been in opera and on the concert platform, the evidence of these recordings is that she has little to bring to the performance of the most profound works of Wolf other than a coyness more at home in *Der Rosenkavalier* and a crooning more suitable for the singing of lullabies. And even there, in *Wiegenlied im Sommer* ("Summer Lullaby"), one of Wolf's best nonweighty songs, her preciosity destroys the necessary feeling of tenderness so marvelously conveyed by Tiana Lemnitz in the Society recording.

Elsewhere, where the great emotional chips are down, Schwarzkopf proves entirely inadequate. In her performance of *Anakreons Grab* ("Anacreon's Grave"), a setting of Goethe's poem about the final, protected resting place of the Greek poet, vocal imitations of turtledoves cooing and grasshoppers jumping only detract from the idea of a divine reward for one fortunate artist. In *Schlafendes Jesuskind,* what is for Janssen a picture of wonderment becomes for Schwarzkopf merely another lullaby. Her *Herr, was trägt der Boden hier* communicates, instead of Gerhardt's nobility under suffering, nervousness and self-pity. *Ganymed,* under Schwarzkopf's ministrations, fares as badly; the beautiful, doomed youth of Goethe's poem emerges rather as a sophisticated lady quite conscious of her own attractiveness.

With Dietrich Fischer-Dieskau, we face an artist at once more penetrating and more troubling. By no means as vocally gifted as Schwarzkopf—or as most of the singers on the Wolf Society discs —he has made a career out of substituting guileful thought for physical strength. It is an important part of his achievement that when he sings, no word goes unillustrated by a twist of vocal color, dynamics, or phrasing; it is as if he had developed some special gift for musical onomatopoeia, enabling him to act out the words rather than merely deliver them.

The effect of all this artfulness is an overwrought absorption in the material. Everything seems to verge on the hysterical, an impression unavoidably heightened by Fischer-Dieskau's lack of vocal amplitude, which frequently—and in *Prometheus* unpleasantly —reduces him to a mere shout. In quieter moments, he too, like Schwarzkopf, croons; indeed, both singers often seem all too aware of the potential of the microphone as an aid to vocal color and contrast.

Fischer-Dieskau's recordings of the *Harfenspieler-Lieder* are, it must be said, attractive on first hearing. Together with pianist Barenboim, he projects a concern with each note and word; here, one feels, are performers who really care. Compared to Fischer-Dieskau and Barenboim, Janssen and his pianist, Coenraad Bos, seem at first—but only at first—a bit cautious and unbending. Then, as the second song follows the first, and the third the second, the plenitude of Fischer-Dieskau's emotion becomes a surfeit, and Janssen's restraint can be experienced as a form of wisdom.

In other songs, too, the contrast is unfavorable to the younger singer. In *Anakreons Grab,* Fischer-Dieskau seems uncertain whether he is expressing Goethe's view of life or singing about the dissolute minor poet of the title; *Ganymed* is tortured and mannered, verging occasionally on rhythmic unsteadiness; *Auch kleine Dinge* ("Even Little Things"), another of Wolf's most successful lighter songs, is done in the stylized manner of the best cabaret singers with no trace of the gentility that marks the performance of Gerhardt.

Such a negative judgment of what may be the two most highly regarded German singers of the post–World War II era cannot fail to provoke objections in general and a particular question concerning their performance of Wolf. How can anything vital be lacking in artists who have sung Wolf's songs in concert or on records so successfully to an audience vastly larger than any who heard this music in the preceding fifty years?

The answer, I believe, is that a basic constituent in the success of these artists in this repertory is precisely the flaws in their approach to it—the charming shallowness of Schwarzkopf and the overwrought, fussy delivery of Fischer-Dieskau.

Describing Hugo Wolf's audience, Walter Legge has written:

> Nowhere today is there a society like that Wolf moved in. His Vienna circle was a mixture of up-and-coming conductors, writers, doctors, university professors, government officials, and fairly rich business people all interested in the arts— particularly music—and nearly all of them capable amateur performers.

It goes without saying that this audience was German-speaking, able to understand the words being sung and the musical idiom in which the songs were written, and alive to the literary nuances and context of the poetry Wolf was setting.

In important ways this enclosed cultural milieu lasted well into our century. But the past thirty-five years have seen the rise of a new kind of audience for high culture—wider, thinner, less knowledgeable, less discriminating. To please such an audience performers must become more approachable and more immediately comprehensible. Legge himself admits as much in speaking of Schwarzkopf (though he draws a different conclusion):

At performances I sat whenever possible in a stage box to watch both what she was doing and how the audience reacted —the exact moment when women fumbled in their handbags for handkerchiefs and men tugged them from their breast pockets. This is *not* calculation; it is in my view obedience to composers' intentions, to involve the audience in the action.

With Schwarzkopf, this emphasis on manipulating the audience's emotions results in the charm and coquetry that mar her performances of Wolf. With Fischer-Dieskau, a more intelligent performer in command of great histrionic gifts, playing to the audience has involved fastening on the one part of Wolf's art that is most readily accessible to the contemporary listener—the pathology that so marked the composer as a man. But the hysteria and instability Fischer-Dieskau thus communicates is not all, or even the best part, of what Hugo Wolf's art is about. At their greatest, Wolf's songs are about the victory of Wolf as an artist over his madness as a man, not about his capture by it. Wolf is so important because in some obscure way—made even more enigmatic by the sparse nature of his music—he sublimated his madness in his songs, just as he sublimated his despair, his suffering, and his hope. This miracle produced, in the end, a detached wisdom, gloriously exemplified in the Michelangelo *Lieder*.

Kipnis on the Society records could communicate this spirit because he had confidence in the ability of his audience to understand and appreciate it. Fischer-Dieskau lacks such an audience and such confidence, and therefore his art is lacking as well.

[*1981*]

# Getting on the Record

Once there was a time when recording was in flower. No longer a toy, but not old enough to be predictable and boring, the phonograph was seen as a unique repository of musical greatness, protected against the ravages of time by preservation on shellac discs. These noisy and imperfect replicas of live performances served for countless sensitive souls as the stimulus of fantasies both aesthetic and personal. What Thomas Mann wrote in *The Magic Mountain* about Hans Castorp's discovery of the phonograph summed up what a whole generation felt about—and through—this primitive technological marvel:

> The carrying power of this ghostly music proved relatively small. The vibrations, so surprisingly powerful in the near neighborhood of the box, soon exhausted themselves, grew weak and eerie with distance, like all magic. Hans Castorp was alone among four walls with his wonder-box. . . . Those singers male and female whom he heard he could not see, their corporeal part abode in America, in Milan, Vienna, St. Petersburg. But let them dwell where they might, he had their better part, their voices, and might rejoice in the refining and abstracting process which did away with the disadvantages of closer personal contact, yet left enough appeal to the sense to permit of some command over their individuality.

For such magic to exist, there must always be magicians. Until the beginning of the twentieth century, the phonograph's magicians were the inventors of the process itself; what they recorded—whistlers, maudlin ditties, dialect routines—was hardly as important as the fact that it was recorded at all. But with the new century came a new era in phonographic musicality. With Caruso's first discs for the Gramophone and Typewriter Company Ltd. in 1902, sound recording came of age.

All the world now knows the name of Caruso. Beefed-up and de-scratched by the latest electronic treatment, his records still fill the corporate coffers of those companies who had the foresight to get him on wax. The requisite vision for the Gramophone and Type-writer Company came from Fred Gaisberg, a young American present in Washington, D.C., at the birth of the flat recording disc (as opposed to Edison's cylinder). In 1902, talent scouting in Milan for his English bosses, Gaisberg signed Caruso in defiance of a home-office veto on the whole project and entered phonographic history as the first real producer of art music.

Until recently we knew rather more about Gaisberg than we did about any of his successors. In 1942, rich in honors even if borne down by cardiac infirmities, he published a rambling book of memoirs, *The Music Goes Round.* In 1976, the English critic Jerrold Northrop Moore brought out a biography of Gaisberg called *A Matter of Records.* Both books project an appealing picture of an unassuming but firm fellow cast among giants.

Giants they indeed were. They included tenor Francesco Tamagno, who created the title role in Verdi's *Otello,* part of which he sang for Gaisberg's clumsy machinery in 1903. In 1905 and again the next year Gaisberg recorded Adelina Patti, whose fabled career as a diva went back to the 1860s. Others whom Gaisberg snared for the early phonograph recording were Ignace Paderewski, singers Nellie Melba, John McCormack, Feodor Chaliapin, and Mattia Battistini, and conductor Arthur Nikisch. In between bouts of headhunting for famous artists, Gaisberg traveled to India and Japan, recording local color; he often went to prerevolutionary Russia as well, both to record the flourishing Russian school of operatic singers and to oversee his employers' business affairs.

Important as were Gaisberg's activities during the acoustic era— the years before the introduction, in 1925, of the electrical recording process still in use today—his work thereafter is more relevant to our present musical life and also more musically valuable. The late 1920s were a time of great Wagner singing, and the records Gaisberg made then document the work of those who remain today the ideal interpreters of this demanding music: Friedrich Schorr as Wotan and Hans Sachs, Frida Leider as Brünnhilde and Kundry, and Lauritz Melchior as Siegfried, Parsifal, and even Walther (a role he never sang in the opera house).

Except for the career of Kirsten Flagstad, the golden age of Wagnerian vocalism was as short-lived as it was glorious. Even so, Gaisberg continued to go from strength to strength. In the 1930s he recorded almost the entire repertoire of the pianist Artur Schnabel, including both Brahms concertos, several Schubert sonatas, all the Beethoven concertos, variations, and sonatas. He recorded as well three Mozart operas, *The Marriage of Figaro, Don Giovanni,* and *Così fan tutte,* and even Mahler's Ninth Symphony in a live performance by Bruno Walter and the Vienna Philharmonic that took place just two months before the *Anschluss.* As Gaisberg points out in his memoirs, his recording diary for the month of February 1939 alone included—in addition to Schnabel—such artists as Fritz Kreisler, Adolf Busch, Alexander Brailowsky, and Andrés Segovia. After his retirement in 1939, Gaisberg continued to scout artists for EMI, the successor of his English employers; his last accomplishment was to sign for the company the marvelously gifted though immensely temperamental pianist Arturo Benedetti Michelangeli.

To list Gaisberg's triumphs, however, hardly does justice to his abilities. Undoubtedly, he had a nose for talent, but so do many concertgoers, who show their discernment by buying tickets intelligently. Gaisberg did far more than just pick wisely and back his choices with contractual commitments. He was in fact an *impresario assoluto,* a title given him within his own organization and by implication in the wider world.

Like every successful impresario, Gaisberg was ruthless in dealing with failure. In his own memoirs he is too cautious to show much of this side of himself. But Moore, in quoting David Bicknell, Gaisberg's successor at EMI, makes the man's mettle clear:

Once I went with him to meet a very grand mezzo-soprano, who said to him in a very hoity-toity sort of voice:
"Oh, Mr. Gaisberg, you *must* tell the Manager at Covent Garden—with whom you have so much influence—to engage me for *Carmen.*"
To which Fred replied: "Oh, but I thought that you had abandoned opera."
"Abandoned opera?" she said. "Why, I am the greatest exponent of the part!"
"Oh," he reiterated, "I heard that you had given it up—at last."

With the great, however, Gaisberg saw his proper role as being friendly. Sometimes, friendliness consisted in at least the appearance of abject slavery, as it often must with artists. A passage Moore quotes from the autobiography of Landon Ronald, an English pianist and conductor who accompanied Patti during her recordings for Gaisberg, offers one example of the kind of performing personality Gaisberg was so deft at accommodating:

> [Patti] had never heard her own voice, and when the little trumpet gave forth the beautiful tones, she went into ecstasies! She threw kisses into the trumpet and kept on saying:
> "Ah! mon Dieu! maintenant je comprends pourquoi je suis Patti! Ah, oui! Quelle voix! Quelle artiste! Je comprends tout!"

Gaisberg seemed to understand that if in such a personality there was megalomania, there was also the very stuff of artistic performance.

Gaisberg's tasks were many. Sometimes, for the aging Luisa Tetrazzini, for instance, he acted as an ambassador to nosy reporters; sometimes, as a homely studio photograph with Schnabel in the Moore biography documents, he was an ingratiating host over coffee and cakes. Bicknell described the lesson Gaisberg taught those around him:

> [Gaisberg] believed profoundly that the success of the Company could only be maintained if the artists were generally contented. He rubbed into me and everybody who worked for him that we were—well, I suppose we were first servants of the Company—but above all we were servants of the artists, and it was our job to help them in every sort of way. And he was a living example of how to do it.

Gaisberg himself put his operating philosophy clearly: "In my dealings with celebrities," he wrote, "I have adopted the attitude that be they ever so stupid or unjust I, the mere mortal, must bow down to the god."

What astonishes us today is how little Gaisberg affected the musical outcome of recording sessions. He selected the artists and plainly chose much of their repertory but for the rest he functioned as a kind of simple photographer, reflecting through his primitive equipment what the artist wanted to do and did.

Gaisberg was to be the last nonintrusive producer. The two great figures who came after him were to make their marks on the recording of classical music by spectacularly intervening in the content of the recording itself. These two men were Walter Legge (1906–1979) and John Culshaw (1924–1980). While much of what they did was known and talked about in the musical world while they lived, the recent publication of a book by and about Legge[1] and an extended set of recollections by Culshaw[2] makes a new kind of consideration of their work possible.

Gaisberg was an American who lived most of his life in England; Legge was born in England and remained throughout his life deeply English, not least in his ability to combine an amateur preparation with a professional career. Although musically more or less untrained, he could sight-read at the piano well enough to get an idea of the music that interested him.

In 1927 Legge went to work for His Master's Voice (a successor of the original Gramophone and Typewriter Company and a predecessor of EMI) writing what today would be called liner notes. He was quick to see that one way to increase the supply of serious recorded music during the Great Depression was to form societies of subscribers who would put up money in advance to support the recording of interesting repertory.

After beginning with the songs of Hugo Wolf, Legge went on to organize the Beethoven Sonata Society, for which Schnabel performed all the major Beethoven solo piano music. The first four volumes (of fifteen) brought in £80,000, a sum equivalent to perhaps two million dollars today. Other subscription projects included the Glyndebourne Mozart operas, Bach and Scarlatti played on the harpsichord by Wanda Landowska, Bach's *Well-Tempered Clavier* played (on the piano) by Edwin Fischer, twenty-nine Haydn quartets played by the Pro Arte Quartet, all the Beethoven violin sonatas played by Fritz Kreisler, and several orchestral works of Frederick Delius conducted by Sir Thomas Beecham.

During much of the 1930s, while working for EMI, Legge served as a deputy music critic for *The Manchester Guardian;* in 1938 and

1. *On and Off the Record: A Memoir of Walter Legge,* by Elisabeth Schwarzkopf, Scribner's, 1982.
2. *Putting the Record Straight,* by John Culshaw, Viking, 1981.

1939, again without leaving EMI, Legge served as Beecham's assistant artistic director at Covent Garden. During World War II he directed the Entertainments National Service Association concerts for the armed forces and war workers. These wartime concerts used all the better English musicians and orchestras. Legge was thus placed, in his own words, in a "unique position to find out who and where the best players were." He was determined that after the war there should exist in Britain "*one* orchestra at least equal and in certain sections, superior, to the best European orchestras. All these players must be in one orchestra—the Philharmonia." For this orchestra Legge wanted no contracts for players, and no permanent conductor. "The Philharmonia Orchestra," he felt, "must have style, not a style."

The orchestra made its debut less than three months after the war ended. Legge soon arranged for Schnabel to play all the Beethoven piano concertos with the Philharmonia, and in 1947 Richard Strauss came to London to attend its triumphant concert of his works. The same year Legge was able to combine his EMI work with the promotion of the Philharmonia by bringing over Herbert von Karajan, perhaps his greatest find, to conduct the orchestra in London. A subsidy from the Maharajah of Mysore, obtained by Legge, enabled the Philharmonia to continue until the large royalties from its work as the EMI house orchestra in the early 1950s allowed it to stand by itself.

By 1951 Karajan had decided to limit his recording activities to the Philharmonia in London. In 1952 the orchestra began to tour in Europe. Legge arranged for Toscanini to conduct the Philharmonia in a 1952 series (there were more than sixty thousand applications for the six thousand available tickets). Though many great leaders conducted the Philharmonia, Legge's greatest (and last) managerial coup was in October of 1954, when Otto Klemperer, famous in Germany in the late 1920s and early '30s as a proponent of the musical avant-garde, emerged at the helm of the Philharmonia as a high priest of Mozart, Brahms, and (especially) Beethoven.

All of this managerial activity has of course long been credited to Legge. What has only recently become clear in detail is the extent to which Legge involved himself in the musical outcome of record-making, something Gaisberg had always avoided. An article by Legge in the English magazine *Opera* (reprinted in Elisabeth Schwarzkopf's *On and Off the Record*) makes clear what his role was in Beecham's 1937 Berlin recording of *The Magic Flute:*

> Before we started the recording I had gone ahead to coach and rehearse the singers. We had an admirable chorus of student and young professional singers . . . and I spent untold hours finding the right singers for the three ladies and the three boys. . . . Now, more than forty years later, it can be told that one side of this set was *not* conducted by Beecham and *not* played by the Berlin Philharmonic; neither was free when the hall was available and I desperately needed all three. It was Bruno Seidler-Winkler, Electrola's house accompanist, who conducted the Berlin State Opera Orchestra and followed Beecham's tempi and nuances through headphones. No prizes are offered for identification of which 78 RPM side!

A deceived listener might comfort himself by remembering that, whatever else had changed between the recording sessions, the producer had remained the same.

Legge's determining role in Schwarzkopf's career has already been discussed in connection with her singing of Wolf *Lieder.* Not only did Legge shape his wife's art; his attentions naturally extended also to her accompanists. In a memorable passage from a letter to a music critic, Legge wrote:

> My wife is going to the USA on Sunday and I follow twelve days later to extract from an American accompanist some of the sensitivity I squeezed out of Gerald Moore and more recently Geoffrey Parsons. Accompanists are made, not born.

Something of what Legge could do with his wife and with those who were assisting her was possible with other artists as well. Thus, according to record critic and musicologist Edward Greenfield:

> The stage of preparation immediately before a major recording project generally took place at Legge's North London house in Oakhill Avenue, Hampstead. There, in the music room, he would supervise piano rehearsals. It was at this house too that he would entertain all the major artists, and a conductor like

Karajan would frequently be staying as the guest of the Legges. That factor alone put Legge on a different footing when he talked to artists. He himself, with long experience of the major areas of the repertory, caring passionately, often had very positive ideas on interpretation. It made an important difference being in a position to state them without giving offense, if necessary to argue them from personal strength as a friend. A positive artist like Karajan or Dietrich Fischer-Dieskau might very well counter what Legge suggested, but Legge's word, particularly if it had a bearing on the presentation of an interpretation on record as such, was not easily ignored.

As often happens with a man so used to getting his own way, a time came when even successful autocratic behavior found its limits. In the early 1960s some control of the Philharmonia passed from Legge into the hands of London's Royal Festival Hall; competing orchestras won away some of the orchestra's key players. EMI, beguiled by the profit stream generated by the Beatles, began to lose interest in classical recordings in general and the Philharmonia in particular. Legge decided to resign from EMI so that he could find work for the orchestra from other companies; the result was unhappy: he fought with Klemperer, and the orchestra suspended its existence in 1964 despite his efforts to save it.

From this point until his death fifteen years later, Legge was a man without a position. He promoted concerts, he acted as a musical consultant, and he gave advice on a lavish scale. His major recording activity was supervising his wife's performances. At the very end, spurred by the prospect of her inevitable retirement, he was engaged in giving joint master classes with her; on one such occasion, at the Juilliard School in 1976, he made clear the extraordinary extent to which he had been the animating intelligence that underlay Schwarzkopf's great career. As far as his relations with other musicians were concerned, they are best expressed by his witty reworking (inserting his own name) of Wagner's famous line for Loge, the crafty god of fire in the *Ring: "Immer war Undank Legges Lohn"*—ingratitude was always Legge's wage.

Walter Legge's musical tastes had been formed by the glittering albeit fast-fading world of interwar celebrity culture. By contrast, such an education was largely denied to Legge's only real competitor in the modern European world of record producing, John Culshaw.

Culshaw came to music through childhood piano lessons. His struggles at the piano provided a direct road to records:

> [Playing] the simplest piece gave me no reward compared with the experience of hearing it played by a great pianist, which in turn produced a severe inhibition: I lost my nerve if I had to play in front of anyone else. You don't want to hear *me* struggling with it, I wanted to say; let me play you a record by Cortot or Schnabel or Backhaus, which will show you what the music is really all about.

Whereas Legge had come of age in the audience of concert halls and opera houses in London and on the Continent, Culshaw, almost twenty years younger, came of age as a crew member in the wartime British Royal Naval Air Service. From flying and from the new technology of radar he learned to think technologically; he also studied music in his spare time.

Upon demobilization, Culshaw worked as a writer on the fringes of the recording world. By 1946, he had found a job with Decca writing short biographies of their classical artists. Except for one short interval spent working for Capitol Records, he was to stay with Decca until 1967. On their behalf Culshaw changed, not the way artists performed on records, as Legge had, but rather the way the records they made *sounded*.

Culshaw's Decca was indeed a far cry from Legge's EMI. In the classical recording industry, no less than in the book publishing industry, the greatest riches reside in a backlist. EMI, now including within itself both HMV and (English) Columbia, owned the treasures of the German Electrola catalogue, and by marketing agreements it had access to all that had been produced in the United States by RCA Victor and (American) Columbia. Not only were the greatest performers of the past on the EMI backlist; at the end of World War II it had available to it the services of the most distinguished contemporary soloists, conductors, and ensembles of the day.

Decca had virtually no classical backlist. Its roster included few well-known names: the conductors Enrique Jordá, Karl Rankl, Ernest Ansermet, pianists Clifford Curzon and Georg Solti (not yet a conductor), violinists Ida Haendel and Georg Kulenkampff, and singers Paul Schöffler and Peter Pears (along with Pears's longtime associate Benjamin Britten). As worthwhile as these artists might be, their work hardly placed Decca in a position to compete with EMI.

But Decca had an ace up its sleeve—not musical but technological. It has since become famous as FFRR—Full Frequency Range Recording. Developed as an outgrowth of Decca's wartime work on submarine detection, FFRR brought a new realism, presence, and clarity to sound recording. At first, the benefits of this new technology were limited by the inherent defects of the 78 RPM discs then in use. All this was changed by Columbia's introduction of the long-playing record in 1948; by 1949 Decca was marketing the quiet new discs, each containing as much music as five of the old noisy 78s, in America through its new subsidiary, London Records. Here, then, was the marketing window for both Europe and the United States. Symphonies, full-length operas, the complete works of composers—all these were clearly and brilliantly reproduced with few side breaks. The whole process was helped along significantly by concurrent introduction of easily spliced magnetic tape for the master recording.

Because of EMI's initial hesitation over the introduction of the LP, Decca got the jump on the market in England and in Europe; in the United States, RCA too made EMI's mistake, and Decca/London found itself with only American Columbia as a major competitor. Decca expanded, and Culshaw, now a producer, found himself increasingly responsible for the recording sessions of such conductors as Sir Malcolm Sargent, George Szell, and Solti, whose star was on the rise. In 1951 Culshaw worked on the now classic recording of Hans Knappertsbusch's live performances of *Parsifal* at Bayreuth.

Whatever the merit of the work Culshaw did at this time, it pales by comparison with what he was to accomplish after the introduction of stereophonic recording in the mid-1950s. This new process completed the sonic revolution that had begun with FFRR, the LP, and magnetic tape. Recorded sound could now be heard to come from different points in a room; musical transparency and a concert-hall atmosphere were audible as well. Culshaw was among the first producers to realize the importance of stereophony for the recording of opera, and to understand fully just how traditional procedures at recording sessions would have to be altered to give the illusion of a live performance.

Culshaw made experiments in this direction with the Flagstad/ Knappertsbusch recording of Act I and the Flagstad/Solti recording of Act III of *Die Walküre* in 1957. But these were only first steps toward his real goal: the first complete recording of Wagner's *Ring*. For this project he enticed Kirsten Flagstad, perhaps the greatest Brünnhilde ever and by this time at the end of her long career, to sing Fricka in *Das Rheingold*. To this representative of the musical past he added as the conductor the man who would become his own choice as the great Wagner conductor of the 1960s and beyond, Georg Solti. He chose the Vienna Philharmonic not only because it was the brightest jewel in Decca's orchestral crown, but also because it was undoubtedly the best orchestra in the world with day-to-day experience of playing Wagner in the opera house. In each of the four operas the casts were the best available; in Birgit Nilsson, Culshaw cast the only postwar Brünnhilde worthy of being spoken of in the same breath with Flagstad.

It is a measure of Culshaw's achievement that now, eighteen years after the conclusion of the project, the clear musical virtues of the Decca *Ring* still seem outweighed by Culshaw's contribution as producer. He used modern stereophonic techniques to provide direction and movement to the music and to isolate performers in special acoustical environments suggesting balances and timbres impossible in live performance; he created ear-catching nonmusical sound effects and crowd noises as well. In this way Culshaw fashioned a *Ring* which exists only on records. His book on the making of the Decca recording, *Ring Resounding,* tells the whole story, and remains essential reading for an understanding of Culshaw's craft.

Culshaw's *Ring,* much to the surprise of his employers, was a huge commercial and critical success. After *Das Rheingold* came out in 1959, he was emboldened to record Richard Strauss's *Salome* and *Elektra* (both with Nilsson, Solti, and the Vienna Philharmonic) in a similar way. Decca's marketing experts called the acoustical result "SonicStage." Some leading critics now objected to Culshaw's work. In a notable article in *High Fidelity,* Conrad L. Osborne accused Culshaw of a "violation" of *Elektra* through his acoustical interventions. Culshaw defended himself against this accusation, but for many music lovers the mud stuck.

Culshaw's memoirs are remarkably free of any bitterness toward this kind of reaction to his work. Much more pervasive in the book —and it seems to be a theme in the ruminations of later producers, including both Legge and Toscanini's producer, Charles O'Connell —is a tone of bitterness toward artists and higher-ups in corporate management. On the evidence of *Putting the Record Straight,* Culshaw was afflicted with a stupid tenor who couldn't get his words right and a great tenor who drank himself to death; his employers, in their shortsightedness and greed, emerge from his description as characters out of the monster and dwarf cast of the *Ring.*

So in the end Legge's joke about the ingratitude he suffered applies also to Culshaw. In 1967 Culshaw left Decca and went to the BBC, where he served as director of music for television. After 1975 he worked as a writer, adviser, and free-lance recording producer. He contracted hepatitis in 1979 while on a consulting trip to Australia, and in March of 1980 he died.

Death affects only record producers and other living things; recordings live on, defying time and decay. By the magic of which Mann spoke, we can now compare the work of Gaisberg, Legge, and Culshaw. What can be said about the value of the quite different work of these quite different men?

Sadly—and it is a conclusion one feels sure none of these producers would object to—it is the quality of the performer, not the quality of the recording procedure, that counts when the historical record is tallied. Gaisberg's artists were the very stuff of legend; their fortunes were made in concert hall and opera house. From Caruso and Patti to Beecham and Schnabel, they learned their art before a living, immediately reacting public. Gaisberg's task was to make them feel good, and to ensure that his employers made money in the process. As a result of his labors a period that may well have been only a silver age of musical performance became most assuredly a golden age of musical recording.

Legge, of course, somewhere saw recordings as a kind of replacement for musical performance on stage. He described how artists should view records:

After the war I found in Schwarzkopf, Karajan, and [Dinu] Lipatti (to mention but three) ideal and incurable perfectionists—self-critical, hungry for informed criticism, untiring and acutely aware that their recorded performances were the true proof of their qualities and their careers.

When the artists were fully formed, as in the case of the tragically short-lived Lipatti, the results of Legge's ministrations were valuable—because limited. When the artists were callow, as in the case of the young Karajan, most of Legge's work has proven eminently forgettable. As for Legge's effect on Schwarzkopf's *Lieder* singing, where he put in the most time over the longest period, the overall result now seems to many cute, labored, and artificial.

A word must be said too about Legge's attitudes in the vexing area of contemporary music. He loathed Schoenberg, and made no bones about it:

> I have sat through most of Schönberg's output without being convinced that he is a major composer—and sitting patiently studying his scores has done more to convince me that he does not deserve that epithet . . . Schönberg's eccentricities were the fruit of his own realization that he was incapable of writing a natural melodic and original line.

Legge was almost equally dismissive of Stravinsky, talking of "the nadir to which Stravinsky has straggled from the apogee of *The Rite of Spring*." The result of his taste, of course, was that Legge missed an opportunity (which his position of influence might have made possible) to record a great deal of contemporary music of the 1920s, 1930s, and early 1940s in historically authentic performances.[3] In this oversight Legge seems more culpable than Gaisberg. Gaisberg at least did what the celebrity wanted, Legge always tried to do what he himself wanted—even when he was wrong.

Because Culshaw arrived on the scene at the end of a great procession of individual performers, it is hardly surprising that overall, his work seems the most timebound. He made, it is true, a valiant effort to replace musical greatness with technological in-

3. Culshaw—although hardly a fan of new music—managed to persuade his superiors, after a battle, to allow the recording of almost all the works of Benjamin Britten in the composer's own performances.

novations. Just how far he failed in this quest may be heard by comparing his electronically marvelous *Ring*—the best thing he ever did on records—against such a primitive phonographic product as the disc transfer of radio broadcasts of Furtwängler's musically unsurpassed 1950 La Scala performances. One passage deserves special mention: the transformation from storm to the rainbow over which the gods cross to Valhalla at the end of *Das Rheingold.* In Culshaw's version, the climactic ring of Donner's hammer and the answering thunderclap can clearly be heard to come from different speakers, creating an effect that might well match the "real" life of Wagner's imagination; in Furtwängler's performance, one hears everything from the same source. But Furtwängler wins the prize, not because he beats Culshaw, but because he beats Solti in creating the *musical* impression of excitement and then repose contained in the notes.

The classical recording business is now in a parlous state. Here in the United States, CBS and RCA, for many years our two great companies, have practically ceased to make domestic large-scale recordings; CBS has now even given up its exclusive and long-standing contract with the New York Philharmonic. Abroad, power lies in the hands of a colossus uniting Deutsche Grammophon and Philips on the Continent with Decca in England; this merger, because it involves Decca's American subsidiary, London Records, has resulted in a further contraction of the available repertory in this country. The highly trumpeted digital recording has proven both slow in coming and remarkably insignificant once it has arrived. The frontier of new repertory seems closed for the time being, and the frenzied drive to redo the performances of older artists in new technology seems to have aroused little interest either.

Is this, then, a time for a new Gaisberg, Legge, or Culshaw? Perhaps so; talent does tend to create its own employment. But the odds rather seem to favor a continuation of the downhill curve we have been following for so many years—at least until we have new music capable of arousing a public demand for its recording, new performing artists, and an audience both cultivated and serious. Until then, we can always read about—and listen to—the past.

[1983]

II

# MUSICIANS

# Glenn Gould

## 1. His Dissent

From the standpoint of originality and imagination, instrumental performance today is a pretty dull affair. Influenced by the widespread diffusion of music and the easy availability of recordings, recent performers of the most diverse intellectual and cultural backgrounds strive mightily to approach a common standard of accuracy, textual fidelity, and unobjectionable musicality. And it must be said that they succeed. Wherever one attends concerts, whichever records one buys, the result is the same: an international, received style of music making. Laudable though this is, it is only in rare cases exciting, provocative, or even capable of inspiring rejection.

But there is one consistent exception. Of the current generation, Glenn Gould has been without doubt the most interesting—in every meaning of that valuable word—pianist the public has heard. From his eruption into fame with an unheralded 1955 concert at the Phillips Gallery in Washington, D.C., to the present day, when he lives reclusively in Toronto, this Canadian has stimulated and offended musical taste in North America and Europe, and through his continuing stream of recordings he bids fair to remain for some time to come the magisterial bad boy of serious music.

How can one man's piano playing stand out so definitively from that of his colleagues? How can one man have escaped the becalming influences to which everyone else has succumbed? The answer to the first question flows in a reasonably straightforward way from a consideration of Gould as a pianist; the answer to the second involves issues of talent, psychology, and nurture that are less accessible to the ordinary procedures of criticism.

Any discussion of Gould's playing must begin by acknowledging the sheer quantity of musical evidence. In the past twenty-five years he has made more than sixty separate records, almost never record-

ing a work more than once. All these discs have been made for CBS/
Columbia Records, which had the good sense to begin a long-term
exclusive contractual relationship with him only days after his
Washington debut. And, what is remarkable in this period of short-
term marketing, more than two-thirds of Gould's records remain
in print to this day.

The pianist's vast recorded repertory ranges in time from the
Elizabethan to the contemporary, and in scope from the most famous masterpieces to unknown Canadian music composed between
1948 and 1964. Nor is it confined to music originally written for
the keyboard; in recent years Gould has busied himself with the
playing of orchestral transcriptions, including the Liszt arrangement of the Fifth Symphony of Beethoven and the pianist's own
reworking of the prelude to Wagner's *Die Meistersinger*.

Not only has he chosen widely, but in the case of several of the
greatest composers he has chosen in depth: among the works of
Bach he has recorded are six of the seven harpsichord concertos, all
the partitas, the English and French suites, the inventions, and the
forty-eight preludes and fugues of *The Well-Tempered Clavier*. He
has recorded all the solo keyboard sonatas of Mozart, and of Beethoven all the concertos and fourteen piano sonatas as well. And in
a praiseworthy service to the music of his own time, he has over a
period of years recorded almost all the piano music of Schoenberg,
including the keyboard parts of his songs and chamber music, and
the still knotty Piano Concerto (1942).

Out of all this music it seems that the pianist's favorite remains
what it has been since the beginning of his career, the compositions
of J. S. Bach. And happily, it is Bach who has occasioned Gould's
greatest successes and most favorable critical responses. His Washington debut recital, repeated nine days later in New York's Town
Hall, included the G-Major Partita; the critics were rapturous. Still
more importantly, his first recording for Columbia, made just five
months later, was nothing less ambitious than the "Goldberg"
Variations, then widely known only in the classic 1945 harpsichord
recording by Wanda Landowska (an earlier one had been made in
1933). It is a tribute to Gould's early mastery—he was twenty-two
at the time—that his "Goldberg" record has remained with Landowska's the yardstick against which all others must be measured.

In that recording, now released again in a version satisfactorily
rechanneled for stereo, may be found all the most attractive quali-

ties of Gould as pianist and musician. The listener's immediate impression is of a lightness of touch and quickness of movement, as if the piano keys were being played on an upward rather than a downward stroke. All the notes seem distinct and yet connected by phrasing and pulse, the result of the pianist's emphasis upon perfect articulation and a legato produced by the fingers rather than the damper pedal. Out of this remarkable technical virtuosity emerges a performance freed both from the authentic twang of the harpsichord so palpable in Landowska's version and from our notion of the piano as a heaven-storming vehicle for romantically plunging hands playing richly crashing chords.

Elsewhere among Gould's Bach recordings, the riches, though numerous, seem hardly as fresh. The very act of executing so many integral performances has unavoidably involved him in playing on each disc at least some works that do not engage his full sympathy. Although he never gives less than full concentration to anything he plays, sometimes in his traversals of Bach love seems to have been replaced by duty, with a resultant monotony of texture and a mannered repetition of phrasing. Yet such cavils cannot be applied to those important works with which he identifies completely; his recording of the D-Minor Concerto, made with Leonard Bernstein in 1957, remains to this day gorgeous in its simplicity and, as always with Gould, remarkable in its technical finish.

At the other end of the repertory, Gould's playing has been equally distinguished, though hardly so successful with the public. His first venture into the music of the Second Viennese School began with a 1958 recording of Schoenberg's Three Piano Pieces, opus 11 (1909). The same year, he recorded Alban Berg's Sonata, opus 1 (1908), written while Berg was a student of Schoenberg. Ironically, while the teacher's work seems today mostly of historical interest, the student's has become a staple of the repertory. It is a mark of a profound performer that he plays better music better than he plays inferior music, and Gould's performance of the Berg sonata, which fully plumbs that work's luxuriant Viennese hothouse atmosphere, is now a standard; by contrast, the Schoenberg performance seems gray and stale. His other performances of Schoenberg, despite the loving care he has lavished on them, give the impression of sharing the same unhappy fate. Only in the accompaniments to Schoenberg's early songs is Gould's playing marked by the same sparkle and vivacity that informs his best Bach playing.

But in Bach and Schoenberg, Gould is hardly performing works central to the piano; Bach's music was not written for the piano at all, and Schoenberg was almost totally unconcerned with the sound quality and technical characteristics of the piano as an instrument. The music that most pianists spend their time on was written from the last quarter of the eighteenth century to World War II, and to be a pianist in the public mind is to take a musical position on how these works should be played. It is Glenn Gould's position on these central works that has made his playing a matter of supreme interest in terms of its originality, freedom, and imagination.

If the word interesting can be defined to mean different, none of Gould's playing is more interesting than his Mozart. As if to counter the notion of Mozart as the epitome of grace, delicacy, and gentle charm, Gould exaggerates the contrasts suggested in the music, employs a dynamic scale unknown in Mozart's time, and plays fast movements at the limits of speed but at the same time heavily. One's impression can only be that Gould dislikes the music, an impression confirmed by his remark in an interview with Jonathan Cott that he does not "really . . . like Mozart as a composer." Whatever his reasons for playing the music, the intended rebuke to a sainted figure is plain. Yet perhaps it is just because of Gould's distortion of the "proper" view of the composer that his Mozart emerges as a figure of bones and guts, driven by ambition to challenge later, larger-scaled composers on their own terrain.

The gentleness so lacking in Gould's Mozart is surprisingly present in his recorded Brahms. Ten *Intermezzi,* recorded in 1960, show the pianist to be a master of the miniature and fully at home in Brahms's rich but bittersweet harmonic progressions. The result is extraordinary, and the best Brahms playing to be heard today. The reasons for Gould's triumph in these gems surely have to do precisely with the absence in them of fustian rhetoric and structural pretension; it would seem that Gould is perfectly willing to be restrained so long as the composition matches that restraint.

Such self-limitation cannot be said to operate in the case of Beethoven, a composer to whom Gould has paid almost as much attention as to Bach. His recordings of the five concertos were made between 1957 and 1966; in addition to his sonata performances, he has more recently recorded three sets of variations and two sets of bagatelles. Gould has made no secret of his admiration for Artur Schnabel, who recorded all Beethoven's piano music almost two generations ago; it is likely that before he is through, Gould will accomplish the same task.

The Beethoven recordings Gould has made so far have been the most controversial of his career. The initial storm broke with his recording of Beethoven's last three sonatas—opus 109, 110, and 111—made in 1956 as his second disc for Columbia. This album has long been out of print, and by now has attained something of the status of a camp classic. Notwithstanding Gould's positive feeling about Schnabel, the recording bears little resemblance to the elder pianist's playing. The chief difference is Gould's inability —or more likely, his unwillingness—to play naturally, to avoid harshness, extreme contrasts, and awkward transitions. It was in giving an impression of flow that Schnabel was a master; the easy *Gemütlichkeit* of his conceptions has long seemed the way a sophisticated musician went about being profound. But in Gould's conceptions what stands out is a frequent brusqueness verging on flippancy. Tempos are often terribly fast—in the slow movement of opus 109, for example, sometimes startlingly so. It is not that Gould takes more liberties with the pulse or always plays faster than Schnabel; it is rather that the liberties he does take intrude themselves on the listener by their unexpectedness.

If Gould's attitude toward these last three sonatas is apparently one of devil-may-care—in the program notes that accompany the recording he writes deflatingly that the sonatas "perhaps do not yield the apocalyptic disclosures that have been so graphically ascribed to them"—toward some earlier sonatas he has felt free to express outright hostility. In describing the famous *Grave* opening of the opus 13 (*Pathétique*), for example, he writes in disparagement of "the somewhat stage-struck character of its doom-foretelling double-dotted rhythm." And of the opus 57 ("Appassionata") he writes:

> . . . [T]here is about the Appassionata an egoistic pomposity, a defiant "let's just see if I can't get away with using that once more" attitude. . . .

What kind of performance can come out of such a conception of the music? The answer is simple: where Gould finds bluster, he adds

rodomontade; where he finds structural weakness, he chooses particularly slow tempos—the snail's pace at which he plays the entire
first movement of the "Appassionata" is surely unparalleled for
audacity in the entire history of recorded piano music. It is all done
without sympathy and yet with a peculiar kind of intimate understanding which conveys at every moment a real, if hardly attractive,
picture of the music.

Gould gives more comfortable performances of other Beethoven
sonatas, in inverse proportion to their fame and the scope of their
ambition. The same can be said of his playing of the bagatelles.
One set of these miniatures, opus 126, which is not only Beethoven's last major solo piano music but is also widely regarded as his
most simply wise, he plays heavily and humorlessly, but the altogether less demanding and less highly regarded set, opus 33, receives from him a bright and lively treatment. Nor is the story
different with the variations, for despite many individual felicities
in his performances of the massive "Eroica" and the smaller C-
Minor set, it is only in the relatively unknown F-Major Variations
that Gould allows listeners to feel relaxed and protected from the
surprises he regularly administers elsewhere.

Paradoxically, but in a manner consistent with his general line
of development, Gould's finest Beethoven is not a piano piece at
all, but the Fifth Symphony. Though Gould has always eschewed
the music of Franz Liszt, he nonetheless chose to record the Beethoven Fifth in Liszt's monumental transcription. As a transcriber,
Liszt often felt free to "improve" compositions by the less great,
but here he is remarkably faithful to Beethoven in notes and spirit,
and so is Gould: in this work he seems fully in his element, playing
brilliantly, directly, and powerfully—perhaps because, in this Beethoven at least, he feels an emotional effect produced by content,
not rhetoric. Musically his conception of the work bears comparison
with the performances of the greatest conductors, and pianistically
only Horowitz has brought equally impressive command (but in
musically less demanding material) to the playing of compositions
already famous in their original form.

Another of Gould's ventures into transcriptions has turned out
less happily. Something of a Wagnerian, he himself, in 1973,
transcribed some of the best-known of the composer's works: the
*Siegfried Idyll,* the Dawn and Siegfried's Rhine Journey from *Götter-*

*dämmerung,* and the prelude from *Die Meistersinger.* (Considering the many notes Gould added, adapted is perhaps a better word than transcribed.) But whereas the Beethoven Fifth Symphony is "pure" music in that it is not bound to the specific timbres produced by the instruments for which it is written, Wagner's operas are a different matter; their musical and emotional effects are closely linked to the individual sounds and capabilities of the exact instruments Wagner had in mind. Thus, the inevitable outcome of playing Wagner on the neutral and in any case different-sounding piano is that the *Siegfried Idyll,* for example, sounds (in Gould's performance) like static musing rather than the ecstatic serenade Wagner wrote to celebrate the birthday of his wife, Cosima, who had six months earlier given birth to the son of his old age. And toward the end of the *Meistersinger* prelude, after having been required at the opening to replace orchestral majesty by pianistic clatter, Gould is forced to resort to the practice of overdubbing (the combination of two separate "takes") to make possible the simultaneous performance of the three main themes as set forth by the composer. And yet, regardless of these shortcomings, who but Gould in the contemporary musical world would have made such an attempt?

Glenn Gould today is solely a recording artist, his playing confined to those discs he wishes to make and have issued. Indeed this has been the case ever since his retirement from the concert stage in 1964, at the age of thirty-one. Yet fortunately more survives than the memory of concertgoers to make clear just what Gould was as a live rather than a record performer. One document in particular fittingly preserves the last time he appeared with an orchestra in New York City, which was also one of the most significant performances of his entire career: his playing of the Brahms D-Minor Concerto with Leonard Bernstein and the New York Philharmonic.

Simply put, this performance (in existence today because the concert was broadcast and preserved on tape by collectors) was a scandal. It began with a disclaimer from the conductor, who spoke to the audience of irreconcilable differences with the soloist. Bernstein then wondered aloud why he did not get another soloist, or an assistant to conduct in his place. He answered his own question by explaining that Gould's performance was a chance for a new look at a familiar piece, that sometimes in Gould's playing the music emerged with force and clarity, and that everyone could learn from an artist of Gould's caliber. These noble sentiments were somewhat vitiated by the final reason he gave, to the accompaniment of occasional muted laughter from the hall, for going ahead with the concert: there was a "sportive" element in music and it had been an adventure collaborating for one week with Gould.

Judging now from the tape, one can see why Bernstein was concerned. The familiar opening movement (marked *Maestoso* though customarily played in a much faster *Allegro*) is begun by the orchestra—plainly at the soloist's desire—in a strong six beats to the bar instead of the customary two. So unused is the orchestra to the initial tempo that the players have difficulty at first keeping together. Although by the time the piano enters the pace has been firmly established for several minutes, the first solo bars are still a shock. Then, at least for some, the shock wears off, to be succeeded by an appreciation of Gould's courage in approaching the music as a symphony rather than a pianist's vehicle, as if what counts are the notes and not the brilliance with which they are gotten through. All in all, the performance—including Gould's beautifully serious playing of the slow movement, and despite Bernstein's heavy-handed conducting—remains a moving as well as a spectacularly individual execution of the work.

But for those who, at the time, had in their ears the ruling memory of countless traditional performances, the whole thing was too much to bear. One of the enraged was Harold Schonberg of the *New York Times,* whose sarcastic review took the form of a report to an imaginary piano fan named Ossip, and was written in a dialect approaching that of the Lower East Side. Throughout, Schonberg refers to the pianist as "the Gould boy." About his choice of tempos, the critic writes that "The reason he plays it so slow is maybe his technique is not so good." Some difficult passages Schonberg "couldn't hear so good, but the inner voices . . . he played good and clear. He should be proud, Ossip. He invented them." Schonberg ends the review by complimenting the assistant who had conducted a Nielsen overture at the concert; he calls him "very good. I mean, Ossip, he's a professional. Not like some pianists I could name."

While the tone of the *Times* review may disqualify it as a reasoned statement about a musical event, Schonberg's response was no doubt reflective of a large section of sophisticated musical opinion, and can hardly have been without effect on the artist who thus found himself held up to derision and obloquy. Only Glenn Gould himself knows what the reception accorded his Brahms Concerto did to his own attitude toward his career and his future. He had often talked of giving up the concert stage some day, but the actual chronology is suggestive: his decision to stop playing at the end of the 1963–64 season must have been made, given the customary lead time in booking and contract signing, about the spring of 1962, the same time as the Brahms incident. But whatever the real state of affairs may have been, there can be little doubt that the incident surrounded Gould's retirement from concert life with an aura of failure rather than triumph.

Nevertheless, by any standards wider than those of the concert business, Glenn Gould has triumphed. And unlike those who have made great careers by pandering to their audience, Gould has had his success on his own terms. To an even greater extent than the publicly touchy Vladimir Horowitz, Gould plays the music he wants to play in the often deeply unsettling way he chooses to play it. Given the pressures to conform in the musical world, one wonders how he has found the resources to be different and to survive in that difference, and what accounts for his unique public acceptance.

Material to answer the first question—only supplementing, of course, Gould's playing itself—lies primarily in his large and windy mass of written and spoken words. The spoken words are most easily available on a Columbia bonus LP (1968) entitled *Glenn Gould, Concert Dropout,* and his written words are frequently on the jackets of his records. Excerpts from all of this, along with copious analyses and philosophical speculations, have been assembled in a recent book by the Canadian musician and academic Geoffrey Payzant, *Glenn Gould, Music and Mind.*[1] This wealth of explanatory material provides a rare opportunity to understand a performing artist's work from the human and intellectual as well as the musical standpoint.

Before the sources and significance of Gould's dissent can be discussed, though, a subsidiary (and perhaps ultimately misleading

1. Van Nostrand Reinhold, 1978. Payzant's book includes a thorough listing of Gould's writings and a complete and informative catalogue of the pianist's records.

and irrelevant) matter must be disposed of. Much has been made, by Gould as well as by his admirers and detractors, of his choice of recording over concerts. The pianist has not been bashful in urging recorded music as the wave of the future, replacing the old-fashioned and moribund concert atmosphere with a medium in which music can find continued and new life. In addition, of all artists he has been the most frank in discussing the manipulative and transforming procedures used in making recordings. These procedures can only be described as unprecedented in the degree to which they disregard the old ideal of a recording as a copy of a continuous, real-time musical performance. To Gould, splicing is king, for it permits, without any audible evidence of the fact, the linking at will of elements of any length from any number of different "takes."

The purpose of this splicing is not just to remedy errors, though Gould does use the technique to produce a note-perfect result. More importantly, multiple "takes" enable him to approach a recording session with no fixed conception of a work; at the session he can try out a variety of conceptions and afterward, during the editing process, select what seems to him to have worked well. He is thus fully free, after the physical act of playing is over, to yoke passages from radically opposed views of the music and forge them into one final performance. It is an article of faith with him that the listener is not only unaware of all this chicanery—Gould calls it being "creatively dishonest"—but is actually the beneficiary of a more integrated, because more consciously put together, performance.

Still, Gould's preference for recording and its technology aside, it cannot be said that there is any fundamental discontinuity between what is remembered of his concert playing—and confirmed by the Brahms Concerto tape—and the evidence of his records. If one ignores inconsequential finger-slips, Gould's playing in both formats is identical in its characteristic features of freedom, discipline, and originality, and also in its ability to charm the receptive listener and infuriate the nonreceptive. All in all, it is likely that Gould's love affair with recording turns on personal factors; there seem to be no overriding musical reasons for the choice.

Any attempt to analyze the real wellsprings of Gould's special position in music must begin by recognizing the imponderables of a musical talent verging in many respects on genius. At the foundation of his great abilities lie almost unrivaled digital skills. Exemplary among these are effortless clarity and evenness in running passages, and seemingly total control over the touch and dynamic level of separate thematic lines being played simultaneously. In particular it is this technical control over melodic material that makes for the most notable feature—at least to nonmusicians—of Gould's playing: his delight and sometimes trancelike absorption in pure melody.

On a more self-conscious level, Gould is a calculating thinker whose decisions, though arising out of fundamental musicality, are informed by a streak of healthy perversity. His recorded answer to the question of why his tempos are always different from those of other pianists is relevant: "If there's any excuse at all for making a recording it's to do [the composition] differently . . . as if it's never been heard before." In some cases—such as the recordings of Mozart and Beethoven discussed earlier—his playing is instantly recognizable for its audacious idiosyncrasy. And even where the differences from tradition are not so blatant or where, as in the case of the Brahms Concerto, they are respectfully based on the composer's own directions, Gould's individuality remains unmistakable.

Perhaps too little attention has been paid to the way in which Gould's characteristic orientation to performance tradition has been shaped by the fact that he is a Canadian. What discussion there has been of nationality as a musical influence on his development has too often been restricted to a stereotyped view of Canadians as moody loners given to introspection and misanthropy. It seems more pertinent to link Gould's freedom from the crushing weight of musical convention to the relative lack of sophistication in Canadian musical life a generation ago, and its resultant powerlessness to exert a conforming influence on this extravagantly talented man. It was precisely the provincialism—so amply documented in Payzant's book—of the world in which Gould grew up that allowed him not only the freedom to develop in his own way but also the ability to retain a primitive and childlike faith in his own rightness vis-à-vis his contemporaries.

All these factors are, however, no more than necessary preconditions for survival; Gould has now been showing for a full quarter-century that he has the staying power to remain at the top in a fiercely competitive world. How has he managed this victory so completely on his own terms? Basically, by his willingness, which sometimes seems to verge on compulsion, to go beyond the piano to express his talents. This internal compulsion may well explain his notorious habit of singing as he plays, a habit that has required the use of special recording techniques to minimize the resultant intrusive noise and still causes much negative critical comment. Many explanations, fancy and homely, have been advanced to account for this mannerism, which the pianist himself would like to conquer. Most pianists sing because their fingers won't obey them; it seems that Gould sings because the piano is inadequate to express his musical vision, and his voice serves him in fantasy as a fulfilling instrument.

More constructively, Gould has gone beyond the piano and its traditions by spending a considerable part of his energies in exploring the wider musical repertory. Besides unfamiliar piano music, he has played more of the Bach harpsichord literature than any other famous virtuoso pianist in memory. In addition, he has recorded part of Bach's *The Art of the Fugue* on the organ and some Handel suites on the harpsichord. In this connection one can understand the importance for Gould of his performance of the Beethoven Fifth Symphony in Liszt's transcription and Wagner's works in his own. Indeed, should he wish to continue along this line of development and become a conductor—even if only on records—his qualifications would be high.

In considering Gould's ability to transcend the piano, it must not be forgotten that he is also that rarity among today's performing musicians, a composer. Unfortunately, only a single major work of his can now be heard, the String Quartet, opus 1 (1953–55). One large work is hardly enough to make a serious reputation as a composer; still, this unfairly neglected quartet, obviously derived from romantic early Schoenberg but no less beautiful because of that derivation, is sufficient to demonstrate that Gould's compositional talent is major. And as in the case of such gifted predecessors as Schnabel and Wilhelm Furtwängler, there can be little doubt that thinking as a composer has provided Gould the performer with a range of musical choices hardly available to artists whose mental horizons are limited to the more or less accurate re-creation of the works of others.

Moreover, as a creative artist, Gould has gone entirely beyond music itself. Since his retirement from the concert stage, much of his time has been spent on nonmusical activities. As one of Canada's favorite cultural sons he has had easy access to the state-run broadcasting system. For the CBC he has made innovative radio programs about the Canadian heritage, using montage techniques derived from his own recording experiences, and for both the CBC and the French ORTF he has produced television films on music and related subjects.

Despite all these activities Gould is still best known as a pianist, and the clearest sign of his public acceptance is his commercial success as a recording artist. Such success requires an enthusiastic public of a size possessed by few serious artists today. Yet it is strange, given the size of his public, and given the present concentration of performers on audience response, that Gould's following among music lovers should not be matched by a commensurate favor with those for whom music is a profession. It is not simply that the reviews, after the early years of his concert career, have so often been mixed and grudging. It is rather that Gould's playing has been largely without influence on colleagues and the countless piano students of his generation. Even where he might be thought at first glance to have had such an influence—in the tendency toward drier and clearer performances of Bach—the trend was present and gaining strength long before him and stemmed more from general musicological and technological considerations than from the work of any one person. Where Gould's playing has been totally and startlingly original—the Brahms Concerto may serve as the supreme if not the only example—his contribution has been ignored by musicians where it has not been reviled. The reasons for this rejection—often, lack of imagination or courage—hardly do credit to today's musical world.

Many theories have been advanced to explain Gould's success with the wider musical public: his personal eccentricity, the memory of his tortured platform demeanor, and the general fascination of the contemporary audience with stage figures who can be viewed as being in some kind of emotional trouble. But another possibility must be considered—namely, that relatively unsophisticated listeners are capable of responding strongly and enthusiastically to what they can perceive as musical power, commitment, and skill. That the untutored should, on occasion, reach sounder judgments than professionals should not be all that surprising. Indeed, colleagues, critics, and students are not the only judges of music, for the very conformity to tradition that makes them indispensable as conservers can function both to rob their own work of interest and to disable them as judges of a single, enormously rare, enormously gifted individual.

Still, to hail Gould's achievement is not to suggest that its particular substance should be imitated. For what Gould has done is not to give definitive performances, but to prove again that old pieces, no matter how great and how familiar, can be seen as new and heard as if for the first time. For this he deserves the gratitude of all who still cherish a vision of musical performance as an independent art.

[1979]

## 2. An Obituary

Glenn Gould is dead. He was the most individual performing musician of his generation, and his passing at the age of fifty removes the one pianist from the musical scene who seemed to have the ability to say something new and interesting about familiar— and overfamiliar—music.

When he gave concerts—which he did widely until 1964—they were wildly successful with audiences and often even with music critics. For almost twenty years thereafter, until his death in Toronto last month, he confined himself to recorded performances. The records he made sold steadily, in quantities far surpassing those of his colleagues.

Gould's recording career began in 1955 with the monumental "Goldberg" Variations of Bach; it ended (at least as far as releases during his lifetime were concerned) with the same work, recorded in 1981 and made available to the public in September to coincide with the pianist's fiftieth birthday. The first recording created nothing short of a sensation; the second has received critical approval no less favorable, though understandably less surprised. What had seemed serious in the new performance when heard before Gould's death now seems premonitory. The news that he had planned to give up the piano after he turned fifty—because he felt he had nothing further to say—can only intensify the impression of heaviness and doom that Gould's last rethinking of the work makes.

In between these two Bach recordings Gould made tens of discs, delving heavily not only into Bach but also into Mozart and Beethoven. At his hands the solo pieces of Brahms were a rare combination of charm and seriousness. He recorded piano works of Schoenberg and of Hindemith, and even music as far away from his affinity for Bach as Scriabin and Prokofiev. He did a brilliant performance of such a virtuoso task as the Liszt transcription of the Fifth Symphony of Beethoven; he made his own striking version of the *Meistersinger* prelude and recorded it. He was a composer, too, and his String Quartet, recorded many years ago but now out of print, remains an enormously talented reworking of early Schoenberg, deeply moving, for all its derivativeness, and never less than brilliantly accomplished as a composition.

Though his playing of Bach was widely admired—at least by those who admit the possibility of performing such music on the piano—and though his recordings of late romantic and contemporary music were appreciated, his conceptions of Mozart and Beethoven hardly fared as well. His way of doing these universally admired works seemed to be a throwing of so many red flags in the faces of our musical arbiters. Slow where custom decreed fast, fast where it decreed slow, staccato where everyone played legato, such music played in this way seemed to many unrecognizable.

But so strong was Gould's musical spark that what began as shock for his listeners ended, at least for many, in acceptance. Part of his ability to convince undoubtedly lay in his manifest conviction about the supreme value of what he was doing. This aura of conviction was strongly reinforced, as is often the case in major performing-arts careers, by the personal idiosyncrasies he so prominently flaunted. All of his many quirks were exploited by his commercial agents and seized upon by the press.

But to stop here and identify Gould the musician with Gould the neurotic would be to miss what made him a great artist. He possessed an unparalleled ability to shape the musical line and to articulate complex contrapuntal patterns at the same time; all that he did was always at the service of what can only be called his fancy. How he was able to accomplish all this, music teachers will puzzle over for decades to come. There is little doubt that they will fail to unlock the puzzle.

Now that he is dead, the predictable tributes—this one among them—are rolling in. He received the accolade of a front-page obituary, continued on a full inside page, in the *New York Times*. The *Times* properly stressed Gould's accomplishments, including his making of radio documentaries. Unfortunately missing, here at least, was an account of the famous performances by Gould of the Brahms D-Minor Concerto with Leonard Bernstein and the New York Philharmonic in 1962. Here, in Carnegie Hall, Gould made his most courageous attack on received opinion; it was the last great moment in his public performing career.

He had the temerity to play the first movement of the concerto slowly, in accord with Brahms's own tempo designation of *Maestoso*, rather than the customary *Allegro*. Bernstein was so aghast at this iconoclasm that he spoke to the audience just before Gould came on stage, abjuring all responsibility for the enormity that was to come. No one felt this enormity more than Harold Schonberg, then music critic of the *Times*.

Schonberg wrote his review in dialect, in the form of an imaginary conversation with an old colleague. He accused Gould of having invented nonexistent inner voices, of playing the concerto at slower than practice tempo because, in Schonberg's words, "maybe his technique is not so good." And he called him "the Gould boy." Heard today, on a broadcast tape, Gould's conception seems viable, thought out, magisterial—and his own.

For music lovers everywhere, his death will be a loss. For Canada as a nation the loss will be especially keen. Gould was by far the most important musician Canada has ever produced, and perhaps its most important artistic figure of any kind whatever. These are difficult days for Canada, racked by structural economic woes, sluggish foreign markets, insecure nationalism, breakaway provinces, and the extremes of bilingualism. Partly as a response to internal problems and partly out of the usual governmental attempt to force-feed cultural growth, Canada has been involved in a lavish and ultimately disappointing program of supporting the arts. There will now be an understandable tendency to react to Gould's death by hatching the usual halls and scholarships and archives in the name of the departed.

But all these projects will inevitably have the effect of replacing one great artist with many little ones. What Gould did with his art is not replicable; he was an original, and those who will follow him must be original as well. They will not become so by being told to worship at a shrine, nor will they become so by being urged to see in Glenn Gould an example of a specifically Canadian art. The influences on Gould were international; they were the great composers. It seems he responded to them so strongly because Canada provided him with the freedom to react in his own way to the material he chose for himself. This is the way, if not to make artists, to allow artists to make themselves. This Gould richly did, and one can only hope that those responsible for Canadian cultural life will continue to allow his successors to do as much.

[1982]

# Karajan:
## The Berlin Philharmonic on Two Coasts

The Berlin Philharmonic, under the direction of Herbert von Karajan, came to our shores in October to play eight concerts. The first four of these concerts were given in New York's Carnegie Hall; the last four took place in an auditorium in Pasadena, California.

Orchestra touring is hardly a rarity today. American groups—notably the New York Philharmonic and the Boston Symphony—regularly tour the United States, and circle the globe as well. Foreign orchestras too come here regularly. Already, during October and November, the Vienna Symphony Orchestra, the Amsterdam Concertgebouw, the Netherlands Chamber Orchestra, the Gewandhaus Orchestra of Leipzig, the Orchestre Philharmonique de France, the Prague Symphony Orchestra, the Chamber Orchestra of Turin, and the Polish Chamber Orchestra have appeared at Carnegie Hall. Indeed, so frequent is the phenomenon of the traveling orchestra that local orchestras now seem increasingly national and international.

Even so, an American tour by the Berlin Philharmonic remains a special attraction. The contemporary manifestation of a great tradition, the Berlin group is now one hundred years old. Its first chief conductor was Hans von Bülow, the son-in-law of Franz Liszt and later the cuckolded disciple of Richard Wagner. The orchestra's second leader was Arthur Nikisch, who succeeded Bülow in 1894. In 1913 the Berlin Philharmonic, under Nikisch's baton, made the first recording of a complete symphony. From 1922 to 1954, Berlin's chief conductor was Wilhelm Furtwängler, the master of a particularly German emotionalism in the performance of the great romantic masterworks.

Under Bülow and Nikisch, the orchestra's glories were musical, its problems financial. Under Furtwängler the musical glories and the financial problems remained, but to them was added the new and almost lethal contribution of Hitler and Nazism. Though Furtwängler attempted to perform such "degenerate" composers as Paul

Hindemith despite the Nazi ban, and though by most accounts he attempted to protect non-Aryan members of the orchestra against the provisions of the Nuremberg laws, in the end he too capitulated, neither retiring from public life nor choosing, as did such famous musicians as the brothers Adolf and Fritz Busch (and Hindemith himself), to join the "other Germany" in exile. Under Furtwängler the orchestra continued to play even after its concert hall was bombed out. Though the quality of its work suffered from the expulsion of Jewish players, it continued under Furtwängler to give concerts notable for their passionate commitment and air of high tension. Recordings of live performances from this time, many of them still available, constitute a peculiar testimony to the ability of great musical performance to exist with every kind of tyranny.

Furtwängler's last years with the orchestra before his death, in 1954, were marked by some great music making, though his most significant work—the performances of Wagner's *Ring* at La Scala and in Rome—was done with other orchestras. These declining years were marred by his gathering egomania and a progressive deafness (his podium in Berlin had to be wired for sound). So strong, however, was the Berlin Philharmonic's dependence on Furtwängler that his death on the threshold of the orchestra's first American tour threatened to be catastrophic. Fortunately, Herbert von Karajan was ready and willing to assume Furtwängler's mantle; so ready was he, in fact, that as a condition of his coming in he insisted on being made conductor for life. He got his way. For close to thirty years he has been identified with the Berlin Philharmonic.

Karajan was born in 1908. He first came to public attention in the small town of Ulm, where at the age of twenty-two he became the head of the local opera house. From Ulm he graduated to Aachen, where both his responsibilities and the standards of performance were on a much higher level. In 1938 he conducted the Berlin Philharmonic as a guest and caused something of a sensation. An invitation from the Berlin State Opera soon followed, but the successful young conductor was unwilling to accept the offer of a debut in a lightly regarded modern opera. Instead he demanded—and got—performances of *Fidelio, Tristan,* and *Die Meistersinger.* Here, in an important review perhaps owing something of its enthusiasm to Nazi backing (Karajan had, for opportunistic reasons, joined the party in 1935), he was hailed in an important Berlin newspaper as *Das Wunder Karajan*—"the miracle Karajan."

He was now securely established. During the war, he continued to conduct at the Berlin State Opera. At the end of the war, not surprisingly, he was seen as something of a Nazi sympathizer and was therefore initially unacceptable to the victorious allies. But in 1946 he conducted the Vienna Philharmonic. Then he came under the patronage of Walter Legge, the powerful head of artists and repertory for English Columbia, a branch of EMI. In 1947 Karajan first came to London to conduct Legge's newly founded Philharmonia Orchestra. Here, as in Vienna, he made a series of well-received recordings, including a famous rendition of Strauss's *Der Rosenkavalier* with Elisabeth Schwarzkopf (Legge's wife) as the Marschallin.

At the same time, too, he was conducting at Bayreuth, where his 1951 performances of *Die Meistersinger* and the *Ring* set standards of orchestral playing that remain to this day. Along the way he became head of the Vienna Opera. His seven-year tenure there, from 1957 to 1964, was stormy and finally ended in acrimony. He conducted often at Salzburg, at La Scala in Milan, and at most other centers of European musical life. So busy was he that he was called the *Generalmusikdirektor* of Europe. It was told of Karajan that upon being asked by a taxi driver where he wanted to be taken, he answered: "It doesn't matter. They want me everywhere." And he made records by the score, at first for EMI, then for Decca, in recent years for Deutsche Grammophon. These discs have sold in the millions and have carried the gospel of Karajan worldwide.

Karajan's activities these days are fairly restricted, and his association with the Berlin Philharmonic takes precedence over everything else he does in music. Though it is a cooperative orchestra in which new members are chosen by the incumbents, subject only to the conductor's veto, the ensemble plainly reflects the care and thought Karajan has given it, especially in lavish rehearsal time, during which he has been able to instill in minute detail his musical conceptions.

The programs announced for the four Carnegie Hall concerts did not, on their face, seem terribly exciting. Strauss's *Alpine Symphony*, an overlong potboiler in the guise of a virtuoso showpiece, was mated on the first concert with Stravinsky's chaste and refined ballet score *Apollo*; the four symphonies of Brahms were divided between the second and third concerts; the final concert was devoted solely to Mahler's Ninth Symphony. The Pasadena programs presented the Strauss and the Stravinsky, two Brahms symphonies, the Beethoven Fifth and Sixth Symphonies, and, once again on the final night, the Mahler Ninth.

Because the Strauss is such meager music, because the Stravinsky is hardly a German romantic specialty, and because the Brahms symphonies are so often done, the most interesting program in New York seemed to be the Mahler. Here was one of the best of Mahler's symphonies played by a great orchestra under the leadership of a conductor who, for whatever political and musical reasons, had come late to that composer's music. The work had been remarkably suited to the conducting abilities and the personal style of Pierre Boulez; his performance of the work during his sojourn with the New York Philharmonic had presented the orchestra in a flattering and unaccustomed light. The piece was one of Bruno Walter's favorites, too, and his performances of it, in some sense profiting from Walter's early association with Mahler and his music (he had conducted the work's premiere in 1912), are still to be found in record catalogues.

Heard playing the Mahler in Carnegie Hall, the Berlin Philharmonic seemed nothing less than a revelation. In smoothness alone the orchestra seemed to invite immediate comparison with an expensive automobile. For those used to the harsh, rough sounds of the New York Philharmonic the Berlin string tone appeared almost supernatural. *Pizzicati* were always together, and sudden dynamic contrasts were achieved with an ease that only increased the impression of suddenness. First-chair string players performed their solos not only with absolute security—that, with the Berlin, is quickly taken for granted—but also with such sweet comfort and effortless virtuosity that characteristic sonic differences between violin, viola, and cello were almost obliterated.

Among the winds, the emphasis was on lightness and grace. The bassoon playing in particular was delicate without any concomitant loss in strength. The flutes too were remarkable; the oboes, *mirabile dictu,* completely lacked the coarse and aggressive tone so much in favor today with larger American musical institutions. The brass played penetratingly without being in any way forward; the trumpets in particular were models of discretion. Missing everywhere was any hint of the musical conception so widespread in our own national style of orchestral playing: the idea that large-scale symphonies are in fact concertos for brass and tympani masquerading under another name.

The total effect of it all was to make Carnegie Hall sound like the great hall that it is, but that it rarely (given what takes place on its stage) has a chance today to be. Here were the glorious acoustics one never gets in Fisher Hall. Here was strength, clarity and lightness, fullness without vulgarity. One's gratitude was so strong that one could not help feeling that the Berlin Philharmonic is the greatest orchestra before the public today.

Without doubt, the lion's share of responsibility for the triumphant impression the Berliners made in this concert must be assigned to its conductor. The physical bearing alone of the string players, sitting at the front of the stage, their legs uncrossed, their bodies taut with anticipation, their expressions conveying eagerness and commitment, proclaimed that here was an orchestra with a respected and vastly powerful director. Given the orchestra's important role in personnel decisions, this power clearly does not stem, as it does in other groups, from the conductor's power to hire and fire. It plainly comes from musical authority, constantly exerted and willingly accepted. The achievement of such an ascendancy over a body of musicians, by itself, securely establishes Karajan as a great conductor. He is certainly the most important conductor to have emerged since World War II.

Such high praise hardly requires that Karajan's conception of orchestral playing remain beyond critical comment. In music, as in life, achievements are made at the cost of other achievements. In the case of Karajan and the Berlin Philharmonic, the striking prominence of rounded melody is often the result of the suppression of inner, less obviously important, parts. These parts are purposely played so softly and so gently that they cease to be heard as distinguishable lines and can only be felt as harmonies. The orchestra itself is capable of remarkable clarity, as explicitly contrapuntal passages frequently demonstrated. It is rather Karajan's musical decision that the audience be given at almost all times only one thing to listen to; that one thing is properly, by his lights, the most easily perceptible melody.

As if to prove that not even Karajan—and a Berlin Philharmonic —is perfect, on one important occasion in the Mahler performance the orchestral leadership and performance were flawed. When a sudden change from a slower to a faster tempo was called for, neither the conductor nor the orchestra seemed in control of what was happening. At one point in the symphony's second movement, Mahler requires a second tempo *Poco più mosso subito* (a small amount faster immediately) and then, after several tempo changes and a *ritardando,* a sudden return to the *Poco più mosso subito,* this time *aber etwas schneller als das erstemal* (but somewhat faster than the first time). All went well enough at the first speedup, but at the further increase in tempo, the ensemble was ragged, the effect both heavy and tacky. The responsibility was obviously Karajan's. In this case, his method of communicating (eyes closed) expressive intentions rather than rhythmic directions hardly sufficed.

Beyond this instance of the failure of directorial control and orchestra response, there was a wider problem of Karajan's conception of the Mahler symphony. Enormously attractive as it was, it all seemed an approach to Mahler for people who (like this writer) don't really like Mahler. Karajan seemed at pains to avoid what might be called a "woodsy" Mahler, a musical evocation of Vienna and Austria at once sentimental and rustic. This kind of Mahler was the specialty of, among others, both Bruno Walter and the Dutch conductor Willem Mengelberg. Even Boulez, through a certain roughness, paid tribute to this idea of the composer. But for Karajan, Mahler seems a species of Bruckner, or rather a domesticated version of Bruckner's idol Richard Wagner. Indeed, Karajan plays Mahler the way he plays Wagner: classically, symphonically in an older, pre-late-romantic sense, emphasizing a surface delicacy and transparency. Real Mahlerians doubtless find this approach reserved, cold, and even bloodless.

But whether one adores Mahler or not, Mahler still remains Mahler: romantic, not classical, peripheral to the orchestral repertory rather than solidly at its core. For this reason, one of the subsequent Pasadena concerts—the third—seemed particularly significant. Here, in the Beethoven Sixth, followed by the Fifth, Karajan and his orchestra confronted undenied musical greatness. Here also, as in the other Pasadena concerts, one had a chance to hear this magnificent orchestra in a small, 1,200-seat hall (at Ambassador College). Because the symphonies of Beethoven were not written to be heard in such enormous halls as Carnegie, with its capacity of 2,800, Pasadena provided an opportunity to evaluate the conductor and his players intimately, to find out whether they sounded as good up close as they had from afar.

At this concert at least, the verdict must be mixed. On the positive side, it must be said that the sounds the group made at the Ambassador Auditorium were never too loud, despite the large size of the orchestra. Still, the close-to-perfection of the New York performance of Mahler was missing in the Pasadena performances of Beethoven. Part of the disappointment lay in the orchestral execution itself; string intonation was sometimes wayward, and the horn and trumpet playing displayed some of the clumsiness often found in the brass choirs of lesser ensembles when they play Beethoven. Rhythm—particularly in the differentiation between eighth and sixteenth notes—seemed often so slack as to verge on sloppiness. Sometimes too the orchestra seemed sluggish in those loud passages that also were fast, as if it was too much of an effort to do both at the same time.

Some of the orchestra's problems in this concert were doubtless due to an understandable letdown after playing to such acclaim in New York. Some of this listener's reaction too was undoubtedly caused by the paradoxical acoustics of Ambassador Auditorium, where the X-ray effect of closeness in making mistakes audible was not balanced by a parallel gain in clarity. But even on this less than ideal occasion, some of the playing was miraculous. The marvelously clear and unforced but always projected execution of the fugato by the cellos and basses in the third movement of the Fifth Symphony was a case in point; another was the remarkable wind playing—again from the bassoons—in the fourth movement of the Sixth Symphony.

Beethoven, of course, is more difficult to play than Mahler, and not just for the orchestra. Not only must the conductor compete against every great recorded predecessor or present performing colleague; he must manage to perform the music straight, without noticeable divergence from the composer's written directions; at the same time he must suffuse everything with his personality in a way that marks off his realization of the music from that of everyone else. So difficult is this to do that it often seems we are living in a time of no great Beethoven conductors at all.

It can hardly be said that Karajan, at least in this particular concert in Pasadena, satisfactorily met the challenge. At the very beginning of the concert the first movement of the Sixth Symphony seemed to go even faster than Beethoven's already quick metronome indication. Karajan's tempi were fast throughout the evening, but their speed did not guarantee any real quality of excitement. The famous transition between the third and fourth movements of the Fifth Symphony, for example, was singularly ineffective. This passage, which conductors as different as Toscanini and Furtwängler have managed to make spellbinding, seemed in Karajan's treatment perfunctory; the famous arrival in C Major at the beginning of the fourth movement was spoiled by a straight-ahead pace and an even further bit of rushing on the downward curve of the opening phrase. And all Karajan's haste exacted a heavy toll at the end of the symphony. The *Sempre più allegro* and the subsequent *Presto* that closes the work were both ragged, with syncopations late and the general effect turgid rather than stirring.

And one feels that even had everything gone perfectly with the orchestral execution and Karajan's leadership on this warm Southern California evening, there would still have been something lacking. The lack may be in Karajan's idea of Beethoven. He seems to approach this music—and this approach is audible on his innumerable Beethoven recordings as well—with a peculiarly mixed style, as if he were not playing Beethoven but rather a music by someone else, which looks and sounds like Beethoven. That someone else may well be Wagner, whose *Ring* (along with the operas of Strauss) Karajan does better than any other conductor alive. Indeed, several passages in the Beethoven Sixth were reminiscent, in Karajan's rendition, of famous places in Wagner: the quiet end of the second movement seemed an anticipation of the end of Act II of *Die Meistersinger,* and the famous storm music later on in the symphony seemed straight out of the musical weather preceding the gods' entrance into Valhalla in *Das Rheingold.*

It must be said that Karajan's magnificent conception of Wagner is not a simple matter. He seems to treat this music as if it were a kind of Mozart, requiring not primordial weight and seriousness but rather translucence, lightness, and grace. But what is successful in Wagner's overwritten music is not so apt for Beethoven. The Beethoven of the largest symphonies is in dead earnest, the very epitome of musical (and moral) seriousness. To rush Beethoven, as

Karajan often does, is to lose touch with the music's general elevation, and not even to be able to project the excitement contained in
the specific passages Beethoven meant to go like the wind. Toscanini too, toward the end of his life, often lost contact with Beethoven when he rushed, but Toscanini at least always seemed totally
involved. Karajan, by contrast, often seems to be imperfectly committed to Beethoven.

On the next night, the first three movements of the Mahler
Ninth seemed to take up where the Beethoven had left off. The
orchestra did not seem as sharp as it had in New York, and total
integration which had characterized the earlier performance was
lacking. The orchestral tone, so marvelous in Carnegie Hall,
seemed both bottled up and grainy in the smaller hall; the important harp parts, so audible in Carnegie because of the instruments'
position at a front side of the stage, almost disappeared because of
the players' relegation back into the orchestra. And the places that
had suffered in ensemble in New York fared no better in Pasadena.

But then came one of those extended moments concertgoers
dream of but rarely experience. The fourth movement of the Ninth,
more than twenty minutes long, is distantly derived from the sublime slow movement of Beethoven's final string quartet, opus 135;
the two movements are even in the same key of D-flat Major, and
their melodic shapes (though not their prevailing emotional character) often seem close. But whereas Beethoven goes on from this
fairly brief lyrical episode to end his work with wit and even gaiety,
Mahler chooses to end his symphony with this slow movement, in
all its self-indulgent melodic concentration. In a great performance,
the result, though hardly life-inspiring, can be shattering.

Karajan's performance of the last movement of the Mahler in
Pasadena was indeed shattering. Seamless, breathless without being
hurried, gloriously played by the orchestra as a whole and at the
end by its solo strings, the total impression was not just of a
supreme orchestra playing under the inspired direction of a conductor of historical stature. Even more, one felt in direct contact with
the German approach to music as a whole, stressing at every moment the art as an ontological reality transcending the earthly
world. Here was not merely a *Liebestod,* a death through love, like
that with which Wagner provided *Tristan und Isolde.* Here was a
veritable *Musiktod,* a death through music.

That this stupendous achievement, so central to the idea of *deutsche Kultur,* came about in the playing of depressing music by a Central European Jew, by an orchestra that now looks back proudly upon its continued existence even during the satanic period of World War II, under the direction of a man whose past is not clean of Nazi affiliations and who himself came only very late to Mahler, should not surprise connoisseurs of the relationship between art and life. Painful though the experience may have been, it was better to have heard it than not.

[*1982*]

# The New Wave of Emigrés

For some time the papers have been full of stories about the flight of Soviet performers from their homeland. Consistent with the central role of ballet in Russian official culture and the recent dance boom in the West, most of the coverage has gone to the defection of well-known dancers from famous companies; merely to mention the names of Nureyev, Baryshnikov, and Makarova is to convey how great has been the Soviet loss. But celebrated though they are, only a few dance stars have defected. In fact, by far the greatest number of artists leaving the USSR have been musicians.

It is difficult to know just how many musicians have been involved in the current emigration. The process has been going on for the past ten years or so, and many countries have provided havens for the refugees. In the United States alone, enough émigrés have arrived to have already made their presence felt in the best orchestras. Furthermore, an orchestra consisting largely of these new arrivals appeared in Carnegie Hall last July to enthusiastic critical response. In the world of free-lance musicians the story is the same: competition from the ex-Soviet musicians in New York is now sufficiently noticeable to cause the beginnings of resentment from their native American colleagues. And on the educational level, similar developments are taking place. Our music schools, in New York and in the country at large, are hiring formerly Russian faculty, and at such distinguished institutions as Juilliard in the winter and Aspen in the summer, young Russian students are proving both ambitious and highly talented.

Most of these newcomers, of course, will of necessity find themselves filling the same kinds of subordinate and supporting roles they would have filled had they remained in the Soviet Union. A few, however, are aiming at nothing less than the highest artistic renown and commercial success. A spectacular case in point has been the triumphant career in the West of Mstislav Rostropovich, the world's leading cellist both before and after his enforced per-

manent exile from Russia. Now increasingly active as a conductor
—he is the music director of the National Symphony Orchestra in
Washington, D.C.—Rostropovich has been joined on this side of
the Iron Curtain by one of the most famous Soviet musicians, the
conductor Kiril Kondrashin. Indeed, this new defection must have
been particularly galling to the Russians, for Kondrashin had been
a popular cultural ambassador for the USSR since his collaboration
with Van Cliburn in Moscow and later in New York at the time of
the 1958 Tchaikowsky contest.

In an as yet less stellar way several other highly touted emigrés
have begun making careers as soloists in America. Among them are
the pianist Bella Davidovich and the violinists Nina Beilina and
Albert Markov. And there are former Russians now embarking on
careers who, in their homeland, were too young to have been anything more than students—for example, the pianist Youri Egorov
and the violinist Dmitri Sitkovetsky, Davidovich's son. Both of
these artists owe their prominence to contests in the West. Sitkovetsky recently won the important Fritz Kreisler Prize in Vienna,
and Egorov was so successful with the audience at the 1977 Cliburn
competition in Fort Worth that his exclusion there from the final
round (due, some said, to Soviet pressure) made him an instant
celebrity.

Why have so many representatives of an important musical culture left their country to seek refuge abroad in a different and
perhaps even alien world? In general, of course, it can hardly come
as a shock that some people want to leave the Soviet Union. The
uncomfortable conditions of daily material existence must be increasingly difficult to bear as knowledge of life in the West becomes
more diffused throughout Soviet society and the realistic possibility
of foreign travel increases. And among Jews—who are heavily represented in the musical life of the Soviet Union—the desire to leave
can easily be understood, as can the grudging willingness of a
suspicious government to let them go.

Still, one might have thought that musicians, because of their
special position in Soviet life, would prove a group at least reconciled to making the best of the opportunities offered them at home.
These opportunities are great, and all the more impressive for being
a feature of Russian life going back to the half-century before the
revolutions of 1917. The Czarist government encouraged music on

a large scale, both through official support of institutions and through personal, aristocratic patronage. Russian conservatories—chief among them those in Moscow and St. Petersburg—became models for the world; foreign specialists were brought in as needed, and for native Russians—indeed, especially for Jews—music quickly became a field in which rapid social advancement was possible in a notably stratified society. And increasingly, private, non-aristocratic philanthropy became effective and publicized, as the rising new middle classes entered on the stage of Russian economic and political history.

Going hand in hand with all this support was the magnificent achievement of Russian prerevolutionary music. Building upon a solid folk and church foundation, Russian composers from the middle of the nineteenth century on felt free to import what they needed from European models and at the same time, as in the case of Mussorgsky, were able to express something of the real national soul. Since Rimsky-Korsakov and Tchaikowsky in the last decades of the past century, Russian works have been a central part of the world repertory. Russians were also in the forefront of musical modernism; Scriabin, for example, was an avant-garde hero at home and abroad. By the time of World War I, leadership in Russian music had passed from the hands of the conservative melodist to the controversial Stravinsky and, somewhat later, to the *enfant terrible* Prokofiev.

As performers, Russians were even more prominent. In Anton Rubinstein they had produced a keyboard virtuoso in the class of Liszt, and such of his successors as Sergei Rachmaninoff maintained the standard. Russian violinists were just as important: Mischa Elman and Jascha Heifetz were only the brightest of the many stars produced by Leopold Auer, the St. Petersburg teacher who founded what has remained to this day the most influential school of violin playing the world has known.

Whatever the nihilistic implications of the Bolshevik revolution for other previously established economic and social classes, the new regime soon made clear that art in general and music in particular were more than ever to be nurtured by the state. Strenuous attempts were made to bring great music to the masses, both at their work sites and at the concert halls and schools from which they had, it was felt, formerly been excluded.

In the decade after 1917 many different approaches to composition, both Left and Right, continued to flourish in the Soviet Union. The meteoric rise of Dmitri Shostakovich began with his graduation piece (the First Symphony) from the Leningrad Conservatory in 1925. The new regime now had its first major composer, a world figure who had been trained since the revolution. And upon the return of Prokofiev in 1932 from self-imposed exile, the USSR was in the enviable position of having not just one but two celebrated artists able and seemingly willing to provide exciting new repertory for performers and audiences alike.

Though the purge years of the 1930s were felt in music, it seemed that musicians were less affected by physical violence and incarceration than other comparable groups in the USSR. Not only was Shostakovich quickly taken back into the fold after severe criticism from the highest levels in 1936; after some earlier difficulty, Prokofiev also found a warm welcome with his 1939 score for Eisenstein's film *Alexander Nevsky*. Throughout World War II—called in the Soviet Union "The Great Patriotic War"—musicians were protected, encouraged, and widely used as morale builders at home and propagandists for their country's cause to the world.

Similarly, while musical life once more felt political pressure after the war in the Zhdanov antiformalist campaign in 1948, musicians were still treated rather leniently, especially compared to writers. And after the death of Stalin, in 1953, Soviet composers began feeling freer to write a reasonably modern-sounding music. With the slightly later thaw in East-West relations, Soviet performers began to travel, and still may be the most frequently exported element of Russian society.

In the past thirty or so years the list of fabulously successful Soviet musicians on the world scene has not only included Shostakovich and (posthumously) Prokofiev, but also Khachaturian, whose "Sabre Dance" from the ballet *Gayane* became an international hit. Even more successful abroad have been Soviet performers, such as pianists Emil Gilels and Sviatoslav Richter and violinists Leonid Kogan and the late David Oistrakh. The supply of young Soviet performers following in the footsteps of these four masters has seemed unlimited, a sure sign of Soviet musical accomplishment and of the large-scale efforts in education and patronage devoted to its support.

Partly as a spin-off from the foreign success of Russian musicians and partly as a result of public policy and the operative values of Russian life, musicians, whatever their level of accomplishment, are highly respected members of Soviet society. They live, it would seem, somewhat better than comparable members of the Soviet nonscientific intelligentsia. In theory at least, they suffer no unemployment; the privileges and perquisites open to the ambitious and the competent range from housing through vacations nearby and travel abroad. To Soviet Jews in particular these opportunities are attractive; unlike many other Soviet professions, music remains at present open and even hospitable to them.

But if the musical state of affairs is seemingly desirable in the Soviet Union, why do so many musicians leave? Beyond the stereotyped bits seized upon by journalists and the private testimony of émigrés, little detailed, solid information about the daily lives and thoughts of Soviet musicians has as yet been published. But fortunately our knowledge about the conditions under which Soviet musicians work has been richly supplemented by the recent publication of the extraordinary memoirs, called simply *To Dance*, of Valery Panov,[1] the brilliant *demi-caractère* dancer of the Kirov ballet who with his wife, Galina, emigrated to Israel in 1974 after many years of suffering and struggle.

The picture that emerges from correlating Panov's experiences in the related field of ballet with the scattered comments of émigré musicians adds up to vastly more than the petty annoyances and irritations inevitable in a flourishing bureaucratic state. Indeed, it soon becomes clear that every putatively favorable feature of official policy toward the arts in the USSR is balanced and most often overbalanced by the use of support as a means of control and of the denial of support as a means of enforcement and punishment.

Thus, state-supported music schools, so lavishly endowed, are the only music schools; denial of admission to them, or failure after entrance, effectively closes off the possibility of a musical career. Composers must write to please the state or find their works unperformable. Even pieces written more than a half-century ago by such giants as Strauss are frequently banned. Concerts subsidized and presented by the state, though their ticket prices may be trifling,

1. This book is now available in paperback, Avon, 1979.

must feature state-approved performers; the audiences themselves at these concerts may, at the whim of the state, be restricted to notables and functionaries. Foreign tours scheduled by the state concert management take place in the context of official foreign political and economic policy; participation in them, perhaps the most desirable plum available today to Soviet citizens, may be, and frequently is, arbitrarily denied to anyone suspected of independence or political unreliability. Plainly, under socialism as under capitalism, those who pay the piper call the tune; but where there is only one payer—the state—there all too easily can be only one tune.

All this would be bad enough if bureaucratic enforcement and caprice were, in the post-Stalin years, limited to persuasion and the provision of enticing rewards. But in fact there is abundant evidence that behind the mechanisms of economic pressure and patriotic exhortation lies the ultimate sanction—the threat of terror. To assume, as is so often done, that the death of Stalin marked a fundamental structural change in the wielding of Soviet power is to forget that the organs of state security remain in place, and continue to employ methods of provocation and incarceration. The hands of both the Communist-party apparatus and the KGB are never far from any Russian citizen, and vastly closer to the members of as public a profession as music. And there is also memory: the generation slaughtered by Stalin and his henchmen was that of the parents of the middle-aged Russian of today.

Such a state of affairs applies with special force, as Panov stresses, to Jews, who at the best of times in Russia have been seen as inherently untrustworthy. When a Jew announces his decision to emigrate, the possibility of further life in the Soviet Union is snatched from him as he waits; and as is also true in the case of defectors, his family and former associates are forced to abase themselves publicly by condemning the renegade. Predictably, the ripple effect of such intimidation and humiliation is one of heightened fear and increased desire to leave.

Remarkably, this new musical emigration is not the first but the third in our century. It was preceded by the flight of artists from the Bolshevik revolution and its bloody aftermath, and then only a few years later by the exodus from Nazi Germany, Austria, and the lands overrun by Hitler.

The emigration from the fledgling Soviet Union after 1917 of composers alone was of the highest significance. Stravinsky, resident abroad during World War I and the 1917 revolutions, did not return to his homeland. Rachmaninoff, after a brief taste of life under the Bolsheviks, left at the end of 1917, never to return. Prokofiev left in 1918 and did not, as has been noted earlier, return until the 1930s. Sergei Diaghilev—important because of his energizing effect on musicians as well as on dancers and painters—also refused to return home to his country under Bolshevik rule. In the world of performance, Soviet losses were equally severe: such prodigious artists as the legendary basso Feodor Chaliapin, violinists Jascha Heifetz and Nathan Milstein, cellist Gregor Piatigorsky, conductor Serge Koussevitzky, and pianist Vladimir Horowitz were all exiles from Bolshevism.

The post-Hitler wave encompassed just about every well-known Jewish musical figure in continental Europe as well as some non-Jews endangered by marriage or advocacy of modernism. The composers included Arnold Schoenberg and Paul Hindemith from Germany and Béla Bartók from Hungary. The performers included such singers as Lotte Lehmann, Friedrich Schorr, and Elisabeth Schumann; pianists Artur Schnabel and Rudolf Serkin; violinists Adolf Busch, Bronislaw Huberman, and Joseph Szigeti; cellist Emanuel Feuermann; harpsichordist Wanda Landowska; conductors Bruno Walter and Otto Klemperer. And these artists were only the visible tip of the iceberg. Less well-known soloists and conductors, orchestra players by the hundreds, distinguished teachers, musicologists, and historians all fled the immediate threat of violence and death.

More was involved, of course, than all these many individuals; as a group they brought with them the heritage of the nineteenth-century golden age of music. Thus the Russian emigration provided the West with virtually the last composers to have written what are today widely accepted as classical masterpieces. Among these works are the three famous ballets of Stravinsky—*Firebird, Petrushka,* and *The Rite of Spring*—and Rachmaninoff's Second and Third Piano Concertos and his Second Symphony. Though these pieces were all done before the revolution, they were widely disseminated only after their composers had left Russia. Especially in the United States, their influence—conservative with Rachmaninoff and modernist with Stravinsky—was enormous in the sense both of inspiring imitators and of helping to close the classical canon.

The influence of early Russian émigré performers has been similarly great. The names of Horowitz and Heifetz are synonymous with musical stardom and its attendant riches and publicity, solidly based in both cases on the highest technical and musical accomplishment. Like Chaliapin before him, Horowitz in particular has been associated with Russian music; his playing of concertos by Rachmaninoff and Tchaikowsky has produced perhaps his greatest commercial success in concerts and on records.

If the genius of the post-1917 émigrés lay in an all-conquering and sometimes even exotic musical romanticism, the post-1933 émigrés specialized in high seriousness and profound intellectuality. Both Schoenberg and Hindemith, each in his own different way, were "pure" musicians, composers for the highly tutored. Deeply opposed to—and unfitted for—popular success, Schoenberg was the last great system builder music has known, and his mental constructs were to rule most of the world of musical composition for a half-century after he first promulgated them in the early 1920s. Hindemith's functional compositions, written respectfully in the musical spirit of J. S. Bach, were greatly effective, especially in the United States, in combating the public perception (itself to some extent a legacy from the earlier Russian émigrés) of music as an arena of tumultuous emotion and gladiatorial combat.

This predominantly cerebral quality extended to the performers of the Hitler emigration as well. Not only was Artur Schnabel celebrated for his programming of composers—Beethoven, Schubert, and Mozart—who made the greatest demands of concentration on the audience; he was known to an even more devoted audience as the scholarly editor of the most influential performing edition of the Beethoven piano sonatas produced in this century. The violinist Adolf Busch, brother of the brilliant Mozart opera conductor Fritz Busch, father-in-law of Rudolf Serkin (important both as pianist and director of the Marlboro Festival), and teacher of Yehudi Menuhin, used his performances of great music as if they were sermons on the superior morality of art. Equally high-minded was Wanda Landowska, a non-German émigré from Hitler: her famous remark to a colleague, "You play Bach your way, I will play him his way," epitomizes both her musical character and her public function.

Nor, in this context, can the nonperforming and noncomposing musical refugees of the 1930s be ignored. In Germany Alfred Einstein had been music critic of the *Berliner Tageblatt,* editor of the *Zeitschrift für Musikwissenschaft,* and editor of three revisions of Riemann's standard *Musiklexicon.* In the United States among his many writings were two widely read musico-historical classics: *Mozart, His Character, His Work* (1945) and the still-used textbook *Music in the Romantic Era* (1947). Going beyond music in itself, Theodor Adorno, a music critic as well as an exponent of the Frankfurt school of sociology, advised another Hitler émigré, Thomas Mann, on the passages in *Doctor Faustus* that are based upon Schoenberg's twelve-tone system. And as in other areas of music, every major American educational institution—and hundreds of minor ones—felt the analyzing and cataloguing presence of émigré European-trained musical minds.

Another factor, often overlooked, is that the Hitler emigration of musicians brought its own audience along with it. All over the United States, attendance at musical events was quickly marked by increasing numbers of refugee cognoscenti. In New York, for example, the Hunter College Saturday Night Series, until its demise in the 1970s the most distinguished recital series in America, was founded by and for these émigrés. As early as 1936, the New Friends of Music had been established in New York City not only as a successor to the old Friends of Music but also as a copy of and replacement for the *Gesellschaft der Musikfreunde* in Vienna; so successful was it in replicating European traditions that it was soon wittily christened the "Old Friends of Artur Schnabel."

What of the latest musical emigration? Is it bringing with it a glittering culture new to us, of a stature comparable to its illustrious predecessors? The answer, alas, seems to be no. At the outset it is clear that no composers of stature are included among the new arrivals. Though this absence is only consistent with the general paucity of such figures the world over, the lack means that the primary requirement of musical significance—important new music—can hardly be satisfied. Those who have left, in any case, are essentially performers.

The first major figure of the wave to leave the Soviet Union was the pianist Vladimir Ashkenazy, who departed in the 1960s. As a technician he is brilliant, and in the past has been infallible; as an interpreter he is satisfying in a restrained way; as an influence on either music or its performance he has not been important. The massive réclame surrounding Rostropovich (and his wife, soprano Galina Vishnevskaya) makes sound judgment of musical value more difficult than in the case of the rather colorless Ashkenazy. Yet even here it can be said that Rostropovich's conducting—with the extravagant gestures and bearlike personal charm that have won him so much public affection—falls far short of his cello playing in musical depth and technical skill. And even in the cello world, where Rostropovich has for many years been king, Pablo Casals (a refugee in the 1930s from Franco's Spain) remains the most significant influence on both his colleagues and the aural memory of the audience. As for the newest star arrival, Kondrashin, he is still an unknown creative quantity, all too firmly associated to his detriment with the overplayed Russian classics.

This general estimate seems to hold true for the less famous émigré musicians as well. Such, at least, was the depressing conclusion produced by the past fall concert season in New York, which featured major recitals by at least five of these new arrivals. Of the three pianists involved, Bella Davidovich (now in her early fifties) was the oldest, the possessor of the largest Soviet reputation prior to her emigration, and the first to appear this season in New York; Oxana Yablonskaya, in her thirties, had a smaller though important career in the USSR; Sergei Edelmann, in his teens, had come to the United States with his family while still a student. The two violinists involved in this unplanned festival were Nina Beilina and Albert Markov (Yablonskaya's brother-in-law), both in their forties; Beilina in particular had been the recipient of critical praise placing her in the top rank of world violinists.

Davidovich's recital took place at Carnegie Hall in early October. For a large and sophisticated audience she played the twenty-four Chopin *Preludes* and the *Arabesque* and *Carnaval* of Schumann. This program of famous pieces was enthusiastically received by the audience, and only slightly less so by the daily New York press. The predictable commercial success followed on schedule: within a month she had future bookings running to well over a hundred thousand dollars in fees. Such success seemed reasonable. Davidovich had in fact played a technically demanding program with pianistic solidity and musicality and had exhibited an immensely attractive stage bearing.

And yet her concert, which was for this listener the high-water mark of the recent émigré musical activity, was hardly reassuring when considered from a standpoint more profound than pleasing sounds, audience success, and commercial potential. The choice of program itself was disquieting. To call the pieces Davidovich played famous is not to disparage them. It is only to state the obvious fact that they have been, for more than a hundred years, in the ears of every music lover and the fingers of every pianist. One consequence of such familiarity is that an artist playing them in an important debut puts himself up against memories of great performances past. But this risk affects the performer alone; just because the field in which the risk is taken is so familiar, it lacks musical significance unless the artist takes the further—today almost unimaginable—gamble of playing those pieces in a new way.

This Davidovich did not do. Her playing fell comfortably within the mainstream of contemporary pianism. Slight (and not important) technical roughness was easily balanced by her ability to keep the melodic line clear at all times in these supremely melodic works. The only distracting feature of her playing was a marked tendency to stress the beginnings of phrases and then gently back away from their climaxes and natural endings. In so doing, she was representative of a widespread tendency in solo performance today —the understatement of high points and an almost apologetic refusal to underline dynamically the basic structural features of romantic favorites.

It was thus the very conventionality of Davidovich's playing that made her choice of program seem uninteresting. Even in the light of the present full-scale retreat from both contemporary and less familiar older music—nowhere more marked than in the case of star instrumentalists and singers—it still comes as a surprise that a not yet aged artist can choose for her American debut a program consisting entirely of chestnuts.[2]

2. That this choice was not a one-time occurrence is shown not only by a hackneyed Los Angeles program the following month but also by her selection of repertory on her first records to be released in the West: on one record the

Perhaps most significantly missing from Davidovich's program was any sign that she is a Russian artist, and any sign of her Russian musical heritage—no Shostakovich (whose piano music is neglected), no contemporary Soviet music, either conservative or avant-garde, written by either supporters or opponents of the present regime. Nor was there a trace of earlier twentieth-century Russian music—neither the famous Scriabin nor the ignored Glazunov and Miaskovsky nor any of the earlier music, as yet undiscovered in the West, of Balakirev, Liapunov, and their predecessors, including Glinka.

It would be pleasant to report that matters improved in the subsequent New York émigré concerts. But the musical weaknesses of the other artists seemed more marked than Davidovich's, and their programming, even when on occasion it included Russian or Soviet virtuoso war-horses, seemed equally vapid.

It might be objected that the recital in mid-October, also in Carnegie Hall, by violinist Nina Beilina, was a special case; observers familiar with her playing felt that she had an off night. However this may be, her performance was rigid and heavy, her stage bearing frightened and artificial. And as with all these Russian artists, the choice of familiar program material—the Beethoven Sonata, opus 30, no. 3, the Bach C-Major unaccompanied Sonata, the Brahms Sonata in D Minor and three Hungarian Dances—only concentrated maximum and unflattering attention on the soloist.

The last of the three Carnegie Hall recitals featured violinist Albert Markov. In at least a bow to our century, Markov began with the *Suite Italienne,* Stravinsky's 1933 arrangement for violin and piano of *Pulcinella,* his 1919–20 reworking of the music of Pergolesi. This composition, however third-hand it may be, makes major demands on the technique and wit of the violinist. These demands were hardly met by Markov, who throughout the recital seemed to be searching for something solid and comfortable. The Bach D-Minor Partita (including the famous Chaconne) disclosed a magnificently steady bow arm as well as flawed intonation, and it was only the Second Sonata of Grieg that finally provided Markov with the toothsome material he evidently craved. Still more to his

---

Chopin *Prelude* again, and on the other the familiar Beethoven Sonatas, opus 31, no. 3 and the "Moonlight," along with the famous *Für Elise.*

taste was the closing work, a rhapsody "in the manner of Paganini" of the violinist's own composition. Sadly, all the whoops and slides, no matter how fiery of execution, only confirmed the impression of the entire recital, one of lurking bad taste searching for public expression.

Two additional New York recitals by émigrés, less ambitious because given away from the world stage of Carnegie Hall, told much the same story. Oxana Yablonskaya demonstrated—in a program of piano favorites drawn from Beethoven, Chopin, Prokofiev, and Mussorgsky—a conventional musical personality tolerably well served by a brilliant-sounding but often unreliable technical equipment. Sergei Edelmann's recital, if only because of the artist's youth, was more encouraging. Obviously a major talent, he performed familiar Beethoven, Chopin, and Prokofiev in a manner that retained excitement and even individuality despite a glassy and forced piano tone. It is not clear from this concert whether Edelmann will be able to control his youthful excesses and at the same time keep his present liveliness; still less is it clear that his personal potential can be realized in the present stultifying cultural, pedagogical, and commercial ambience of New York.

The saddest aspect of all these concerts—and of the work of more famous ex-Soviet musicians—was how little the musicians involved seem to have brought over with them besides their own personal abilities. Because these abilities have been cultivated within the parameters of the current international style of musical performance, none of the émigrés has affected musical attitudes in the West toward the familiar music upon which they have concentrated.

But even though they have failed in this test of significance, they might have attempted a task vastly more important than any mere alteration in styles of performance. They might have presented us with a Russo-Soviet musical heritage that, except for a few famous works, is still unknown in the West, insufficiently written about by our scholars and historians,[3] and essentially unavailable (one assumes at the decision of the Soviet government) outside Russia on Western phonograph records.

3. It is significant that the only available material in English on the Soviet musical world was for many years Boris Schwartz's *Music and Musical Life in Soviet Russia 1917–1970*, Norton, 1972. It has now (1983) been brought more or less up to date and reissued by the University of Indiana Press.

It may be unfair to blame the Soviet émigrés—or their colleagues who have remained at home—for failing to accomplish this mission. Possibly they have made an unfavorable aesthetic judgment on this music, or perhaps their neglect of it is part of a wider rejection of Soviet life and culture as a whole. But whatever their reasons, and however justified they may be, the failure of the Soviet emigration to bring us, as the two previous emigrations of this century did, either new music or a new way of playing old music, severely limits the musical interest and artistic significance of the entire phenomenon.

Nevertheless, if the emigration lacks aesthetic importance, it possesses political and human significance. It demonstrates once again that totalitarian societies can neither procure the loyalty of their subjects with carrots, nor compel their obedience with sticks. And it suggests what is so often forgotten: that beyond the ideology of distributive justice and subsidies to artists and intellectuals lie the need and desire for simple freedom. In the last analysis it is freedom, not music, that the new Soviet musical emigration is about. And that is both its own justification and justification enough.

[*1980*]

# Stravinsky: Rerecording History

Not surprisingly, the present centennial of Igor Stravinsky's birth has brought forth a variety of historical documentation on the composer's life and work. Some of this documentation has extended as far as gala performances of the Russian master's music: the Metropolitan Opera performed a Stravinsky triple bill, beginning with *The Rite of Spring* (1911–13), continuing with an opera, *Le Rossignol* (1908–14), and concluding with the semi-staged oratorio *Oedipus Rex* (1926–27). And commemorating its long association with the composer, George Balanchine's New York City Ballet put on a Stravinsky Festival in June including some of the later and less appreciated compositions.

Major celebratory attention, however, was focused on Stravinsky's career and life, the story of which comes to us again, as it has over the past generation, through the mind and pen of the master's faithful amanuensis and factotum, Robert Craft. Following on the heels of Craft's enormous—and handsome—1978 collection of letters and memorabilia, *Stravinsky in Pictures and Documents* (assembled in collaboration with Stravinsky's widow, Vera), three volumes of the composer's Craft-assembled recollections have been reissued in paperback: *Conversations with Igor Stravinsky* (1958), *Memories and Commentaries* (1959), and *Expositions and Developments* (1962).[1] While these books will remain of great interest to connoisseurs of artists' lives, the extent of Stravinsky's participation in them—and therefore their exact authenticity—seems in as much doubt as ever.

Whatever their historical validity, the picture of Stravinsky these autobiographical productions conjure up is of a grandly charming man whose genius is only highlighted by his capricious irascibility.

1. *Stravinsky in Pictures and Documents*, by Vera Stravinsky and Robert Craft, Simon & Schuster; *Conversations with Igor Stravinsky*, by Igor Stravinsky and Robert Craft, University of California Press; *Memories and Commentaries*, by Igor Stravinsky and Robert Craft, University of California Press; *Expositions and Developments*, by Igor Stravinsky and Robert Craft, University of California Press.

A rather different picture of Stravinsky emerges, however, in the first volume of the *Selected Correspondence.*[2] Although Craft served as editor here too and supplied commentaries, the authenticity of this material at least seems unquestionable. The bulk of the book is composed of letters between Stravinsky and such notables as the French composer Maurice Delage, the Swiss conductor Ernest Ansermet, the Russian editor V. V. Derzhanovsky, Jean Cocteau, Nadia Boulanger, Lincoln Kirstein, W. H. Auden, and Craft himself. Through excerpts from the letters of Stravinsky's first wife, Catherine, the first section provides a glimpse into the composer's tangled personal life; the remainder gives tedious coverage to a lifelong obsession with questions of business and career.

As our picture of Stravinsky gains in authenticity it loses much of its charm. Stravinsky seems to have been as concerned with himself as was even that colossal egoist Richard Wagner; like Wagner, he was calculating in money matters and given to using for his own purposes anyone who came into his line of sight. Craft has devoted many years to justifying this egoism at the same time he has copiously described it. It is a mark of both Craft's intellectual skill and his love for his mentor that the reader now ends up almost granting the basic premise: great composers have a right to be money-grubbing and to expect unlimited personal services from colleagues and friends as well.

If in matters of business and companionship Stravinsky emerges as no less blameworthy than other composers and musicians of his time, the fragments of the composer's correspondence with Catherine Stravinsky (1881–1939) are vastly damaging to our respect for the composer as a moral being. Marital infidelity is hardly unheard of among composers, but Stravinsky's was far from casual: for the last eighteen years of his marriage he carried on a barely clandestine affair with the woman who would become, scarcely more than a year after his wife's death, the second Mrs. Stravinsky. To make matters worse, the affair was in progress while Catherine was suffering from the ravages of tuberculosis, which finally ended her life just before the outbreak of World War II.

Craft's description of the situation, though it hardly does justice to the ethical issues involved, epitomizes his cleansing approach to the flaws he finds in Stravinsky:

2. *Stravinsky: Selected Correspondence,* Vol. I, edited and with commentaries by Robert Craft. Alfred A. Knopf, 1982.

Fifteen years after wedding Catherine, Stravinsky met and became infatuated with Vera de Bosset Sudeikina. Telling Catherine that he could not live without this other woman, he expected his wife not only to accept the triangular relationship but also to join him in admiring and befriending the younger woman. Since Catherine had always subordinated her wishes to her husband's, he correctly anticipated that she would do the same in this new situation. It may be said that she had no alternative, for her illness precluded a full participation in his life, and divorce between two people so closely united was unthinkable. But these pragmatic explanations are less important than that of her absolute devotion to Stravinsky and to what she saw as his divine creative gift.

To this redemptive story of the sacrifice woman pays to genius has now been added, to commemorate the centennial, a picture book documenting the idyllic relationship between the composer and the real (albeit belated) love of his life. Simply entitled *Igor and Vera Stravinsky: A Photograph Album,*[3] this book manages to include a normal-looking snapshot of Stravinsky naked at water's edge, along with many of the blissful couple arriving, departing, and just plain *sur le voyage.* There are studies of the couple at home and in hotels, working and sightseeing, eating and talking, middle-aged and old, sick and well, alone and accompanied by the famous. In a book whose photographs were chosen by Vera Stravinsky (and Rita McCaffrey), one is not surprised to find the composer's first wife absent. Also absent, however, are his four children by his first wife, to whom he was deeply, if capriciously, attached. It seems especially strange, in a book replete with musical allusions, to find no mention—even in the book's captions (written by Craft)—of the composer's younger son, Soulima, who frequently appeared as a soloist in Stravinsky's music, often under his father's baton.

Indeed, so beguiling is this presentation of artistic and personal life in words and pictures that one almost forgets that music is the *raison d'être* of a composer's career. This being so, the first task of a serious centennial celebration would seem to be not providing interesting and decorative books, but rather presenting the master's

3. *Igor and Vera Stravinsky: A Photograph Album, 1921 to 1971,* Thames and Hudson, 1982.

music in such a way that present and future generations may see his achievement both as it was and, insofar as such matters can be reconciled, as he wanted it to be perceived.

In Stravinsky's case, the material for accomplishing such a historiographic task exists in the vast phonographic legacy he spent almost half a century building. Stravinsky took his recordings seriously. There was in this seriousness, it is true, an admixture of commercial motives, but no composer can be expected to deny himself unnecessarily a conductor's fees and royalties. More important was Stravinsky's belief that *his* music could only suffer at the hands of other conductors, whose interpretations he saw as willful distortions advanced by performing celebrities for the sake of their own preferment. To this kind of self-indulgence Stravinsky counterposed an ideal of sober and accurate execution, involving the rigorous observation of the composer's notated instructions. And who could better know the composer's instructions—and their meanings—than the composer himself?

The result of Stravinsky's interest in this regard was the almost complete recording of his entire compositional output in performances in which he participated himself. Many of his works he recorded more than once. *The Rite of Spring,* for example, he recorded three times, in 1928, 1940, and 1960; he recorded *Firebird* (in different versions) four times, first in 1927 and last forty years later, in 1967. Even the less popular pieces of his later years often received second performances under the composer's direction, taking advantage of whatever advances in audio technology had become available.

This nearly complete coverage of a composer's work, under the auspices of the leading record labels of the day, is doubtless due in part to Stravinsky's early fame; it is due also to his long life, which stretched from the beginnings of the recording process into the era of phonographic inclusiveness so characteristic of the 1950s and '60s. Credit belongs as well to the record companies for appreciating Stravinsky's stature as early as the 1920s, and for taking the financial risks that recording his music necessarily entailed.

Now Columbia, the latest and most extensive of Stravinsky's recording affiliations, has issued a luxuriously boxed, thirty-one-record set of almost all his music in his own performances: *Igor Stravinsky: The Recorded Legacy.* The set has been assembled under the direction of Vera Zorina, the widow of Goddard Lieberson, a Columbia Records executive who was close to Stravinsky during the greater part of his association with Columbia. Miss Zorina's contact with the composer had begun even earlier, at the time of her marriage to George Balanchine and her performances as a dancer in *Petrushka* and *Apollon Musagète.*

In general the set comprises reissues of Stravinsky's last attempts to impose his conceptions of his works on posterity. Here, then, are the stereo discs made in the 1960s, most often with orchestras in New York and Los Angeles assembled specially for the occasion. Like all the other recordings of Stravinsky's work in the last twenty or so years of his life, these recordings were made with the help of Robert Craft, who served variously as a musical secretary, the rehearsal conductor who prepared the orchestra, and as a coeditor of the tapes when the final discs were being prepared. To round out the picture, Columbia has given us almost three full sides of Stravinsky in rehearsal and in conversation, talking about his life and work. So that history, too, will be paid its due, we are allowed to hear Stravinsky as a solo pianist in recordings from the 1920s and '30s, and as an ensemble pianist (with violinist Joseph Szigeti) from 1945.

Columbia's presentation is elaborate: the pressings are imported, related works are grouped in separate sleeves, and a glossy souvenir booklet is provided, together with notes on individual compositions (in three languages) and illustrations. Everything necessary to the full appreciation of history and art—at a price of four hundred dollars—is here. Or is it?

The answer is an almost unqualified no. Columbia has promised us Stravinsky's recorded legacy; of this legacy it has given only that part which it was convenient to assemble. As a result, what we are asked to view as history is all too often little more than a repackaging of familiar performances, which are—or recently were—widely available in the United States and (one assumes) in Europe.

The treatment in this set of Stravinsky's most famous work, *The Rite of Spring,* is a case in point. It is represented here by the composer's 1960 recording with a group of free-lance musicians sailing under the name of the "Columbia Symphony Orchestra." This performance has been available as recently as this year in not one but three different packagings. As a musical achievement, this performance of the *Rite* is comfortable and pleasant, tonally lush, rhythmically flaccid, and clearly correct in detail more by virtue of the tape-splicer's art than by virtue of the discipline acquired through concert performance. If we listen to it without the sentimentality with which we customarily regard the productions of age and eminence, we cannot but feel it is an old man's performance (Stravinsky was seventy-seven at the time) of a young man's work.

Was this the most interesting rendition Columbia could find to include in its tribute? There are two earlier Stravinsky recordings of the *Rite,* each with some claim to our consideration—and to that of history. Twenty years earlier he recorded his masterwork, not with a pick-up orchestra, but with the New York Philharmonic. This recording, too, was made for Columbia; it was issued first on 78 RPM discs, and then, around 1949, as one of the first long-playing records. As such it remained available until the advent of stereo recording in the late 1950s. (It was in order to provide a stereo version conducted by the composer that the 1960 record was made.) Tauter in rhythm, more energetic in direction and momentum, leaner in timbre, the 1940 performance is valuable as a document of Stravinsky's earlier and plainer conception of his work, and of his mature abilities as a conductor. It also has much to tell us about the state of the New York Philharmonic, then under the administration of John Barbirolli, as a performer of difficult contemporary music in the time between the strong regimes of Arturo Toscanini and Artur Rodzinski. Keeping in mind that playing errors on a recording could be corrected in 1940 only by remaking an entire four-minute-plus 78 RPM side, the performance remains a credit to both Stravinsky and the Philharmonic.

Vastly more praise, though of a different kind, can be given to Stravinsky's first discs of the *Rite.* They were made in Paris in 1928 and are valuable relics of the heroic age of orchestral recording. It is all too easy for us today to hear in this performance only some errors in execution caused by the relative newness of the work and the consequent insecurity of the players. But to do so would be to ignore much of present value for the sake of mere surface accuracy.

Despite its obvious age,[4] this recording makes clear how different the performance it enshrines is from our customary contemporary fare. Its orientation, after all, is to the past, not the present. It was

4. Heard today, even on adequate equipment, these 78 RPM originals understandably fall far short in sound of what they could be if rejuvenated by sophisticated contemporary reprocessing techniques.

made a scant fifteen years after the *Rite*'s scandalous premiere. Here can be heard an orchestra faced with a modernist adventure rather than with just another performance of a repertory piece coarsened by years of being presented to unsophisticated audiences in the distortions of superstar maestri. Here can be heard as well the transparent sound, in which the French musicians of the time were trained, that must have been in Stravinsky's ears when he wrote the *Rite*. And here too is Stravinsky as a conductor with reserves of youthful energy as yet undiminished by age.

The result is a rendition as dry in sound as the 1960 recording is lush. The opening bassoon solo, for example, clumsy though it must have been to play in 1928, seems to suggest the cold spring of Russian experience, and not, as it often now suggests, the quasi-tropical foliage of southern California. The famous barbaric chords near the beginning do not seem the piquant exercises in mild dissonance they are in today's performances; the French musicians of an earlier day, it is evident, heard them as willful impositions of dissonant sound rather than as logical constructions. As a whole, the orchestral playing on these old records is without that quality of trembling emotion so fashionable on today's concert platforms.

What do these features of performance mean for our understanding of *The Rite of Spring*? The answer is simple. To hear the 1928 recording is to understand something of what caused the uproar when the work was first performed in Paris in 1913 and the combination of shock and delight which marked the *Rite*'s progress through the musical world. The lack of sentiment that can be heard in these grooves must have appeared to the cultivated pre–World War I audience as a taunting rebuke to received nineteenth-century ideas—not just of music and art, but of order, civilization, and human feeling. What seemed a heartless provocation to some members of the musical audience then was a titillation to others, and the civil war in art that ensued is still with us today, fought by different forces on different battlefields. For us to understand Stravinsky's achievement in this way is to raise *The Rite of Spring* from the level of an orchestral blockbuster to that of its true status as a formative element in our twentieth-century sensibility.

On a less exalted plane, something of the same lesson of authenticity can be learned from comparing another set of Stravinsky recordings. Unlike *The Rite of Spring,* the *Ebony Concerto* (1945) is hardly a major contribution to our cultural lives. Written by Stravinsky for Woody Herman and his band, this short three-movement composition is derivative in its evocation of swing and comparatively slight in musical substance. The verve of its syncopations, however, and the easy way Stravinsky manages to penetrate the idiom of American commercial jazz give it considerable charm, and the work justifies frequent performance.

In the new Columbia set, the *Ebony Concerto* appears as recorded by Stravinsky in 1965 with Benny Goodman as the clarinet soloist and the Columbia Jazz Group as the orchestra. The performance is dull and under-rehearsed. Occasionally it lacks even minimal ensemble precision; generally it lacks sympathy for either swing or Stravinsky. By contrast, Stravinsky's original 1946 recording (long since unavailable), with Woody Herman himself as the soloist and his own band as the orchestra, is both an outpouring of instrumental virtuosity and an incandescent reading of the composer's intentions. On page after page of the score, the first recording puts its successor to shame. The performance of a difficult passage in the second movement, for instance, containing a sequence of alternating beats and offbeats, is faster, surer, and more accurate than its later counterpart—altogether a textbook illustration of how to play quick syncopations. Indeed, so poor and unidiomatic is the newer recording by comparison that it may safely be said that to know the *Ebony Concerto* only in its present manifestation is not to know it at all.

Because the musical material is more substantial, the recorded versions of Stravinsky's Concerto for Two Solo Pianos (1931–35) are still more instructive. The stature of this work is incontestable; it remains one of the few great works written for two pianos. Its appearance in the new Columbia package is in a 1945 recording by the team of Vronsky and Babin, then well known. Their playing here is workmanlike, passingly accurate, and, at best, glossy in surface; frequently it is marked by that slight tendency to rush which was often noticeable in this otherwise excellent duo's playing.

There is, however, another recorded version of the concerto Columbia might have chosen, flawed in the extreme though it is. This is of a performance by Stravinsky and his son Soulima made for French Columbia in 1938. Stravinsky seems to have thought that the recording was never released because of the coming of the war. In fact, some extremely rare copies are extant. A tape of the 78 RPM discs has been deposited in the Rodgers and Hammerstein Archives of Recorded Sound of the New York Public Library at Lincoln Center, where it may be heard but not copied.

This recording may be inadequate—because of problems in both recording technology and Igor Stravinsky's piano technique—but to hear it is to experience the same *frisson* of historical discovery provided by the original recordings of the *Rite* and the *Ebony Concerto*. Soulima's playing of the more difficult first part is fluent, sensitive, and elegant; his father's playing, if less accomplished, is distinguished by several marvelous outbursts of melodic projection and rhythmic authority. The Stravinskys play the second movement, a classically influenced *Notturno*, at a markedly quicker pace than Vronsky and Babin. Though the pace may have been chosen in order to accommodate the approximately 4′20″ time limits of a 78 RPM side, it does accord with the spirit of the composer's own metronome directions.

As with the first Stravinsky recording of the *Rite*, the remarkable aspect of the father and son performance of the concerto is the way it achieves musicality without the faintest glimmer of sentimentality. All is direct, straightforward, natural. This, one feels, is the true aesthetic of Igor Stravinsky, so different from the fevered substitute his admirers have been busily creating over the past generation.

Columbia's choices elsewhere in this new collection betray similar vagaries of artistic and historical judgment. Missing is Stravinsky's own solo playing of the Serenade in A, for instance. The presence here of an estimable performance by Charles Rosen and the availability (for the time being) of a sonically inferior pressing of the Stravinsky performance on Seraphim can hardly compensate for its absence in what is putatively the composer's "recorded legacy." The inclusion here of one work unrecorded by Stravinsky deserves comment as well: the Sonata for Two Pianos (1943–44) appears in a 1961 performance by Gold and Fizdale. In this performance Stravinsky's work sounds like high-class cocktail music.

One can appreciate the dilemma posed to the compilers of this set by the existence of not one but two recordings of the *Duo Concertant* (1931–32), both with Stravinsky at the piano but featuring different violinists. The decision was made to use the later, 1945 performance with Joseph Szigeti. It remains a worthy document of Szigeti's playing and of his service to contemporary music. Thus ignored, unfortunately, is the rougher earlier performance (1933) by Samuel Dushkin, who not only played many concerts with Stravinsky but also collaborated with him in writing the solo part of the Violin Concerto (1931). So highly did the composer think of Dushkin that he prefaced the concerto score with the following words, here translated from the French:

> This work was performed for the first time, on October 23, 1931, under my direction at a concert of the Berlin Radio by Samuel Dushkin, for whom I keep deep gratitude and a great admiration for the high artistic worth of his playing.

This being the case, one can only regret that Dushkin's 1932 recording of the concerto, with Stravinsky conducting the Lamoureux Orchestra, has been rejected by Columbia in favor of Isaac Stern's easily available 1961 recording with Stravinsky conducting the "Columbia Symphony Orchestra," this time in its Hollywood manifestation.

Although Stravinsky wrote one of his most important compositions, the Concerto for Piano and Wind Instruments (1923–24), for his own use as a piano soloist, when his son Soulima came of age as a pianist almost a decade later Stravinsky was content to exchange the role of soloist for that of conductor, and with the roles so divided the pair often performed the piece. They were recorded by RCA in 1949, with the backing of yet another New York freelance orchestra. Heard today, this recording remains excellent, despite its ensemble irregularities. It is especially noteworthy for Soulima's piano playing, which is rhythmically alive and yet exact. Here is both a historical document and a vital performance; its supercession in the new set by an undistinguished (and less clear) 1964 recording with an aged Stravinsky conducting for Philippe Entremont can hardly fail to raise the question of whether the difficult personal and financial relationship between Soulima and his father and stepmother during the Craft years may not have exercised an undue influence on Columbia's selection.

There are many other examples of Columbia's having passed over earlier performances of enduring historical importance for recordings now available. Among the recordings that have been over-looked are a restrained and taut 1927 recording of the first suite (and part of the second) from *The Firebird* (1909–10), a 1932 performance of the concert suite from *The Soldier's Tale* (1918), featuring brilliant trumpet playing, a 1931 performance with a Russian choir of the *Symphony of Psalms* (1930), and a 1957 recording of *Perséphone* with the New York Philharmonic. A note of regret should be sounded as well for the exclusion of the 1953 recording of *The Rake's Progress* (1948–51), a fond relic of the days when the Metropolitan Opera from time to time performed new works. Not only is this recording an important historical document, but it employs singers—Hilde Gueden, Eugene Conley, and Mack Harrell—superior to the singers who replace them in the later recording included here. It also offers the listener an opportunity to hear Stravinsky conduct an orchestra prepared by Fritz Reiner, who led the live performances of *The Rake's Progress* at the Met.

It is not difficult to imagine the reasons for the choices made on the Columbia collection: the better sound and more careful editing that later recording techniques afford; the greater accuracy in into-nation and ensemble of later performances; the players' greater ease with the music; and the authenticity supposedly achieved by pre-senting the "last thoughts" of the master as manifested in his last performances. As appealing as these reasons might seem, they are specious when tested against the requirements of history and the responsibilities of historiography.

In present-day recording practice, producing a "better sound" means little more than using space-age recording techniques in order to substitute the judgment of the producer in the control booth for that of the musician in the studio. Recording can be done faster that way, with fewer "takes" and fewer spoiled sessions. And in the control of the outcome by technical personnel can be found the secret of the supposedly error-free rendition of later recordings: they have been produced not by musicians playing perfectly but by editors splicing together the fragments of many different "takes" in order to produce a superficially integrated and continuous product. The greater ease doubtless afforded musicians by their increasing experience with Stravinsky's music is corrupted by the fact that they have often heard that music in meretricious performances.

The value of preserving Stravinsky's final conceptions of his music is, at least at first glance, a more compelling reason for preferring his later recordings to his earlier. Who, after all, would not want to know what Beethoven thought at the end of his life about how the *Eroica* Symphony or the *Pathétique* Sonata should be played? Who would not be interested in hearing how the Wagner who had completed *Parsifal* would conduct *Lohengrin*? But wouldn't it be even more valuable to hear how Beethoven, in the full flush of his virtuoso pianism, performed the *Pathétique,* or how Wagner regarded *Lohengrin* at the time of its composition, when his belief in salvation through love had not yet been transformed by the physical apathy of age?

Because Stravinsky recorded his music throughout his career, we can see both the vigor of relative youth and the possible wisdom of age. The evidence suggests that in Stravinsky's case the vigor of youth is musically preferable, whatever the fruits of his later rethinking. And here a consideration of reality intrudes as well. The last decade of Stravinsky's performing life, the decade of his greatest phonographic activity, was also a time of ill-health, increasing infirmity, and dependence upon others.

Beyond these artistic considerations, an identifiable attitude toward history and its preservation connects the various literary and musical productions that now constitute these Stravinsky centennial celebrations. This attitude is nothing less than the instrumental use of the past to further the interests of the present. In the case of the books under discussion here, the interest cannot but be seen as the image of Vera Stravinsky and Robert Craft, controllers until now of the valuable Stravinsky material. In addition, in the case of the Stravinsky recordings, the interest is profit—or, more accurately, the lessened loss—for Columbia Records and its parent, CBS.

In the gathering together of masses of biographical trivia and countless photographs of the same people doing the same things, in the luxurious packaging of a spuriously "complete" (and musically often dubious) group of recordings, truth is submerged in a welter of detail and of consumer goods. Lost only—and how strange it is to say this, considering the historical importance of this material—is history itself: the past as it happened, nothing more, nothing less.

In Stravinsky's case, the tasks of historiography are still to be accomplished. The recent death in New York of Vera Stravinsky will doubtless create a new situation as regards the administration of the Stravinsky papers; whether new hands in control will bring a further objectivity and completeness in their treatment remains to be seen. The situation of the early records is rather more clear, for the rights to them remain in the control of the record companies— chiefly EMI in Europe, and, to a lesser extent, RCA in this country. Their opportunity to give us the heroic Stravinsky remains. They should seize it.

[1982]

III

# GROUPS

# Great Orchestras Today

## 1. Mehta's Philharmonic

When Leonard Bernstein stepped down as music director of the New York Philharmonic in 1969, to everyone's surprise—and to the dismay of many—the Philharmonic chose as his successor Pierre Boulez, a French avant-garde composer only recently turned full-time conductor, famous both for the forbiddingly cerebral quality of his music and for a certain aesthetic, social, and political radicalism, which he frequently expressed in harsh and biting polemics.

Boulez was at this time, however, in the process of becoming widely known and respected as a conductor; he was even—compliment of compliments—greatly admired by George Szell, a man who specialized in contempt for his colleagues. From a start in the 1950s conducting first avant-garde music and then more generally the music of the twentieth century, Boulez had during the 1960s fulfilled extended engagements with the BBC Orchestra in London and later with the Cleveland Orchestra in this country. Here his success in modern music made him someone to watch (although his conducting of Wagner at Bayreuth during this decade did not make anything like so positive an impression). Boulez's first appearances with the Philharmonic took place during March and April of 1969; the public announcement of his appointment as music director came less than three months later.

Why did the Philharmonic make what was, on its face, so astonishing a choice upon so limited an acquaintance? From what little has been written and from much more that has been talked about, it is possible to conclude that Boulez was hired because he was felt to represent the wave of the future. In those days it was widely believed that youth was taking over the world, and the culture that would "turn them on" was the culture of the avant-garde. Established arts institutions, then, could only survive by preempting both the new audience and the new aesthetic. To accomplish this task, Boulez—a kind of domesticated Stockhausen—must have seemed an inspired choice.

During Boulez's tenure, the Philharmonic, which had always played a large amount of new music, played even more. In addition to tilting the balance of programming at subscription concerts away from the famous classics toward unknown works both old and new, Boulez instituted avant-garde concerts at which he attempted to help unpopular new music along by introducing it himself in his personally charming manner. Each program he conducted was stimulating in conception, precise in direction, at all times original, and even memorable for those of intellectual bent.

But the hoped-for young came to his concerts only in small numbers, and even then on a very selective basis. For Boulez as for everyone else, the Philharmonic audience turned out to be composed of the same middle-class stock that has supported music for the past 150 years.

These worthy burghers, however, were not entranced by Boulez's choice of repertory or by his essentially uninvolved and strangely rootless conceptions of music written before this century. Subscriptions to the Philharmonic dropped; among the audience that came, discontent was expressed in lukewarm applause and even booing. Orchestra members, unhappy with the personal attention he lavished on a few favorites and with his strict and frequently curt criticisms of their playing, furthered the opposition to Boulez by calling him "the French correction." Toward the end, standards of performance slipped, as the orchestra found itself playing music that seemed either uninteresting or actually loathsome. And the press, led by the *New York Times,* retracted its early favorable judgment and strongly suggested that in spite of Boulez's admirable performances of new works, his inability to conduct romantic music in a traditionally satisfying way made him unsuitable to be head of the Philharmonic.

For despite Boulez's undoubted musical and intellectual strengths, what brought him down in New York was, in reality, a double failure. In the widest sense, the youth movement of the 1960s, far from heralding a cultural and social utopia, turned out to be a descent into apathy, anarchy, and even, from the cultural point of view, barbarism. Parallel with the fall of the youth ideology was the perceived collapse of the musical avant-garde publicly represented and championed by Boulez, marked as it was by a progress from dissonances to the use of nonmusical sounds, ending finally in works of absolute silence. To be sure, as a composer Boulez himself had drawn back from the abyss, continuing to write music marked by organization and coherence. But the audience rejected his music as decisively as it did that of his more abandoned colleagues.

Recognizing what was happening, Boulez wisely did not postpone the inevitable. In 1974 he decided that he would leave at the end of the 1976–77 season; since his departure from New York he has not conducted in the United States.

Finding a conductor to replace Boulez was a problem simple to formulate and difficult to solve. The affections of the public, alienated during the Boulez years, must at all costs be recaptured. The paying customers in the hall, record buyers everywhere, and the hoped-for millions of viewers on television must be given what they wanted.

In a sense it was vastly more natural for the management of the Philharmonic to accomplish this task than it had been, in hiring Boulez, to predict the future. No one at Lincoln Center, after all, had possessed any special knowledge of the tastes of the young; no one, it must be assumed, had had much liking for the avant-garde music championed by Boulez. But in the post-Boulez era, management and audience could once again be united; everyone could join in the love of a repertory of romantic blockbusters leavened by the great classics, all performed with commitment and involvement. All that was needed was a conductor who could play the pieces people liked the way they liked them played.

It was Zubin Mehta's fortune to fit this recipe to perfection; and so was consummated what has been called "the musical marriage of the decade."

Born in Bombay in 1936, Mehta is the son of an American-trained violinist who himself wanted to conduct. The father led a semiprofessional orchestra in Bombay, and through hearing it rehearse, the son early became acclimated to Western classical music. So complete was his orientation to this repertory that on his own testimony he remains to this day little more than a mere listener to his own, Indian, music.

In 1954 Mehta jumped at a chance to go to Vienna to study conducting, learning the double bass as a sideline. He speedily impressed his teachers, both by his quickness and by his will.

While in Vienna he formed many friendships, including one with the *Wunderkind* pianist—and later conductor—Daniel Barenboim. By 1958 Mehta had emerged as the winner of an international contest for conductors in Liverpool. In 1960 he was named music director of the Montreal Symphony Orchestra and soon made his debut with the Vienna Philharmonic. Almost immediately thereafter, in 1961, he became music director of the Los Angeles Philharmonic, then about to move into its highly touted new hall. Mehta was lionized in Los Angeles, where the full resources of Hollywood-style publicity were mustered in his behalf.

Abroad, too, his career prospered. He was made the Director of the Israel Philharmonic, a position he still holds. He made many records, not only with the Israel and Los Angeles orchestras, but also with the Vienna Philharmonic and several groups in London; these records were consistently strong sellers. In the fullness of his success he dropped some disparaging remarks in 1967 about the New York Philharmonic, but following an apology he was eventually welcomed to the orchestra as a guest conductor. His appointment as music director, to begin in 1978, was greeted with enthusiasm and relief. After the six-year "plague" of Boulez, the audience could come home again.

A quick look at the repertory Mehta has decided to conduct during his first three seasons begins to suggest the magnitude of the change he has brought to the orchestra since Boulez. On subscription programs Mehta has scheduled about as much twentieth-century music as Boulez did, but his choices have been on balance less provocative in the case of the avant-garde and less didactic in the case of works by accepted historical figures. On the other hand, Mehta has greatly increased the percentage of the repertory chosen from romantic composers—a category that includes music from Schubert and Mendelssohn to Brahms, Tchaikowsky, and Mahler. One change in the repertory in particular stands out: while Boulez played a great deal of French music and little late romantic music save Mahler, Mehta almost completely ignores French music (except for the showy aspect of Ravel) and instead specializes in Strauss, and does a good deal of Mahler as well.

As the repertory has been changed under Mehta, so has the sound of the orchestra. Boulez had favored clarity, astringency, and even delicacy, as if the ensemble were some kind of electronic instrument, which could be programmed to make every detail simultaneously audible. Mehta has, by contrast, shaped a warm, lush, opulent, and even thick sound, which in its richness suggests the tone of the Vienna Philharmonic rather than either the dryness of Boulez or the virtuoso brilliance historically associated with many top-rank American orchestras.

Sometimes the mood on the stage seems to have changed as well. As against the seriousness of the Boulez days, a performance last season of the Rimsky-Korsakov *Capriccio espagnol,* for example, was marked by a palpable air of relaxation and even a bit of clowning from some first-chair players during their solos.

The public reaction to all this has been enthusiastic. Subscriptions are on the rise, and individual tickets for many concerts are often hard to come by. Press comment has been on the whole favorable, though much praise has been qualified by caution and a general air of surprise. Publicity, generated by the Philharmonic's energetic hired hands and gladly featured by the media, has been extensive and usually tasteful. At concerts, instead of the pained looks so evident in the days of Boulez, smiles are now the rule.

So comfortable is the public mood, so charming the atmosphere in which Philharmonic music is now being made, and so natural and unassuming has Mehta been in the numerous interviews he generously gives on radio and television, that it seems almost churlish to ask just how well he conducts, and just how good a musician he really is.

Without doubt, Mehta is a dependable professional conductor, well-organized and efficient in his use of rehearsal time. He also possesses a strong memory, feeling free to conduct long and complex works without a score. It is, however, said by some not so docile back-chair members of the orchestra that such manifestations of derring-do rarely pass without troubling, even if only occasional, lapses.

His Beethoven is undistinguished, managing to seem at once cautious and mannered. A case in point was his performance of the Fifth Symphony in November 1978, just after he had taken over the orchestra. It is a work to which he must have given much thought; he has many times mentioned the structural necessity not to make a break after each of the statements of the four-note motto that begins the first movement. Because of this concern for the

niceties of phrase length, one would have expected a taut, integrated, cohesive performance. Instead it all seemed flabby in conception and erratic in pacing, gotten off to a bad start from the very
first note, which Mehta stressed as the first of a triplet rather than
treating it as it is written, as an unaccented upbeat. The result,
predictably, was shaky ensemble throughout the first movement
and a sense of unease everywhere in the piece.

Much the same can be said about Mehta's performances of such
different composers as Mozart and Brahms. His Mozart G-Minor
Symphony was slick and pretentious, as were his accompaniments
of Mozart works for soloists like Shirley Verrett and Leontyne Price.
As for his Brahms, it seemed as upholstered as his Mozart had
seemed heavy. In his hands the Brahms Fourth Symphony began as
badly as did his Beethoven Fifth, and by the time the long work
was over, the cushions of Mehta's conception had obscured much of
Brahms's detail without managing to hide the raggedness of the
playing.

A noteworthy exception to Mehta's stilted relation to the classics
has been, oddly enough, his performances of Schubert. An account
of the Fifth Symphony, for instance, was gently lyrical, unforced,
and simply expressive. Similarly, Mehta's Haydn seems straightforward and sturdy. Perhaps the reason for his good results with
Haydn and Schubert lies in some awareness that these composers
can be played without any attempt to make the kind of big statement Mehta finds necessary in Mozart, Beethoven, and Brahms.

While Mehta has played a great deal of romantic music—including the accompaniments to many concerti eschewed by Boulez—
his heart plainly lies with that part of the repertory centered around
Richard Strauss. The Strauss Mehta loves is evidently the composer
of the sensual tone poems and *Salome*, rather than the composer of
the neoclassic *Ariadne auf Naxos* or the resigned and gentle *Capriccio*.
Given Mehta's penchant for the immediately affecting, audience-
moving big statement, it is easy to see why he prefers the earlier to
the later Strauss. The Strauss Mehta likes best combines enormous
scale with an infinite number of momentarily attractive details—a
gigantic mosaic of emotions, expressed in the richest of harmonies
and the most vibrant and varied of orchestral colors. These Mehta
exploits to the hilt, producing from *Also sprach Zarathustra* and *Ein
Heldenleben* a result that for his adoring public constitutes something
close to signature tunes.

Successful though he is in this music—and in the operas of Puccini as well—it is hardly a happy sign that he finds his home in what, for all its attractiveness, remains lesser music of vulgar and somewhat dubious taste. Moreover, there is something disturbing in how seriously he takes these works, how highly he values them, and how much he plays them. To treat such music in this way is to credit it with a stature even Strauss himself scarcely had in mind.

Mehta's approach to music is, in general, thoroughly modern—a statement that will surprise only those who confuse contemporary performance styles with the avant-garde in composition. In fact, executants today make every effort not to sound dry, cold, and hostile; their stated goals are feeling, expressiveness, and, for want of a better word, "humanity." To modern performers—regardless of the cultural and intellectual inhibitions they feel because of the doctrines of authenticity and exactitude—notes are shells to be filled with personal meaning through rhythm, tempo, dynamics, phrasing, and all the various permutations and contrasts thereof.

But in addition to these old standbys, one expressive device, because it can be indulged in without doing obvious violence to the composer's notation, is a special favorite. This device involves playing as warmly as possible at all times; the slang expression current among musicians is "playing with feeling." The greatest contemporary masters of such affective technique are string players, led by Mehta's close musical associates Isaac Stern, Pinchas Zukerman, and Itzhak Perlman. To hear them all together—described in the publicity as "The Fiddlers Three"—with Mehta conducting in a nationally televised Pension Fund Concert this past September was to hear modern playing at its height. So much emotion so constantly exhibited, not only in Brahms but also in Bach, Mozart, and Vivaldi, is for the majority of the audience the sound of gold; to other, perhaps more discriminating, tastes it all seems like molasses.

For no matter how great the gain in immediate audience satisfaction, raising the emotional temperature so high by means of this indiscriminate approach requires the performer to slight such classical virtues as contrast and repose. In this hyperemotional musical world, every moment is equal to every other moment; emotion itself becomes a style rather than a bearer of meaning. And eventually where everything is hot, everything is cool. The end can only be boredom, and indeed such boredom is characteristic of today's world of serious music. Never have so many striven to be so vital, and never have so many been so uninteresting.

No matter how great his audience success and his present superstar status, it is precisely this kind of boredom that Mehta is courting. The conclusion cannot be avoided that for all his eloquent posturing on the podium, Mehta brings no distinctively personal musical qualities to his work. As a result, he has during his period in New York been utterly without effect on musical life either in styles of performance or in repertory. He has discovered no important new music, he has rediscovered no hitherto little-known music, and he has had no noticeable influence on the way anybody plays anything. Notwithstanding the press comparison of Mehta with Toscanini and Furtwängler (a more apt comparison would be with Stokowski), Mehta is all in all of little concern to his colleagues, and even to members of his own orchestra.

Soloists, to be sure, are understandably eager to appear with him; their careers benefit. Orchestra players value both his public kindness toward them and the hope he holds out of increased compensation for recordings and television broadcasts. But none of this has much to do with the influence of a historically great conductor on his times.

Worse still, it seems that the basic hope of New York's many serious music lovers—that the Philharmonic would finally begin to play as well as the talents of its members have long promised—remains unfulfilled. The besetting dryness of tone of the Boulez years has been corrected, only to be replaced by an opaque uniformity of texture and a sloppiness of attack. Despite the changes in first-chair players Mehta has begun to make, no improvement in this state of affairs seems about to take place. The opening concert of the current season was marked in both the Bartók Concerto for Orchestra and the Brahms Second Symphony by imprecise ensemble and an overall air of routinized dullness. And though we are always told that everything is improving, the disturbing evidence of recordings going back a generation and more is that the Philharmonic used to play better.

Any historical consideration of the New York Philharmonic provides ample evidence for the conclusion that Zubin Mehta's tenure as music director represents one pole of the orchestra's repeated alternation between the conception of the conductor as explorer and innovator, and of the conductor as audience success. In the present century the explorers were Mahler, Mitropoulos, and Boulez; their successors were the box-office hits Stransky, Bernstein, and now Mehta.

One can hardly blame the Philharmonic for choosing survival as its primary goal. Orchestra players are expensive employees in today's world of fifty-two-week seasons, high-powered labor negotiations, and the proffered manna of government funding. And the shortage of viable new music has made it harder—some would say impossible—for a new conductor to produce an artistic statement by musical means alone.

But perhaps the most debilitating condition under which the Philharmonic, along with other musical institutions in America, labors is the requirement that it be all things to all men. The demands the orchestra must satisfy are seemingly limitless: they range from the satisfaction of sophisticated audiences to the painless education of the unsophisticated; from the pleasing of private backers to the meeting of the demands from minorities for representation; from the preservation of old music to the showcasing of the new; from the need to bring over European artists for excitement to the requirement enforced by both government and press that American artists and composers be given preferential treatment.

Impossible as might be the simultaneous accomplishment and even the undertaking of all these tasks, they must—to make matters, if possible, still worse—be pursued in the political-cultural atmosphere of today's America. In this world high art is either diverting entertainment for a mass audience or it is nothing: anything that demands more from an audience or is more serious in its goals is open to the twin fatal charges of elitism and social irrelevance. Such an idea of art as amusement is hardly unfamiliar to the Philharmonic. Once upon a time, after all, the orchestra filled four weeks of engagements at the Roxy Theater, and just this past summer, in addition to its usual outdoor, amplified concerts before hundreds of thousands in New York City parks, the orchestra played a concert—also amplified—for the patrons of the Resorts International casino-hotel in Atlantic City.

At the moment the Philharmonic is riding a crest of local popularity, and its status as an established institution gives it a prime claim on the cultural dollar. But the mass public is a fickle master and, no less than private philanthropy, it is both unpredictable and limited. At some point the hard questions will be asked: Does the Philharmonic have an artistic mission, and is it fulfilling that mission in a distinguished manner? These are questions to be decided in musical terms alone. At the moment the answer to both is no. Indeed, under Mehta, the Philharmonic is not even making the attempt.

[1980]

## 2. Room on the Podium?

Public attention is focused at last on the weakened and precarious condition of the music directors (our current euphuism for celebrity conductors) across the entire United States.

Merely to mention the orchestras involved is to convey the magnitude of the problem. Of our six major orchestras—those of New York, Boston, Chicago, Philadelphia, Cleveland, and Los Angeles —only one orchestra is secure and comfortable in its choice of conductor, and that is Cleveland's, largely because Christoph von Dohnányi, the orchestra's new music director, has yet to begin his first season. Elsewhere the situation ranges from troubled to dismal. In Boston, Seiji Ozawa's reign, long under attack from the press, is openly threatened by the popularity of Sir Colin Davis, the orchestra's principal guest conductor. In Chicago, Sir Georg Solti, hitherto the most securely entrenched conductor in America, must contend with extensive newspaper discussion of the choice of his eventual replacement. In Los Angeles, Carlo Maria Giulini is increasingly perceived as a musician of limited repertory, somehow lacking in that "star quality" no less necessary on the West Coast than elsewhere. Even in Philadelphia, where for over half a century Eugene Ormandy appeared to be oblivious to everything but old age, Riccardo Muti seems (despite having just signed a new contract) to have failed to excite his musicians or to provide a new and convincing image for the orchestra.

The most strained situation is in New York. Here Zubin Mehta has in no way succeeded in exerting an influence on the city's musical life. The critics of the *New York Times,* after an early welcome to the conductor, have rarely been able to praise more than one work on any given Mehta program; except for his performances of Bruckner and Mahler, there is in fact no press enthusiasm for anything Mehta conducts. Moreover, Mehta's relations with his players are now in disarray. He has made many changes in orchestra personnel, not all of them by the relatively palatable mechanism of retirement. Stories of harsh treatment, including summary dismissal, are frequent, and no public display of respect for the musicians—as on the recent occasion of the deaths of two of them—can assuage the worry and fear developing in the Philharmonic.

The New York audience seems remarkably cool in its attitude toward Mehta. It is almost always possible to get a ticket to a Philharmonic concert, and, even when the tickets themselves are sold, it seems (to judge by the empty seats) that a number of buyers fail to use them. Perhaps the best (or, from the standpoint of the orchestra management, the worst) sign of Mehta's present difficulties is the Philharmonic's loss last year of its exclusive CBS recording contract, a loss that marks the end of an association of almost fifty years. Mehta's records aren't selling, and no amount of hype in the glossy media has made any difference at the cash register.

Some recent signs of an upturn in the Philharmonic's recording fortunes have only underscored Mehta's plight. In January an official of the orchestra told a group of orchestra musicians during a rehearsal break that Deutsche Grammophon, the German (and world) record industry leader, was going to make recordings of Mahler and Sibelius symphonies with the Philharmonic. Tellingly enough, the Mahler was to be conducted by the recent Philharmonic guest conductor Giuseppe Sinopoli; the Sibelius was to be in the safe hands of the orchestra's laureate conductor, Leonard Bernstein.

But to treat all these problems in terms of press, labor relations, public, and contracts is to ignore what by rights should come first in the discussion: the music and the quality of its performance. In this area, the similarities in the situations of all these great orchestras (Cleveland for the moment excluded) outweigh local differences. We are not in a great era of orchestral performance in this country; if anything, recent years have seen a decline in the musical and technical quality of the best symphony playing.

Fortunately, evidence of this decline exists in some more permanent form than the memories of subscribers. Phonograph records, even though inadequate, document what the better days were like.

In the case of the New York Philharmonic, one does not need to go back to the now mythical age of Mengelberg and Toscanini. A CBS/Columbia disc of the Brahms Second Symphony conducted by Artur Rodzinski, available as recently as the 1970s, and a private-label set of Strauss's *Elektra* from a 1949 performance in Carnegie Hall conducted by Dimitri Mitropoulos testify to a level of ensemble playing never reached at Lincoln Center today. From the Philadelphia Orchestra (also on CBS/Columbia) one can still find in second-hand record stores plush and soulful examples of Russian music recorded in the 1950s, including the Second Symphony and *The Bells* of Rachmaninoff. Fritz Reiner's Chicago Symphony recordings from the Fifties, of music ranging from Beethoven symphonies to the virtuoso *Navarra* of Albéniz, are now heard as classics of the phonograph. Similarly, the Cleveland Orchestra's recordings of Beethoven and Mahler, under the direction of George Szell, demonstrate why the Cleveland Orchestra was the best orchestra in the world just twenty years ago. Little evidence of Koussevitsky's work with the Boston Symphony is available today; a recent Vox/Turnabout rerelease of Arthur Foote's *Suite* (opus 63) and Grieg's *Elegiac Melody* (opus 34, no. 2) reminds us of what aching beauty can be produced by a great string section under a great conductor.

On all these records we hear orchestras that manage, each in its own way, refinement without loss of character, bite without roughness, and unanimity of attack without heaviness and rigidity. And here are conductors who achieve, each in his own style, sentiment without sentimentality and musical personality without eccentricity. The result of it all is real musical interest.

These great conductors were deeply committed to their orchestras. Indeed, wherever they had a permanent job, they ruled the artistic roost. But now, when we survey the American musical scene, we find that the music directors of our greatest orchestras are little more than absentee landlords—if they can be said to be landlords (in a metaphorical sense) at all. Zubin Mehta, Riccardo Muti, and Seiji Ozawa each conducts less than half of his orchestra's concerts. Carlo Maria Giulini conducts about eight weeks during the regular season in Los Angeles, and Georg Solti about the same in Chicago. The rest of the year is taken over by guests, associates, and assistants. Some of them are good, many of them are mediocre; none has responsibility for the orchestra or the musical life of the community.

This problem of American orchestras has been noticed before. As long ago as 1936, the composer Douglas Moore (whose opera, *The Ballad of Baby Doe,* remains a high-water mark of our national folk opera) wrote an article in *The American Scholar* on the problem of finding a suitable replacement for Toscanini at the New York Philharmonic. In his essay—"Imported Virtuosos for American Music?"—Moore made several points that are relevant to our present predicament.

After paying every honor to Toscanini, Moore turned to the shortcomings of even this great man in his American context:

> In one significant respect, however, Toscanini has evidenced the limitations of the virtuoso. Aside from his service in selecting and training the personnel of the orchestra he has shown no interest in exercising his musical leadership in the community. He has scarcely seemed to notice the existence of a musical life in the city. He usually arrives from Europe the day before his first rehearsal and departs at midnight after his last concert. While here he participates in no way in the musical life of the community outside of his concerts. . . .
> He has been the supreme musical authority in the Philharmonic Orchestra but the powers which he should exercise, the responsibility which he would be expected to assume, have gone by default to the management and the board of directors.

And now? Although today's music directors (themselves hardly Toscaninis) often spend their time in the communities where they conduct living in the houses they own rather than in hotels, they all ceaselessly travel the world, conducting other orchestras at will and sometimes holding the music directorships of other institutions. Riccardo Muti, Seiji Ozawa, Georg Solti, and Carlo Maria Giulini all conduct more outside their American home bases than they do within them; Zubin Mehta finds time to be the Director of the Israel Philharmonic. Their influence on local musical life here remains practically nil.

Moore's remark about the responsibility of leadership having passed to management and boards is now spectacularly true. Of this nonmusical pair, today it is management—or, to use the current term, the administrators—who run the show. For them, organized in close alliance with their colleagues at other orchestras, musical life is a public philanthropy to be hawked to every possible corporate, private, and public purse. The particular tool of admin-istrators in this selling job is, of course, glamour: foreign names and career images sell tickets, raise money, and satisfy egos all the way round. American orchestral life resembles nothing so much as a fifty-two-week combination of charity balls for the rich and wine and cheese parties for the middle classes. As is always true with houses of cards, this one has seemed solid—until now. But poorer performances combined with escalating costs (not least of which are the astronomical salaries paid to star conductors) are threatening to bring everything down. Perhaps now is the moment to think of art and not box office, of music and not glamour. Perhaps now we may begin to think—as Douglas Moore did forty-seven years ago—of rooting musical activity in particular civic environments. Perhaps now we can attempt to choose musical leaders who will give their full musical lives to the communities that employ them.

This may even mean (perish the thought) employing American music directors for at least some of our great orchestras. I can at this moment think of at least four Americans who richly deserve this chance. They are Leonard Slatkin, Gerard Schwarz, Michael Tilson Thomas, and Jorge Mester. Not only do these talents deserve such important opportunities, but we too will benefit. For if we will begin to entrust our own musicians with major responsibilities, perhaps they may provide our musical atmosphere with the kind of interest and distinction that comes from dedication and time spent on the task. Will the audience come? To paraphrase Gertrude Stein about Ezra Pound, if the music's good, they'll come. If not, not. It is a mistake to ask for more.

[1983]

# Does the City Opera Have a Role?

The New York City Opera, so the story goes, had its beginnings in a 1943 meeting in Mayor Fiorello La Guardia's office. Interrupting a rosy account of prospects for bringing culture at low prices to a large audience, the mayor—affectionately called "Little Flower"—shouted: "This is all very well and good and I congratulate you, but where is opera for the people?" Posthaste, there was opera, performed by a company that, almost forty years later, is still with us.

It began life, as did the other cultural presentations under city auspices that had immediately preceded it, at the old Mecca Temple on West 55th Street. The first season's offerings were tentative and even a bit vulgar in appeal—Puccini's *Tosca,* Flotow's light *Martha,* and Bizet's *Carmen.* Two aspects of the opening year were significant for the company's future: *Martha* was done in English, in the fashion of a Broadway musical; and the general style of production in all three operas placed theatrical and dramatic values on a par with the music.

The initial success was sufficient to make continuation possible. The City Opera's first four directors were László Halász, Joseph Rosenstock, Erich Leinsdorf, and, from 1957 to 1979, Julius Rudel. All were conductors, each of them with a special interest in opera; the reign of each was often contentious, marked by interesting departures in aesthetic conceptions, and characterized as well by an air of unpleasantness on their eventual supersession. The present general director is the American soprano Beverly Sills, herself a product of the City Opera and one of the small number of native-born opera singers to achieve celebrity status in the world of show business.

Throughout its life the repertory of the City Opera has been carefully chosen in an atmosphere of high hope and even, on occasion, a certain intellectual excitement. It was obvious from the beginning that the new company could never compete with the

Metropolitan Opera, either in sustained presentation of the most important and lavishly produced classics or in the engagement of star singers of international reputation. But it was also clearly perceived that the operatic field remained open to the exercise of daring and wit. Because the Metropolitan, in pursuance of its historical mission of presenting the "best" to a socially and economically elite audience, was ignoring lesser-known and smaller, older works, as well as the entire production of recent years, many worthwhile works cried out to be done. And because of the Met's wholesale importation and employment of European singers, an entire generation of American-born and American-trained singers, at home with both easy dramatic communication on the stage and English as a language of theatrical discourse, was widely available.

Thus, despite the gleam in Mayor La Guardia's eye, there was born a conception of the City Opera as something more than dollar opera for the masses. Here was an idea of a real second major opera company for New York City—a company at once younger, more stimulating, more up-to-date, and above all as American (or, more properly, Americanized) as the Metropolitan was European.

The facts of the repertory testify to the immense efforts the City Opera has made to implement its original goals. By the end of its first quarter-century, in 1968, it had presented no fewer than thirty-five works by Americans, including Gian Carlo Menotti, Carlisle Floyd, Douglas Moore, Robert Ward, Marc Blitzstein, Kurt Weill, and Lee Hoiby. Contemporary Europe was represented as well. In this period the City Opera put on twenty-seven little-known pieces by modern composers; among these were works of Manuel de Falla, Béla Bartók, Richard Strauss, Carl Orff, Maurice Ravel, Igor Stravinsky, Arthur Honegger, Dmitri Shostakovich, Benjamin Britten, Luigi Dallapiccola, William Walton, Alban Berg, and Gottfried von Einem.

Not entirely forgetting its mandate to serve the popular—and to offset the heavy losses that running a serious opera company always entails—the City Opera devoted some of its time to such classic masters of light opera, operetta, and musical comedy as Franz Lehár, Gilbert and Sullivan, and Jerome Kern. For the rest, in this twenty-five-year span, the City Opera did classics like *Rigoletto* and *La Traviata,* and even from time to time such true heavyweights as *Don Giovanni, Die Meistersinger, Der Rosenkavalier,* and *Pelléas et Mélisande.*

Again true to its original conception, in all City Opera productions throughout its history, the vast majority of singers employed have been American. While relatively few of these singers have gone on to the kind of international careers achieved by such American-born products of the Metropolitan Opera as Jan Peerce, Richard Tucker, and Leonard Warren, those who have done so include Sherrill Milnes and, of course, Beverly Sills.

A significant change in the world of the City Opera took place in the middle of the 1965–66 season. On February 22, 1966, the company left its old home at the musty Mecca Temple (for many years called the New York City Center) for the glamorous, newly built New York State Theater at Lincoln Center. The junior company thus became the Met's cotenant in America's most highly publicized compound devoted to the performing arts.

Attractive as proximity to the exciting world of the Metropolitan Opera House and Philharmonic (later Fisher) Hall may have seemed, only those determined to look on the good side of everything could find the New York State Theater an unmixed blessing as an opera house. Because it had originally been designed as an ideal venue for ballet, sight had been given rather more consideration than sound in the building's planning; the aural result is that voices and orchestra alike sound vastly different in various parts of the house, and the direction from which sound seems to come frequently does not relate directly to its true point of origin. Overall, the sound is best downstairs, and becomes progressively nebulous as one rises to the higher balconies. And regardless of where one sits, music in the New York State Theater tends to sound vague and distant.

To the City Opera's credit, despite what must have been temptations, it remains in some measure true to a desire to keep its repertory weighted in favor of both the unfamiliar and the new. In recent years it has continued to stage contemporary opera written by composers as different as the Argentine Alberto Ginastera and the American Leon Kirchner. In the realm of older but nonetheless little-known operas, the company has explored products of the *bel canto* school, originally to exploit the talents of Beverly Sills and, more recently, one must assume, because of a high opinion of the intrinsic merit of these works.

In the present season, for example, the company will have presented twenty-six operas. Of these, eight belong roughly to the twentieth century; of these eight, however, three—all of them American and indeed the only American efforts programmed by the City Opera this season—are short, one-act pieces, meant to make a single evening's bill. Among the remaining works, two—*The Cunning Little Vixen* and *The Makropoulos Affair* (both done in English) —are by the Czech Leoš Janáček; one—*Silverlake*—is a refashioning of a work by Kurt Weill; one—*Mary, Queen of Scots*—is by the English Thea Musgrave; another is an old City Opera standby, Sergei Prokofiev's *The Love for Three Oranges*.

Another group of eight belongs to the category of unfamiliar compositions from the nineteenth century and before. Among them are two operas by Donizetti, and single works by Rossini, Handel, Nicolai, Bizet, Verdi, and Mozart. The conventional works the company is doing include three famous ones of Puccini—*Tosca, La Bohème,* and *Madame Butterfly*—as well as *Don Giovanni, Carmen, Falstaff,* and *The Barber of Seville.* Rounding out the list are three light pieces: *Tales of Hoffmann, Die Fledermaus,* and *The Student Prince.*

The current season is the second under the general directorship of Beverly Sills. Though opera seasons take years to plan, and though the cadres necessary to realize an administrator's goals must be built up over a long period of time, Sills's years of close involvement with the company—and the grooming for the job she was plainly receiving in the years before Julius Rudel's resignation— suggest that it has been possible for her personal artistic preferences to begin quickly taking hold.

As a singer, Sills was known for her dramatic impact, her vivacious stage presence, and her ability to make the maximum use of a large, flexible, but frequently unwieldy voice. Her artistic efforts were generally directed less to the communication of musical values than to the expression of platform personality. Because the world of opera and its fans is so oriented toward star performers, it seemed both proper and natural for her to project the characters she portrayed through the medium of her own marked personality, and equally natural for her to emerge (as her singing career inevitably drew to its end) as a best-selling memoirist and a talk-show host on commercial and public television.

Not surprisingly, in her first years as the general director of the City Opera, Sills has brought the same virtues of inexhaustible energy and public charm to her tasks. As part of running her company, Sills chooses repertory, hears singers, engages conductors and stage directors, and makes all long-range plans. To a degree greater than is the case with most holders of such positions, she is both chief fundraiser and public-relations expert.

In addition, she is the company's chief public spokesman, appearing as either intermission host or guest on the City Opera's nationally broadcast public-television appearances. Even the celebration of her retirement as a performer has provided an opportunity for Sills, as she sings her way across the country for the last time, to spread the gospel of a new era at the City Opera. And only last October, she was both the chief attraction and the guest of honor at an immense benefit for the company, which, it is said, raised one million dollars. The predictable result of all these highly publicized activities is that she has become synonymous with her company in a way reminiscent of the association between Kirsten Flagstad and the Norwegian State Opera for a few years around 1960.

But no matter how prominent the public image of the City Opera is under its present regime, its artistic image can only be formed by what takes place in performances in the opera house itself. Here the just concluded fall season at the New York State Theater—the spring season, of course, is yet to come—provided a unique opportunity to make an aesthetic case for the City Opera without the distraction of the usually overwhelming competition from the Metropolitan Opera, which was closed for the duration of its lockout-strike. Operatically, the City Opera now had New York to itself, a long hoped-for chance to advance the cause of interesting rather than hackneyed repertory, of ensemble productions rather than star turns, of theatrically rather than merely vocally effective performances.

On the evidence of the City Opera's record in the past months, the company hardly lived up to this opportunity. The productions I saw included works characteristic of the City Opera's activities not only during the current season but also during its history. Here was a towering masterpiece of the classical tradition (Mozart's *Don Giovanni*); a tuneful favorite of the lovers of late Italian opera (Puccini's *La Bohème*); a little-known, pleasantly slight work of an older Italian tradition (Rossini's *Cinderella*); a work closer to the later genre of operetta (Nicolai's *The Merry Wives of Windsor*); and finally a gaggle of American works (Stanley Silverman's *Madame Adare,* Thomas Pasatieri's *Before Breakfast,* and Jan Bach's *The Student from Salamanca,* which together make up *An American Trilogy*) illustrative of the new in native operatic composition.

Only two of these works—*Don Giovanni* and *La Bohème*—were sung in languages other than English, while the others were either done in English translation or, as in the case of *An American Trilogy,* in the original English. In solid City Opera tradition, all the singers were important as members of the ensemble rather than as stars, talented musicians rather than operatic heroes. And providing a link with the past, the conductor of *The Merry Wives of Windsor* was the company's former director, Julius Rudel.

Everything about these performances was respectable, professional, adequate—and ultimately dull. From the standpoint of execution, the overwhelming impression was of much talent, hardworking and eager, in the long run going to waste because of insufficient and essentially uninspired direction.

Of all the operas done by the company this season, only *Don Giovanni* incontestably possesses the kind of stature that demands a level of realization taxing to the abilities of even the greatest artists. As if in recognition of this high stature, the performance I saw was sold out—the only such of all the performances I attended—and the audience was both deeply respectful and, one suspects, sophisticated.

What it saw and heard was one singer of undeniable force and personality—the Puerto Rican bass Justino Diaz in the title role. Though neither his appearance and stage deportment nor his vocal style managed to evoke the requisite blend of reckless but melancholy passion and Italianate vocal suavity, his dramatic projection and athleticism were achievement enough. Two other voices—those of Michael Burt as the Commendatore and Faith Esham as Zerlina—were strongly impressive in purely vocal terms. Elsewhere the singing was mostly acceptable, though nowhere distinguished.

The stage production reached its climax in the penultimate scene, when the statue of the Commendatore speaks with terrifying force to the doomed Don. That the final scene, the stage fully peopled and illuminated, seemed anticlimactic is perhaps traceable both to the heights Mozart's music had just previously reached and to a palpable loss of tension on the part of the performers.

Indeed, just that sort of tension—which makes the longest piece of music seem brief—had seemed in short supply from the moment the orchestra began the overture. Save for the scene just before the opera's end, rhythms were slack, instrumental tone lacked vibrancy, and passages of vocal recitative were rushed, their words indistinguishable. During famous arias and ensembles, the tempi chosen by the conductor, John Mauceri, seemed capricious, without necessary relation to what had gone before; it was therefore hardly surprising that the singers were so often at odds with the accompanying orchestra.

*La Bohème,* Puccini's treatment of the contrast between bohemian life and romantic love, made, in the City Opera's current production, a dispirited impression. In theatrical terms, the impression was undoubtedly affected by the unfortunate tendency of the singers to come to the front of the stage to deliver important bits of melody or dramatic business. At all times characters felt free, while singing, to face the audience rather than their partners on the stage.

But even more important than these dramatic gaffes was the lack of compelling musical direction from the pit. The leader once again was John Mauceri, reputedly one of the company's best conductors. The opening half of the first act, for example, was raced through, words and actions seeming pointless and disconnected. When the famous passages took over—those beginning *Che gelida manina, Mi chiamano Mimi,* and *O soave fanciulla*—Mauceri presided over a luxuriant indulgence in Puccini's melodies detrimental both to the singer's comfort and the story's urgency. By the end of the fourth and final act, one's only wish was for something—a faster tempo would have sufficed—to put the drooping lovers out of their misery.

Rossini's *Cinderella,* as televised nationally by PBS on November 6, was, for all the work's essential triteness, more convincing dramatically and musically than most live performances seen in recent years in the New York State Theater. Perhaps because cameras and microphones bring images and voices closer to the viewer than is possible in a large opera house, the broadcast was clear in texture and immediate in impact; the voices seemed strong and fresh, the orchestra tone alive and confident. Because the English words were distinct and natural in sound, the story was communicated plainly and effectively. One's major reservation could only concern the choice of this particular banality for so prestigious an airing.

Nicolai's *The Merry Wives of Windsor,* seen live in the State Theater, did not fare so well. Shakespeare's story of bungled caddishness is always good for a laugh; in the hands of Verdi—as in the hands of Shakespeare himself—Falstaff assumes a certain picaresque grandeur. Nicolai's talent hardly extends so far; both as story and music, his version is of no more than historical interest in the development of light opera. Be that as it may, the City Opera presentation on the occasion I saw it—with, it is true, a replacement cast on the stage—seemed pointless, an effort half-considered and half-worked-out. What appeared to be the production's one set, composed of wall panels and patterned flooring, was forced to make do (with the addition of a few props) as a domestic interior, a tavern, an outdoor square, and, slightly altered, as a forest. Julius Rudel's conducting suffered from the lack of breadth, commitment, and excitement characteristic of the City Opera's conductors in recent years.

All the above works, of course, belong to opera's past; potentially the most significant offering of the City Opera's fall season was its trio of American pieces. Of these three operas—all being given their world premieres—Silverman's *Madame Adare* was directly commissioned by the City Opera, Pasatieri's *Before Breakfast* was written on a grant from the National Opera Institute funded by the National Endowment for the Arts, and Jan Bach's *The Student from Salamanca* was the winner of the City Opera Competition for one-act operas.

The three works are composed in widely differing styles. Silverman utilizes a musical vocabulary drawn equally from Broadway and the classics, and even includes some synthesized tape squeals. Pasatieri, as is his wont, employs a neo-Puccinian idiom owing most, it would appear, to the influence of that composer's *Il Trittico,* and includes as well an extended excerpt from an old Duke Ellington record. Bach's *The Student from Salamanca* is written in the mode of neo-pastiche popular in today's world of liberated compositional styles; his preferred models are Mozart and Rossini, and the whole work is suffused with the flavor of a tasty morsel from *Carmen.*

Not only is pastiche the musical order of the day for all three composers. Despite the varied nature of their subject matter, all three belabor a common theme: the sordidness and absurdity of human striving. Silverman's opera is about a crazed woman, torn between being an actress and being an opera singer, who kills her psychoanalyst because he will not accept the payment for her "cure" which, in her less successful days, he had once demanded. Pasatieri's opera, a setting of Eugene O'Neill's monodrama of the same name, is about a shopgirl, caught amid the squalor of tenement life in a blighted marriage. And Bach's work is an elaboration of the hoary old story of an old miser betrayed by his young wife and her feckless companions.

Musical borrowings combined with the maudlin exploitation of human weakness and suffering could only result in a kind of camp masquerading as high culture—an aesthetic nihilism that views art as entertainment and entertainment only really worthwhile as a mockery of life. Predictably, the performances of this questionable material were not so much disorganized as demoralized. The pacing of actions and gestures seemed wayward, the singers shouting their fragmented pittances into the void of an unresponsive audience. The evening ended up a black eye for American music, for contemporary opera, and perhaps most poignantly, for the City Opera itself.

Need it all have turned out so badly? No one can be under any illusion that the record of new opera in the past quarter-century has been encouraging, and no believer in high standards can possibly be sanguine about the present state of musical composition. Despite several successes among its many efforts at finding new American works—one thinks immediately of Carlisle Floyd's *Susannah* (1955), Douglas Moore's *The Ballad of Baby Doe* (1956), and Hugo Weisgall's *Six Characters in Search of an Author* (1959)—it is surely significant that not one American opera is currently in anything like repertory status at the City Opera, or for that matter anywhere.

But even with all allowances having been made for the present very real difficulties, the impression remains that the City Opera had not, in the case of *An American Trilogy,* made a serious attempt to find and put on worthwile contemporary operas. Over the whole course of the three operas were the signs of a tentative, tremulous attempt to accommodate the present enigmatic cultural *Zeitgeist.* The choice of several small works rather than a single large one suggests a hope on the part of the City Opera administration that boredom at least might be avoided; that the more musical styles, as it were, the merrier, as if in art there were safety in numbers; that the choice of subjects at once so close to the bone of contemporary fantasies and so ultimately trivial in their outcome might titillate an audience drawn from a society of television viewers; that, above all, showing a new work—any new work—was something that could only bring credit on all concerned and especially on the management. These vain hopes, now dashed, suggest that at this point in its life the City Opera, in its search for new music, is floundering.

One would hesitate to criticize the present regime for the choice of the works which make up *An American Trilogy* were it not for Sills's pride in their presentation. And further illustrative of her taste in new works is her intention, announced in an adulatory interview published in *Opera News,* to go "to Holland to see Philip Glass's new work on Mahatma Gandhi" and her disclosure that "she's talked with David Del Tredici [the composer of lengthy settings of *Alice in Wonderland*] and Stephen Sondheim about something new for the company." One need not be a booster of the avant-garde to deplore such aesthetic judgments.

Furthermore, Sills's preference in new works augurs ill for her coming choices in more traditional repertory. It suggests an increased concentration both on *bel canto* operas—star vehicles for which the City Opera does not have the stars—and light music, the entertaining products of the bygone commercial stage. It further suggests that what solid works are chosen will not receive the necessary concentration and investment.

Bad as this weakness in musical judgment is, it becomes all the more troubling when to it is added the present state of conductorial leadership in the City Opera's orchestra pit. Because the heart of opera is musical composition, musical preparation, and musical performance, the real direction of an opera house can only come from musicians. Bringing in an occasional name conductor, which Sills evidently has in mind, is not good enough. What is needed is a resident conductor of high and original gifts presiding over a resident staff hardly less talented.

Whither, then, the City Opera? Neither its choice of repertory nor its present standard of performance can guarantee it an assured place on the artistic and musical scene. Its principal claim to a future is, at the moment, little more than the fact that it already exists. And indeed, the prevailing opinion today among supporters of culture is that no organization of past distinction ought to be allowed to die. But perhaps in our changing national climate a profound and hitherto forbidden question may be asked: Does an artificial prolongation of the life of artistic organizations, by consuming the available resources, close off the possibility of new forms and expressions of significant continuing importance? If its current direction is any sign, a good place to start thinking about an answer might well be the New York City Opera.

[*1981*]

# Rich Met, Poor Met

Our premier opera company will be 100 years old on October 22, 1983. Its history began in the old Metropolitan Opera House on Broadway just below Manhattan's Times Square. The anniversary celebration will take place just twenty-five or so blocks to the north, in the palatial monument bearing the company's name at the Lincoln Center for the Performing Arts. During this first century, the Met has thus had only two homes.

For a long time it has also seemed that the Met's sponsors have been similarly unchanging. The old Met building was put up in the post–Civil War era by New York millionaires angry at being shut out of the more genteel society that then surrounded operatic production in the city. The names of some of these upstart nabobs —Vanderbilt, Astor, Morgan—bulk large in our social and commercial history; so too do such early Met names as Roosevelt, snatched from the camp of the elite Knickerbocker enemy. These notables and their families were eventually succeeded by such equally famous figures as Otto Kahn (a partner in Kuhn, Loeb) and Cornelius Bliss (an associate of J. P. Morgan). To this day, even when the names involved have been less firmly rooted in our past, the financial and business direction of the Met has remained in the hands of those securely occupying the commanding heights of the American establishment.

Beneath the unchanging façade of patrician power, however, lies a quite different picture of adaptation to changing times and conditions.

As recently as the 1920s, the Met made an annual profit. Even before the fat years, the burden on the backers of grand opera had hardly been onerous, either in the demands of the company itself or in the ability of the then almost-untaxed rich to pay. Indeed, it would seem that the individual assessment paid by each founding family from 1883 until the abolition of free box privileges in 1940 amounted to something under a yearly average of $5,500.

The Depression changed this happy state of affairs. Attendance sagged, and with it ticket income. Attempts—brilliantly successful from the beginning—were made to broaden and enlarge the Met's public. In 1935, Mrs. August Belmont (another of the great names) founded the Metropolitan Opera Guild, a national organization built around the listeners to the Met's national radio broadcasts, which had begun in the early 1930s. From an initial membership of no more than 2,000, the Guild now boasts more than 100,000, all of whom receive a copy of the glossy magazine *Opera News,* one of the two leading publications of its kind in the world; it is the achievement of *Opera News* that it both serves as house organ for the Met and provides coverage of opera elsewhere in America and in Europe.

Nor was the Met slow in adapting to the possibilities that developed in the Great Society years for the wider dissemination of culture. After a shaky start in the preceding two decades, the company embraced television, finally emerging in the 1970s as the crown jewel in the efforts of the Public Broadcasting Service to bring culture to the masses and the masses to culture. Using recently developed and relatively unobtrusive camera and lighting techniques, the Met has found it possible to telecast opera under the conditions of live performance; capitalizing on its position in Lincoln Center and in New York, the company has been able to generate viewing audiences of hitherto unparalleled size to watch the famous operas of the repertory. To these audiences it has assiduously spread the gospel of opera at the Metropolitan.

It has been so successful at this kind of evangelizing that if any one thing can be said to be the Met's forte, it is marketing. Master of all the procedures which contemporary public relations has developed and which electronics has made possible, the Met uses direct mailing and computer-based refinements of analysis to identify and reach its potential audience. To that audience it sells opera books and records, an entire range of such memorabilia as posters from the past, calendars, and the inevitable T-shirts and tote bags. A recent "Met by Mail" catalogue offered a Met shower curtain, a *La Bohème* bath sheet, and—a rather more expensive ($3,400) way of showing one's love of art—a seventeen-inch-high replica of a Met chandelier, produced by the Austrian firm that made the originals.

If the Met is up-to-date in its marketing procedures, it has also not lagged behind in that quintessential component of contemporary artistic life, fundraising. The old technique of passing the hat to one's friends hardly suffices under modern conditions of multi-million-dollar budgets. And even the largest audiences, paying the highest ticket prices, cannot fund the demands of artists sought the world over, powerful unions representing musicians, chorus, and technical employees, and the administrative staffs necessary to bring the audiences in. So the net must be cast wide, to catch the small givers, the rich patrons, the culturally disposed foundations, and above all, those Loreleis of philanthropy, medium-sized and large corporations.

Just how well the Met has succeeded in getting money is shown by the current state of its Centennial Fund endowment drive, begun in mid-1980 and scheduled to last four years. By December of last year, only eighteen months after its inception, the campaign had raised more than $54 million in contributions and pledges from 130 individuals, foundations, and corporations. This amount, which averages out to more than $415,000 per contributor, has come from, among other corporations, Exxon and Texaco, IBM and AT&T, Chemical Bank and Avon; among corporate foundations kicking in are those of Mobil, Shell, and Union Oil, General Electric and U.S. Steel, and Metropolitan Life. By late winter it was being said that more than $60 million had been raised, and prospects for the future look so good that a decision may be made to continue raising funds well past the original $100-million target.

The result of all this activity is that the Metropolitan Opera remains today a totally private institution, alone of all the great opera companies in the world—among them Berlin, London's Covent Garden, Milan's La Scala, Paris, and Vienna. Whereas all the others are not only largely funded but indeed made possible by lavish government support, the Met receives only trifling federal, state, and local subsidies; perhaps the most important official help comes from the privileged access the Met has to public television. For the rest of its enormous budget, the Met goes it alone, supplementing earned income (approximately a relatively high two-thirds of the total) with contributions. Governance of the Met is still, as in the old days, in private hands.

Tempting as it must be to those concerned to rejoice in such a staggering accomplishment—all the more remarkable against a general background of gloom in fundraising for the arts and during a time of economic readjustment and possible government-aid cut-backs—the fact remains that the money being raised is for an artistic purpose, and long after contributors and administrators have been forgotten, the reputation of the Met will be determined by what that purpose is and how it has been served.

Like all great operatic enterprises, the Metropolitan Opera has from the beginning been an agglomeration of star singers perform-ing a repertory largely composed of the most popular works. This was as true at the turn of the century as it is, *mutatis mutandis,* today. Just about every great singer of the century, from Caruso on down, has sung, usually repeatedly, at the Met. Not surprisingly, the operas that have been done the most frequently are the most famous ones. Verdi's *Il Trovatore* has been given more than 300 times, and *La Traviata* almost 500. Puccini's *La Bohème* has now achieved almost 600 performances, and even a work so relatively little known (in recent times) as Wagner's *Tannhäuser* is near the 300 mark.

Frequently, though by no means always, the quality of orchestral direction at the Met has been notable. Felix Mottl (a Wagner disciple of Bayreuth fame) and Gustav Mahler appeared with the company before 1910. Arturo Toscanini, first conducting at the Met in 1908, was artistic director of the company until 1915. In the 1920s the Met podium was occupied by, among others, the little-appreciated Artur Bodanzky and the great Italian operatic maestro Tullio Serafin. In the 1930s and '40s, aided by the refugee flight from Europe, the supply of important conductors at the Met included such historic names as Fritz Busch, Fritz Reiner, George Szell, and Bruno Walter, as well as Sir Thomas Beecham. In the more recent period of the 1950s and '60s the famous included Ernest Ansermet, Karl Böhm, Herbert von Karajan, Rudolf Kempe, Josef Krips, Dimitri Mitropoulos, Pierre Monteux, Georg Solti, and Leopold Stokowski.

But all this concerns fame and stars. Music does not live (to quote a witty line from Hugo Weisgall's opera, *Six Characters in Search of an Author*) by *Faust* alone. If an opera company wishes to be more than a platform for artistically safe (even if financially risky) ventures, it has three duties beyond the presentation of the already accepted and acceptable. Simply put, these duties are, first, to present a balanced view of the past; second, to explore the art of the present day; and third, to encourage the art of the company's own place. For the greatest institutions to maintain their reputations, these duties—always in addition to the presentation of those celebrities and their vehicles which alone make everything else possible—must be accomplished simultaneously. To give up on the past and devote oneself only to the contemporary is to lose the perspectives of history and quality; to give up on one's own time is to become irrelevant to changing taste and creation; to ignore one's own place is to become rootless, without distinctive flavor and cultural resonance.

Throughout this century the Metropolitan has compiled a varied record in fulfilling its three duties. In the course of offering celebrity opera it has, over the long run, found it possible to give a reasonably representative picture of the operatic past. Older novelties and revivals, combined with many star singers of idiosyncratic abilities and preferences in repertory, have kept audience and backers happy; normal circulation of the famous repertory, based on the availability of casts, has introduced reasonable flexibility into the choice of works produced.

The Metropolitan's relation to the works of the day has, sad to say, become progressively weaker as the number of new works seen to be commercially viable has steadily dwindled. At the turn of the century, the situation was vastly different. Then, the greatest operas of Wagner were none of them more than thirty-five years old; his last opera, *Parsifal,* had been performed for the first time at Bayreuth in 1882, and received its first showing away from that shrine in a pirated production at the Met in 1908. In 1900, Verdi's *Aida* was only twenty-nine years old, *Otello* thirteen, and *Falstaff* seven; Puccini's *La Bohème* and *Tosca* were contemporary products, hot from the composer's pen. Not only was the freshness of these works no handicap to their entry into the repertory, it was in fact a great point in their favor.

This state of affairs was not to last. While the later works of Puccini continued to receive timely performances at the Met, Strauss's *Salome* (1905), first done at the Met in 1907, was not given again until 1934; *Elektra* (1906–08) did not appear at all at the Met until 1932. Debussy's *Pelléas et Mélisande* (1892–1902) waited for its first Met performance until 1925. Berg's two great operas, *Wozzeck* (1914–21) and *Lulu* (1928–34), did not come to the Met until 1959 and 1977, respectively. While since World War II the Met has made a limited commitment to the new by doing operas of Britten, Poulenc, and Weill, several renowned works, each of them in some way cornerstones of the modern sensibility, have not been put on by the Met until this day. Among them are Busoni's *Doktor Faust* (1916–24), Hindemith's *Mathis der Maler* (1935), and, above all, Schoenberg's *Moses und Aron* (1932). Even Pfitzner's arch-conservative *Palestrina* (1915) has been passed by.

The Metropolitan's record in the development and use of American singers is, by contrast, excellent. For almost three-quarters of a century, native singers have not only been employed in workaday roles, they have achieved major solo careers sufficient to attract large audiences. In the golden age of singing· in the decades around World War I, these stars included Geraldine Farrar, Alma Gluck, Louise Homer, and Rosa Ponselle. Later, during the 1930s, such famous names as Richard Crooks, Grace Moore, and Lawrence Tibbett were on the company roster. In the 1940s and '50s Robert Merrill, Jan Peerce, Risë Stevens, Helen Traubel, Richard Tucker, and Leonard Warren became Met celebrities. In our own time, three of the Met's biggest draws are Marilyn Horne, Sherrill Milnes, and Leontyne Price. And the list goes on: a recent Met program points with pride to the large number of Metropolitan Opera Audition winners appearing this season—among them Grace Bumbry, Shirley Verrett, and Ruth Welting.

The relation of the Met to American operatic composition has hardly been as strong or as consistent. It is true that out of the nearly 250 works in the company's historic repertory, 25 have been American. The list begins with Frederick Converse's *The Pipe of Desire* (1905), performed by the Met in 1910; it ends with Marvin David Levy's *Mourning Becomes Electra* (1967), first given during the inaugural season at Lincoln Center. But most of the Met's American works were done prior to World War II. Though several of these— Victor Herbert's *Natoma* (1911), Deems Taylor's *The King's Henchman* (1927) and *Peter Ibbetson* (1931), Louis Gruenberg's *The Emperor Jones* (1932), and Howard Hanson's *Merry Mount* (1933)—are resonant presences in the history books, they all seem fated, for one reason or another, not to be revived.[1]

In the years after World War II, American opera at the Met was represented by (in addition to Levy's *Mourning*) two operas of Samuel Barber, *Vanessa* (1958) and *Antony and Cleopatra* (1966), and one of Gian Carlo Menotti, *The Last Savage* (1963). Though *Antony* was commissioned by the Met for its opening at Lincoln Center, and performed on that occasion with a notable cast and a distinguished audience in attendance, the opera proved unpopular with public and press; so strong was the reaction of Met management to this failure that the cause of national opera itself was set back many years. Even Stravinsky's *The Rake's Progress*, hardly American but nonetheless written here, in English, and performed at the Met in two seasons during the 1950s, has vanished from sight and sound.

Since the 1960s, there has been no American opera at the Met. Two new works have been commissioned for eventual performance, one from the modernist Jacob Druckman, and another from the rather more crowd-pleasing John Corigliano. But both these works are still in the future, with their completion and performance schedules as yet unclear.

At the heart of all the artistic activities of the Metropolitan Opera, it goes without saying, is the company's management. This management is ultimately responsible for all decisions of repertory, casting, and production. It is a responsibility which is—and must be—delegated, but which cannot long be evaded.

In this century, there have been three important administrative regimes at the Metropolitan. The Italian Giulio Gatti-Casazza (1908–1935) inherited Caruso and brought Toscanini to the company. In addition to his successful work as shepherd of the stars, he showed some interest in new American and European works. Gatti's long tenure was succeeded by the interregnum of the Canadian Edward Johnson; wartime conditions facilitated Johnson's replacement of imported singers by homegrown colleagues. The masterful

1. Given these works' virtually complete disappearance, it is good that a 1978 release brings together early recordings from all of them save *Peter Ibbetson* in performances contemporary with their presentation at the Metropolitan. This LP, New World Records NW 241, makes clear not only what has been lost, but what was never continued.

and voluble Sir Rudolf Bing—knighted in 1971 by Queen Elizabeth II—reigned from 1950 to 1972, bringing to the house a sharpened discipline and a feeling for glittering production values. His clearly announced views on modern music and box-office risks produced a Met up-to-date in every area save repertory.

Bing's retirement (only partly, it would seem, at his own wish) brought on an uneasy situation confused as much by ill luck as by conscious design. The Swedish opera director and administrator Goeran Gentele was appointed in 1970 to take Bing's place; shortly after his term of office began, he was killed in an automobile accident. Schuyler Chapin, Gentele's assistant, was hired first as a temporary and then as permanent general manager. One of Chapin's first acts was to appoint the well-known Czech conductor Rafael Kubelik to the newly created post of music director; Kubelik resigned before the end of his first season because (according to Bing) he did not receive the proper prerogatives his manager desired for him.

In musical decisions, Chapin now relied increasingly on the young James Levine, American-born, American-trained, and certainly the most successful American conductor to come along since Leonard Bernstein. While Levine has lasted at the Met, Chapin has not; he was soon done in by his own lack of decisiveness and, according to some, by a lack of support from the board.

By the mid-1970s, a new administration had come in, and save in one respect it is with us still. At the outset, this new management was a troika. Levine was music director, the English stage director John Dexter was director of production, and Anthony Bliss (who had earlier, from 1956 to 1967, been the Met's president) assumed, as executive director, a position *primus inter pares*. At present Dexter is gone from the triumvirate; Levine's post remains as before; and Bliss, as of January 1981, became general manager, a title the company had supposedly renounced in 1975.

To the Met's present fundraising success has been joined a businesslike management, utilizing every modern technique of financial and personnel administration. Only one mishap has marred the generally refulgent picture of prosperity and progress. A 1980 orchestral dispute lasting almost three months resulted in the cancellation of almost 100 performances. The fracas—usually referred to as a management lockout—ended with a contract that raised wages and sharply reduced the musicians' weekly workload; intemperate statements on both sides added to an already deep labor-management distrust perhaps unequaled in major American musical institutions.

The effects of the 1980 troubles, coming as they did at the beginning of the season, effectively removed the possibility of judging the offerings of 1980–81 on a fulfilled artistic basis. Two productions of that truncated year did, however, earn wide comment. A French triple bill, taking the name of *Parade* from the ballet (1917) of Erik Satie with which it began, also included Poulenc's *Les Mamelles de Tirésias* (1947) and Ravel's *L'Enfant et les sortilèges* (1920–25). Mainly significant for the Met debut (at age seventy-six!) of the French opera conductor Manuel Rosenthal and the presence in the house of an elite and fashionable artist-intellectual audience little seen these days at musical events, *Parade* was ecstatically received by a press anxious to demonstrate that there is *some* contemporary music it likes. In aesthetic terms, it seemed that the only purpose served by the production (other than providing a moderately diverting evening) was that of satisfying some of the Met's obligations to this century in music and art.

If in fact that was the aim, another of last season's offerings accomplished it in a vastly more serious way. The full three-act version of Berg's *Lulu,* completed by Friedrich Cerha, received a visually stunning production, enhanced by not one but two remarkable portrayals of the title role. One was by the role's intended singer, Teresa Stratas; the other, provided when Miss Stratas became ill, was by the Hispanic-American soprano Julia Migenes-Johnson. Both singers triumphed in a work that impressed at least this listener as the last great nineteenth-century operatic masterpiece, though it has earned contemporary classification thanks to its lurid plot and the learned commentaries Berg's closely wrought music has accumulated.

The present season has fortunately been complete. Comprising twenty-seven works by eleven composers, the repertory included two triple bills: Puccini's *Il Trittico,* consisting of *Il Tabarro, Suor Angelica,* and *Gianni Schicchi,* and an homage to Stravinsky, beginning with a ballet performance of *The Rite of Spring,* continuing with *Le Rossignol,* and ending with *Oedipus Rex.* Of Mozart there were *Così fan tutte* in a new production, *The Abduction from the Seraglio,* and *The Magic Flute.* The German heavyweights included

*Fidelio* of Beethoven, Wagner's *Tannhäuser, Das Rheingold, Siegfried,* and *Parsifal,* and Richard Strauss's *Die Frau ohne Schatten.* French music was represented by a new production of Offenbach's *Tales of Hoffmann.* The perennial children's favorite, Humperdinck's *Hansel and Gretel,* was there for the Christmas crowd. The rest was Italian: Bellini's *Norma,* Rossini's *Barber of Seville* (in a new production); Puccini's *Madame Butterfly, La Bohème,* and *Tosca* (in addition to *Il Trittico*); Verdi's *Luisa Miller, Rigoletto, La Traviata, Il Trovatore,* and *I Vespri Siciliani.*

The early part of the season was disfigured by stunningly inadequate performances of *Rheingold* and *Siegfried.* That only these two operas—of the four in the *Ring* cycle, the least able to stand on their own—were performed this season is itself a consequence both of the labor troubles of last year and persistent difficulties in casting major Wagnerian roles. Be that as it may, both operas were poorly sung, conducted in pedestrian fashion by the respected Erich Leinsdorf, and shabbily staged in the old Met "neo-Bayreuth" mode, which has now grown stale and aimless. Perhaps worst of all, the Met orchestra played Wagner's music badly, showing both raggedness and apathy.

Leinsdorf redeemed himself in October with a fine *Frau ohne Schatten,* strongly cast with both Birgit Nilsson and Eva Marton appearing in the same work. The once hugely imposing production has now begun to seem something of a monumental curiosity, but it could be said of this presentation, as of few this season, that musical values were largely well served.

By contrast, Levine's *Tannhäuser* in January, along with his April *Parsifal,* seemed more dutiful than compelling. In *Tannhäuser,* Leonie Rysanek's Elisabeth received the usual plaudits, though she struck me as artificial in stage deportment and out of tune in vocally important passages. The worldwide shortage of tenors capable of strong singing and believable acting made itself felt here, too. Missing in *Parsifal,* as in previous seasons, was any suggestion on Levine's part that he had identified himself either with Wagner's transcendent music or with the composer's more dubious religious conceptions.[2] Moreover, the leading roles were much less adequately sung than they had been in past years.

2. This is no doubt a minority view: Levine has been engaged to make his Bayreuth debut this coming summer, conducting the 100th-anniversary performance of *Parsifal.*

The new Stravinsky triple bill catered to an audience remarkably similar to that served by *Parade* the previous season. Again the evening began with a ballet, and perhaps for a similar reason: minute for minute, ballets are simpler and cheaper to put on than Met-scale opera. But in this case the ballet—the once infamous *Rite of Spring*—is a symphonic showpiece, part of the repertory of every virtuoso orchestra in the world. At the same time it has a long history of unsatisfactory rendering as a ballet. The Met orchestral performance did not, in fact, come up to the standard of the New York Philharmonic, its competition across Lincoln Center Plaza; the dancing was hardly stirring; and English painter David Hockney's much ballyhooed decor seemed both sparse and (dare one use the word?) hackneyed.

Matters improved in *Le Rossignol*. Inspired dancing by Natalia Makarova, and sensitive surroundings created by Hockney, combined with excellent singing and diction (from the pit) by Gwendolyn Bradley and Philip Creech, made the work vastly more affecting than it has often seemed in recorded or concert performance. *Oedipus Rex,* though visually arresting—the narrator was even made up to look like Jean Cocteau, the work's librettist (along with Stravinsky)—seemed to lack the archaic, mythic quality conjured up by the composer. What was substituted instead came closer to being peculiar and even a little nasty.

Without doubt the centerpiece of the entire season was the eagerly awaited Franco Zeffirelli production of *La Bohème*. In its first performance (and as televised) it featured Teresa Stratas as Mimi, José Carreras as Rodolfo, and Renata Scotto as Musetta. Later in the season Teresa Zylis-Gara replaced Stratas, Placido Domingo came in for Carreras, and Migenes-Johnson for Scotto. The original cast, as viewed on television, seemed to be overacting for the camera; the replacement cast, at least as viewed in the house, was less histrionic, and the result therefore dramatically more believable and vocally even superior, though Migenes-Johnson did sound dwarfed by the huge voices of the two stars. Levine's conducting, common to both casts, was straightforward and even compelling in a no-nonsense way. Still, to a listener aware (from records) of Toscanini's burning intensity in this music, of Beecham's unbuttoned lyricism, of the Italian afflatus surrounding the performance of the fabled tenor Beniamino Gigli, conducting and singing alike seemed both unidiomatic and unmoving.

The Zeffirelli-designed sets, on the other hand, were (and are; they will doubtless remain in use for the next generation) a kind of marvel of the age. The first- and fourth-act set, scene of initial joy and final tragedy, used the whole enormous Met stage to present a picture not only of Rodolfo's garret but also of what looked like half the roofs of Paris as well. The third-act set, a winter scene recalling a kind of Franco-Japanese impressionism, was both beautiful and evocative. But it was the second-act set of a street above and the Café Momus below that took the prize: two levels, hundreds of extras, the scene a circus extravaganza dwarfing any conceivable human emotions and relationships. After this miracle of the designer's and carpenter's art, the death of Mimi in the finale seemed so much meaningless bustle, with actions and feelings being worked out on a relatively tiny and unimportant scale.

*The Barber of Seville,* seen in February in a new production by John Cox, also used the Met stage to maximum effect. This time the major attribute was the huge revolving platform (whose malfunction had contributed to the disastrous Met presentation of *Antony and Cleopatra*). Here, in Rossini's comparatively simple piece, several different settings appeared, as if by magic, in the course of a few minutes. Unfortunately, nothing musical came close to this level of virtuosity. Andrew Davis, the English conductor now in Toronto, led a performance that aimed at small-scale elegance and instead managed to be both lifeless and clumsy; the orchestral playing too was sloppy. Vocally the laurels went to Marilyn Horne, now secure the world over as a superstar. She gratified her fans, displaying remarkable agility in complicated passagework. The tenor singing Almaviva, in contrast, sang the opening *"Ecco ridente"* without making even an approach to the required florid style.

With five operas this season, Verdi was undeniably well represented. *La Traviata* and *Il Trovatore,* neither of them characteristic of Verdi's mature genius, received performances that were rewarding, like the curate's egg, in parts. The star in *Traviata* was the production, first seen here last season. The refined and elegant sets advanced the opera's action in time to post-1870 Paris. The resulting polish and sparkle, though attractive, seemed neither natural to the music nor radically new; everything appeared to belong more to the world of Strauss's *Arabella* than either to Verdi or to us. Catherine Malfitano sang Violetta in a soaring and attractive voice, employed to little dramatic purpose; Nicola Rescigno's conducting lacked bite and passion.

James Conlon's handling of *Trovatore,* with Leontyne Price as a vocally commanding if sometimes uneven Leonora, was little better. In the past this talented conductor has shown an affinity for the less earthy Puccini. Here with Verdi he seemed to be attempting a curiously refined orchestral execution. The result most of the time was a loss of tension, and an opaque tone in the work's frequent climaxes. The stage direction too appeared to have gone sour; all too often the stage was populated by posed statues, not living actors.

Vastly more interesting was the new offering of *Così fan tutte,* which made its bow in late January. The sets were dazzling, the singing perky, and Levine's conducting was vibrant and, even more admirable, tightly controlled. In all it added up to a weighty, hearty Mozart, in some places sounding rather like Handel and in others like a Richard Strauss tribute to Mozart. But at least here, as in the earlier *Bohème,* one could see a new operatic style in the process of being born at the Met, a style suited, as perhaps it must be, to the huge expanse of the house and the newly large and largely new audience to which the Met is now catering. The fact that this style at its best is big, brilliant, and brittle may be compliment enough to some; to others it must inevitably seem the technologically efficient product of the conjunction of art and marketing.

*Fidelio,* seen at the end of March in its first performance this season, marked the podium debut at the Met of Bernard Haitink, the permanent conductor of the Amsterdam Concertgebouw and music director of the Glyndebourne Festival in England. Here, at last, was a great name at the helm, an experienced leader of international operatic productions and, to boot, a widely respected interpreter of Beethoven. The result was deeply disappointing, and not only because of the forced and tense vocal production of Shirley Verrett as the heroine Leonora and the wretched singing of tenor Edward Sooter as Florestan.

As so often happens at the Met, the performance failed in the pit. Again, orchestral playing was ragged; again, the conducting lacked drive, passion, and integration. The enthusiastic audience reaction to Haitink's performance of the famous *Leonore* Overture No. 3, between scenes one and two of Act II, made clear how far standards of interpretation and execution have slipped in contemporary musical life.

The season also included three concert performances. One, in February, was a Saturday matinee, also broadcast, of Verdi's *Requiem,* conducted by Levine and starring Leontyne Price; a second, in March, featured Tatiana Troyanos and Placido Domingo, with Levine conducting, in a program of vocal and orchestral excerpts; the third, again in March, not broadcast at the time, presented Marilyn Horne and Price, once more under Levine's baton. Concerts at the Met by company artists are hardly new, but this emphasis on them suggests a decision by management that opera production, clearly a financial loser, should and must be supported by every conceivable attempt to capitalize on the prestige and availability of stars—even at the cost of diluting and changing the public image of the company's mission.

The rest of the year, heard (except for *The Magic Flute*) on radio or seen, as in the case of *Il Trittico* and *Rigoletto,* on television, offered little to conflict with an in-house assessment. Crudely exciting conducting from Levine in *Norma* and *I Vespri Siciliani*; journeyman efforts from all concerned in *Tosca* and *Madame Butterfly*; a heavy *Tales of Hoffmann*; an unremarkable *Hansel and Gretel*; all these added to the impression of a season woefully deficient in precisely those qualities necessary, in the words of a Met radio commercial, to "dazzle the imagination."

The verdict on the season just past must rather be one of a rude plenty in staple items and a tendency to substitute limited novelty for any real discovery at all. Orchestral standards did, on the whole, improve throughout the year from the low estate of the two *Ring* opera performances; as a rule the best orchestra playing came when Levine himself was conducting. Indeed, Levine is undoubtedly the best conductor now working at the Met on anything like a regular basis. His strengths as a musician are brisk confidence and a consistent ability to achieve lively performances. His defects are a sameness of style in Italian music (generally his best) and the lack of an architectural sense in such weighty music as Wagner. It is easy to blame Levine for arrogating to himself the best conducting assignments and bringing too few outside names to the Met, but given the present worldwide dearth of conducting giants, such blame is perhaps misplaced.

Singing levels at the Met—at least apart from Wagner—seem adequate to sustain performances of major works. Though Levine himself has talked of the difficulties he faces in finding voices for such works as *Aida,* superstars like Domingo and Pavarotti, Horne and Sutherland (absent this year but returning next), are still capable of thrilling large audiences. In any case, it hardly seems a tragedy that a few familiar works will retire from the repertory for a while.

The problem of Wagner is rather more serious. Here the Met is in trouble not just in voices. The conducting in these cornerstone works of the repertory is not now adequate for communicating them to an audience that has not been offered a full *Ring* since the 1974–75 season. When these operas return to the Met as a cycle, it must be in a new production taking account of the many changes in the staging of Wagner during the last generation. This is not necessarily to endorse such trendy manipulations of Wagner's original intentions as those perpetrated by Patrice Chéreau at Bayreuth in 1976, or even to agree with the kind of recomposition involved in Jean-Pierre Ponnelle's Met production of *The Flying Dutchman* a few seasons back. The point is not that any particular new production is good, or even that the new is better than the old. It is rather that in opera production, as in music itself, the essential greatness of the old can only be seen against the background of the new; this remains true even where new ventures can realistically promise little hope of wide success.

The Met's unwillingness to take risks is at its most striking in the matter of repertory. Next season, for example, contemporary music will be represented by a revival of the *Parade* triple bill. Elsewhere, the most modern-sounding work will be *Pelléas et Mélisande.* Mussorgsky's *Boris Godunov* will return, as will Strauss's *Der Rosenkavalier* and *Arabella.* Novelty will be represented by Francesco Cilea's *Adriana Lecouvreur* (1902). The great event of the season will be the Met premiere of Mozart's *Idomeneo,* written just over 200 years ago. As has become usual for the Met, nothing will be really new, and nothing, most assuredly, will be American.

One question can hardly be avoided. Given the Met's remarkable affluence, to what use is all this prosperity going to be put? In other times, the answer would have been simple: the business of a performing-arts institution is to put on the art of the day.

Now the function of such an institution, as we have seen in the case of the Met, is museological. Indeed, such curatorial work is seen as the only course consistent with the survival of the institution.

This position of caretaker is one which connects the Met of Bliss and Levine with the earlier reign of Rudolf Bing. But what was acceptable in the late 1940s in New York is not so today. Then the New York City Opera was close to the beginning of its vanguard work in presenting native and imported works of the day. Now, however, the City Opera is weakened, unsure of its repertory, casting about for any possible means of continuing as a functioning enterprise. As a result the Met is more important in New York's cultural life (and, because of television, that of the country as well) than ever before. How will it choose to discharge its responsibilities?

Even on the level of survival, it is clear that the Met plays it safer than it might, and safer than other, not really dissimilar institutions do. The San Francisco Opera, for example, has regularly put on new and controversial works; in the last few seasons these have included such chancy items as Shostakovich's erotically explicit *Lady Macbeth of the Mtsensk District* (1934), Luigi Dallapiccola's twelve-tone *Il Prigioniero* (1944–48), and Aribert Reimann's avant-garde *Lear* (1978). That such adventuresomeness is consistent with high-level performance of the standard repertory is shown by the recent extraordinary San Francisco productions of *Arabella* and Wagner's *Die Meistersinger*.

Clear as are the short-term benefits to the Met of following a cautious strategy, there are other, rather less pleasant, long-term effects. Even more than in the case of new art, the already famous requires freshness, vivacity, and the deeply felt illusion that each re-encounter is a pristine experience. To perform the same—or similar—works in the same way year after year is to become imitative and repetitive. To have no other place to find something new than in previously hidden parts of the old is to exaggerate minor discoveries and discrepancies and to run the risk of violating the one basic attribute of the old—its age. The matter can be simply put: without the new to stimulate digestion, the old loses its power to nourish. Here perhaps is the reason for the present vague mood of dissatisfaction with the Met now noticeable among audience and critics alike: where there is nothing to disagree with, there is nothing to cherish.

Given the present negative attitude toward new operatic and musical art, can one really require that the Met—or any other great performing institution—take remedial action in the almost certain knowledge that the happiest outcome will be no more than a *succès d'estime,* and that the far more likely outcome will be failure with both the press and the public? Can one, in other words, institutionalize risk taking?

Here, precisely, there may well be a priceless opportunity for the Metropolitan Opera to defend and even enhance its unique private status and independence. By showing that a free-enterprise system in art can be just as innovative and creative as it has been in business and finance, the Met might counter the argument that only government support can assist the development of new art. The Met is rich enough to try; is it capitalist enough to pick up the challenge?

[1982]

# Opera Appreciation, Metropolitan-style

Just because so little new creation of high musical art is currently visible, the efforts of performing institutions are increasingly turned toward the more or less distant past. But while such efforts undeniably have the easy virtue of concentrating on the "greats," they present a dilemma as well: How can a knowing and participant audience be found for the cultural products of another time and, as in the case of our country, another place?

This dilemma clearly affects no institution on the American artistic scene more poignantly than the Metropolitan Opera. Well on its way to a $100-million annual budget, the Met has forsaken the cause not only of contemporary operatic composition but even of production. Instead the company has chosen to spend its talent and treasure on the presentation of hallowed works—or occasionally of lesser-known works by hallowed composers. These works are to be produced, it is clear, in a manner going no further in innovation than a bright re-creation of the originally intended style.

But evidently an audience for even this safe museological task cannot be taken for granted, and given the desirability of expanding audience figures for company image and for fundraising, this audience must be both large and patently enthusiastic. So little faith does the Met have in this happening by itself that it has little choice but to add yet one more dimension to its already assiduous marketing scheme: "education." It has attempted to teach its audience many times before, primarily through its radio (and television) broadcasts and their intermission features, and through its publication, *Opera News*. Now a new teaching method is being tried, a method that brings together in book form material on an individual opera, ranging from the libretto and its translation to historical essays, a plot summary, photographs, a discography and bibliography, and, most innovatively, a retelling of the opera's story by a major—or at least famous—author.

The subject of the Met's first attempt in this new line is Richard Strauss's *Der Rosenkavalier* (1910). A success on its premiere in Dresden in 1911, it was first done by the Metropolitan in 1913, the same year as its first performance in London. Since then it has been performed countless times all over the world, and has become known as a solid favorite of audiences everywhere. *Der Rosenkavalier* is one of the major attractions in the Met's especially conventional 1982–83 season, and the release of the present guidebook is timed to coincide with the Public Broadcasting Service's "Live from the Met" telecast of the opera.[1] In line with the Met's general marketing philosophy of making something saleable for every purse, the book is available in three versions: paperback at $8.95, hardcover at $16.95, and a deluxe edition at $75.

One should begin with the good news first. Hugo von Hofmannsthal's magnificent libretto, a spicy mélange of romantic German sentiment and cosy Viennese sentimentality, is included in a reasonably readable format. From here on everything in the guidebook is downhill.

The translation of the libretto, for example, is the dated and even originally inadequate 1912 version of Alfred Kalisch, an early English Straussian. Kalisch's staid rendering, which remains the official translation of Strauss's publishers, Boosey & Hawkes, has here been updated to remove some of the old-fashioned English diction that so disfigured Kalisch's work. But the unaccountable substitution of "Mignon" for "Quinquin," the lover's endearment by which the Marschallin calls Octavian throughout Act I, is retained, for reasons no more persuasive than were those involved in the original substitution.

There is here a wider loss of literal meaning as well. Thus the first four lines of the libretto, which in the original German read

> *Octavian*: Wie du warst! Wie du bist!
> Das weiss niemand, das ahnt keiner!
>
> *Marschallin*: Beklagt Er sich über das, Quinquin?
> Möcht Er, dass viele das wüssten?

is given in the neo-Kalisch translation as

1. Richard Strauss, *Der Rosenkavalier*; libretto by Hugo von Hofmannsthal, story adaptation by Anthony Burgess. The Metropolitan Opera Classics Library, Little, Brown and Company, 1982.

*Octavian*: All thy soul, all thy heart—
    None can measure their perfection.

*Princess*: Why grieve so sorely at that, Mignon?
    Should it be known on the housetops?

It hardly seems necessary to point out that the original German contains no mention, not only of Mignon, but of such words as "soul," "heart," "perfection," and "housetops." Whatever the merit of these words—and of the concepts they denote—there is no reason to think their addition is a service to Hofmannsthal's original creation or to its understanding by an unsophisticated reader.

Present too, in the Kalisch translation—both old and revised—is a kind of bowdlerization that hardly seems necessary in today's world or faithful to a work of art. At the end of Act I, for example, Octavian, realizing that the affair with the Marschallin is at an end, says, *Soll dass heissen, dass ich Sie nie mehr/werd' küssen dürfen, bis Ihr der Atem ausgeht?* Kalisch palely renders this erotic description as "Does it mean that never again—no, never,/I shall kiss you—kiss you in endless rapture?"

There is, fortunately, evidence that a rather more literal—and therefore more informative—version is possible. A translation of the *Rosenkavalier* play, which the poet published separately from the libretto, was included in volume three of the Bollingen *Selected Writings* of Hofmannsthal. This version, by Christopher Holme, has virtues of both plainness and fidelity. The opening lines, for example, are rendered as

*Octavian*: What you were! What you are!
    No one can know, no one can guess!

*Princess*: Is that a complaint? Would my Quin-
    quin prefer that many knew it?

And the sensual lines so misrepresented by Kalisch are given by Holme simply and accurately as "Does that mean I shall never again/be allowed to kiss you till/you gasp for air?"

No work of music appreciation would be complete without written material telling the reader what he ought to like and why he ought to like it. In the Met guidebook this function is assumed by

George Marek, former RCA record executive and record columnist for *Good Housekeeping,* the writer of a worshipful biography of Beethoven and a hostile one of Strauss. For the Met book, Marek has written two pieces, one an "Introduction" to the opera and the other a "Reevaluation" of Strauss and Hofmannsthal. It is difficult to think that either essay will increase a neophyte's comprehension or enjoyment of the opera.

About *Der Rosenkavalier* itself, Marek is by turns lowbrow and dismissive. He asks, in the best style of cookery magazines, "Can anybody resist this inundating feast of melody?" Then, after praising the high points of the work, he goes on to savage Strauss's creation:

> *Der Rosenkavalier* is too long. Worse, at certain moments the music is too fulsome and boisterous and grandiloquent. At others—stretches of the second act and the beginning of the third—it coasts.

So plain are these words that Marek's continuation

> But the defects of the opera can be counted on the fingers of one hand. Its joy remains intact after a lifetime of hearing. . .

can only seem lame and inexplicable. He nowhere can account for the opera's strength in the face of what he sees as its defects, except in terms of peremptory and superficial judgments. Ignored, for example, is the whole question of just why the opera's most salacious feature—the casting of the Marschallin's seventeen-year-old lover as a female role—produces in us an effect not of disgust but rather of charm and even virtue.

When Marek turns to Strauss and Hofmannsthal as artists, this same combination of ambivalence and poorly grounded summary opinion is again in evidence. He admits that Strauss wrote "enough to assure [him] an important place in music's living repertoire"— but his list of what will live unaccountably fails to mention the towering and refined masterpiece of the composer's very old age, the *Metamorphosen* for twenty-three solo strings of 1944–45. Perhaps this work was left out because it accords ill with Marek's judgment of Richard Strauss as a musician:

For such music [the works Marek thinks will last] we are willing to accept the blots that spot even his best conceptions, a touch of vulgarity—indeed more than a touch—an occasional sugariness of melody and harmony, a tumult noisier than the thought warrants, and here and there polyphonic nodules. . . .

From these dicta it is a short jump indeed to some remarkably negative judgments on the permanent value of the Strauss-Hofmannsthal collaboration. For Marek, *Der Rosenkavalier* almost says it all:

> In more aspects than one, *Der Rosenkavalier* marks the apogee of Strauss's operatic creations. *Ariadne auf Naxos* may equal it in charm—it is Hofmannsthal's best libretto—but not in full musical satisfaction. Its end, from the entrance of Bacchus, is a disaster. But Act I and most of Act II are unmitigated joy.[2] Not so *Die Frau ohne Schatten*: the libretto is sesquipedalian with various symbolisms clashing all over the place. *Die aegyptische Helena* is even less convincing, and *Arabella* is a rehash of *Der Rosenkavalier,* where one has to wait until the third act to hear truly fine music.

But all this, I am afraid, is little more than mere like or dislike. To these preferences can easily be opposed other, and perhaps more detailed, opinions. The end of *Ariadne,* though monstrously difficult to perform, is a brilliantly successful example of Wagner's conception of "endless melody." And the first act of *Arabella* contains such touching and beautifully made music as Arabella's *"Er ist der Richtige nicht für mich!"* and the subsequent duet passage with Zdenka.

Having found Strauss lacking as a composer, and having judged the collaboration with Hofmannsthal to have produced only one first-class, albeit flawed, work, Marek is scarcely inconsistent when he passes a negative verdict on Hofmannsthal as a writer. He asks a question, then answers it:

2. A reader might be forgiven here for feeling some worry that Marek has gotten hold of the wrong opera. *Ariadne* is indeed composed of two parts but they are not "acts"; in the score the work is described as *Oper in einem Aufzug nebst einem Vorspiel*—"Opera in one act with a prologue."

Was he a great writer? I think not. His lack of clarity, his inchoate mysticism, and a touch of theatricality in his verses prevented him from being more than a minor, though a fine-grained talent.

But to ground this opinion Marek fails to quote any of Hofmannsthal's great poetry; he fails to mention the *fin-de-siècle* classic of literary self-doubt, the *Letter of Lord Chandos* (1902); he ignores the epic fairytale *The Woman without a Shadow* (1919), a companion to the libretto for Strauss's opera. And he even passes over the very poetry of the Strauss operas for which Hofmannsthal wrote the words. Thus there is no recognition of the great literary merit in the Marschallin's monologues on time in *Rosenkavalier*; unremarked by Marek go the ineffably moving (and in German lyrically tender) lines of Octavian about the defenseless Sophie in Act II of the opera:

Mit Ihren Augen voll Tränen
kommt Sie zu mir, damit Sie sich beklagt.
Vor Angst muss Sie an mich sich lehnen,
Ihr armes Herz ist ganz verzagt . . .

[With her eyes full of tears
she comes to me to complain.
In fear she leans on me,
her poor young heart is quite hopeless. . .][3]

To accompany the text of the guidebook, there are photographs of famous productions of the past in Europe, and of the current production at the Met as well. The photographs of the past are interesting evidence of how anchored to that past the present production is. The discography, adequate as far as it goes, lacks listings of so-called pirate records; thus missing is the George Szell performance at Salzburg in 1949, an important document of how a great modern conductor dealt with this complex score. Missing also from the list of recorded excerpts is the extraordinary performance of the Act III trio by Viorica Ursuleac (Strauss's favorite soprano), Tiana

3. Because the Holme translation is of Hofmannsthal's play rather than of the libretto Strauss used for musical purposes, these words do not appear therein. I have therefore used the Walter Legge version, which is included in the Schwarzkopf-Karajan recording for EMI/Angel.

Lemnitz, and Erna Berger; on the other side of this 78 RPM disc[4] is a ravishing account of the concluding duet by Lemnitz and Berger. Both sides are conducted magnificently by Clemens Krauss, Strauss's librettist for *Capriccio*. The bibliography, though containing many important items, lacks material on Hofmannsthal: missing is mention of the other two volumes in the Bollingen selection from Hofmannsthal, the *Poems and Verse Plays* and the *Selected Prose*. Missing too is any listing of the short works on the author by Lowell A. Bangerter and by Hanns Hammelmann, both entitled *Hugo von Hofmannsthal*.

However undistinguished the material I have so far discussed may be, it is passably earnest and no doubt well-meaning; it is rarely meretricious. But that word is unfortunately the only one that can be applied to Anthony Burgess's vulgar, coarse, cheap, and ill-written attempt to do for the ignorant what Hofmannsthal did for the cultivated audience he knew. Using many of the lines from the opera as dialogue[5] and the stage directions as descriptive material, Burgess shows that what was once done supremely well can be neither improved upon nor even simplified. What began with Hofmannsthal in lyric poetry thus ends with Burgess in leaden prose, all wrapped in the lineaments of philosophy.

Burgess's first lines are a disquisition on history—the kind of disquisition that is all wool and a truism wide. To read it is to recognize the genre:

> History is always the past. We never live through history. When we are old, we discover to our surprise that we *have* lived through it. When we die we join it.

But as Burgess starts to talk about the Marschallin and Octavian as lovers, he quickly jettisons the philosophy:

> Of the movements of history the lovers knew nothing and cared less. The movements of their own bodies were of greater interest.

4. The original appearance of these performances was on Deutsche Grammophon 67075; according to Alan Jefferson in *Opera on Record,* they also appeared on LP as Discophilia KG UI.

5. Strangely, Burgess seems to base his dialogue not on the original German but on the Kalisch translation: thus he uses Mignon instead of Quinquin; like Kalisch, he uses the word "perfection" at the beginning of the story, though it does not appear in Hofmannsthal.

As with history, so with passion; on the next page we find the mood more Noël Coward's bright brittleness than Hofmannsthal's intended gentle spoof on *Tristan und Isolde*:

There was nothing effeminate in his lovemaking. "But when I say *you*," he was saying as he dressed swiftly, "and speak of your this and that, I'm just as foolish as when I say *I*. The words have no meaning. We lose our identities in love and become one being."

"Which means," said the Princess, "that I may not say *I love you*. But I say it. I say it now."

When Burgess gets around to describing Baron Ochs, Strauss and Hofmannsthal's somehow likable comic villain, we are treated to a touch of merrie England at its most repulsive:

His belly was more than Falstaffian: it denoted heavy dinners and heavy bevers before and after them. He would have looked more presentable with a Falstaffian beard, but this was an age of clean shaves and wigs. His nose was a maimed beacon: its red shine was marred by the lumps of good living and a wart on the left-hand slope that sported three filaments which waved in the breeze of his bark. His eyes of a sharp blue were couched in fat.

It seems ironic that poetry as beautiful as that of Hofmannsthal should be represented to an unsuspecting public by a writer capable of such clumsiness and confusion as the following description:

Then there came in Ochs's breakfast, on a tray borne by one of the Baron's own men, an ill-favored starveling with a faint squint. . . . He [Ochs] pointed to a low square stool: he would pick at it later when this mob had gone.

Can this be from the pen that wrote myriad articles in the *Times Literary Supplement,* and even *A Clockwork Orange?*

As the retelling proceeds, the Marschallin ages, Sophie falls in love with Octavian and Octavian with her, the Baron is undone, and the Marschallin gives way to the new reality of love between coevals. But as Burgess tells the story, we have little of the majesty of the Marschallin, the innocence of Sophie, or the maturity of Octavian. Instead we have pasteboard characters and maudlin situations undercut even in their sentimentality by a trite and superficial cynicism never present in Hofmannsthal. Thus when the Marschallin is describing to Octavian her vague presentiments of the future at the end of Act I, Burgess has her say "We're in a banal situation—something out of a play so bad it makes the spectators yawn."

The final proof of Burgess's failure either to penetrate the story or to communicate it is clear at the end, where he slides over the emotions so magnificently presented in the great Act III trio. The Marschallin's resignation, Octavian's transport of love, Sophie's consciousness of wonder and surrender—all this is simply eliminated and Burgess is content with describing the famous concluding episode, in which the little black boy runs across an empty stage to pick up Sophie's dropped handkerchief, as the result of Sophie's having "had the makings of a thrifty housekeeper." O romance, O magic, O art!

Nor is Burgess content to leave matters here. The last paragraph but one tells what happened to the characters after the opera ends.

> Octavian lost a leg and an eye in the war of the Austrian Succession. Sophia died bearing her second child. The widowed Princess entered a nunnery. Baron Ochs married the richest heiress of all Austria and died at ninety-one in his bed. Or, if you wish, none of these things happened.

And the final paragraph makes clear the whole thing isn't worth a hill of beans: " 'It would,' Sophia's father sometimes said, 'have made a rather good comic opera.' "

What are we to make of this effort at music appreciation that contains not one note of musical example? What are we to make of a discussion of the work of a great poet and writer that contains little of his own material and no appreciation of what he wrote? What are we to make of this hack retelling by a popular novelist of a glorious masterwork of European civilization? And what are we to make of the sponsorship of all this by one of America's greatest artistic institutions, which is also one of the world's half-dozen or so greatest opera companies?

The answer seems inescapable. This unworthy production is the result of replacing the goals of art by those of institutional survival and expansion. By this book, the Metropolitan Opera has amply demonstrated that its interest is neither in a living new culture nor in the preservation of a distinguished older one.[6] It has demonstrated, too, a nihilistic lack of faith in the ability of its audience to appreciate and demand art. There will be those who will try to explain the present failure as a democratic degeneration, some loss of taste consequent on the granting of the franchise to a mass citizenry. But the matter is far simpler. It is the old story of the corruption of the weak by ambition, money, and power. It will be tempting to blame all this merely on the artistic personnel of the Metropolitan. To do so would be most unfairly to ignore the fact that the company is run by the board, and by the administrators. Theirs is the decision, and theirs is the shame.

[1982]

6. As if to make clear that this project is no one-time event, the publicity release announcing the *Rosenkavalier* book ends with the ominous words "future volumes in the Metropolitan Opera Classics Library series will include a story adaptation of *La Traviata* by Mary McCarthy and *La Bohème* by V. S. Pritchett."

# The Hollywood and Other String Quartets

Until now chamber music has been booming, or exploding, to choose only two of the military metaphors so often invoked. The proof is in the numbers. A 1981 publication of the National Endowment for the Arts, citing a spokesman for an advocacy group, painted a rosy picture:

> Droves of young musicians around the country are turning to careers in chamber music. There are now more than 1,000 chamber music groups, according to Benjamin Dunham, executive director of Chamber Music America. "More and more talented musicians who would otherwise have gone into symphony orchestras, teaching jobs, or solo careers are now gravitating toward chamber music and creating their own audiences through the force of their own personalities, their energy, their hustle, their exciting programming, and their excellent playing."

And indeed, wherever one looks one finds more small ensembles playing more pieces than ever before in our musical history. What holds true on the amateur level, where more or less accomplished enthusiasts play for fun, is paralleled by similar prosperity in schools, where groups ranging from brass and woodwind quintets to string trios and quartets are being joined "in residence" by combinations (on occasion exotic) of any of these traditional instruments with piano and/or percussion.

At the pinnacle of all this activity, it goes without saying, are those ensembles actually playing numerous concerts, for sizable fees, to audiences across the country. Among such groups are two brass quintets, the American and the Empire, and the Beaux Arts Trio, which has won a large following for its performances of the piano-trio literature. But whatever the success of these interesting combinations, the greatest public renown is, as always, reserved for the traditional string quartet. This combination of two violins, viola, and cello has been hallowed not just by time; it is the medium for performing what many believe to be the greatest body of music ever written: the string quartets of Haydn, Mozart, Beethoven, and Schubert. Of course there are also countless lesser but still imposing works by such composers as Schumann, Brahms, and Dvořák in the nineteenth century, as well as major efforts by Bartók, Schoenberg, and Shostakovich (and their many disciples and opponents) in the twentieth.

Several highly publicized groups occupy the string-quartet spotlight in America today. At their head, by a combination of longevity and the kind of eternal youth that comes from periodically replacing all the players save the original first violinist, stands the Juilliard Quartet. This ensemble, founded in 1946 and associated with the music school in New York of the same name, has specialized from its inception in exciting and energetic performances of a modern repertory beginning with Bartók and Schoenberg and extending as far forward as the last two quartets of the American composer Elliott Carter. All this material the Juilliard has recorded, often more than once, first for RCA and then more recently for Columbia (now called CBS).

Next to the Juilliard in fame is the Guarneri Quartet. This group of experienced musicians—the first violinist was an assistant concertmaster of the Cleveland Orchestra under George Szell, and the cellist was a member of the New Music Quartet, which did many contemporary works during the 1940s and '50s—is associated in the current academic year with the University of Maryland. Though it has played some contemporary music, it tends to eschew the problematic in favor of the solid classics of the repertory. It has a large following, and receives high fees for its many appearances. It is also the subject of a lighthearted but withal adoring book[1] written by a *New Yorker* staff member, much of which first appeared in that magazine.

On a somewhat lower level of status is the Cleveland Quartet, whose members all teach at the Eastman School of Music in Rochester. Recording, as does the Guarneri, for RCA, the Cleveland projects an appealing air of youthfulness. Equal to the Cleveland in

1. *Quartet: A Profile of the Guarneri Quartet,* by Helen Drees Ruttencutter. Lippincott and Crowell, 1980.

popularity and activity is the Tokyo Quartet, whose original members (despite the name of the group) were all trained at Juilliard. Now for the first time with a non-Japanese member, the Tokyo is billed as an American ensemble.

There are many more quartets that are somewhat less active and well known. An older group, affiliated with Columbia University, is the Composers Quartet; it has specialized in contemporary music, venturing somewhat beyond the Juilliard in degree of concentration on the new and in the intellectual difficulty of the works performed. Among the younger groups are the Concord, which has recently won attention for its playing of the complete cycle of the Beethoven quartets, and the Emerson, whose performances of Bartók have similarly brought it to recent notice. There are, in addition, permanent groups being formed (and one assumes, breaking up) all the time, as well as many ad hoc ensembles, some organized by schools out of available faculty members, others the creation of such presenting organizations as New York's Lincoln Center and the 92nd Street Y. These last, essentially audience-oriented, attractions tend to concentrate on a wide choice of well-liked material played, as in the case of Lincoln Center's Chamber Music Society, by different instrumental combinations, rather than on the string-quartet literature by itself. A new trend, though one with solid historical roots, consists of first-chair symphony players appearing under the name of the orchestra in chamber-music concerts; the possibility of such performance opportunities is often an attractive condition of orchestra employment.

It is fashionable to point out that chamber music in general and string-quartet playing in particular inevitably suffer from a built-in economic handicap. Though the number of players is small, the audiences for which such concerts are given are also small, compared to those who patronize opera companies, symphony orchestras, and star recitalists. The houses in which chamber music is played are rarely very large, and devotees of the art are reluctant to allow the music they love and the ensembles they cherish to be presented in roomy but always more distant-sounding environments. Indeed, to do so would be to sacrifice the major selling point advanced on behalf of chamber music: its intimacy.

So chamber music, on this analysis at least, needs large amounts of money for its survival. Since that money cannot be generated at the box office, it must come from subsidies. As in the past, some of the burden can be, and is, borne by schools and institutions. Some too is borne by such profit-making activities—usually well-attended recital series—as still remain in serious music. But school budgets face increasing demands and declining revenues. Musical institutions are themselves always confronting higher labor, administrative, and plant costs. And the fees for star soloists have increased well beyond the rate of inflation, with the resultant loss of the profits from celebrity appearances that could formerly be used to support concerts of more limited appeal. It must be said too that the older kind of music patronage, in which one individual would underwrite a group, is now extinct.

In the case of chamber music, the new money needed has come from a coalition of private-sector philanthropy based on nonprofit foundations and corporations, and an increasingly effective governmental support program. In the 1981 fiscal year, for example, the National Endowment for the Arts granted a total of $476,200 for chamber music (including $23,000 for a program of chamber-music advocacy run by Chamber Music America). In themselves these grants were too small and too widely distributed to be decisive. But as an indication of federal-government approval, they helped to raise vastly larger sums from donors who otherwise might have given less or not at all.

The corollary of all the money going into chamber music is, of course, the money being taken out. Not only are administrators being supported in the style to which they have quickly become accustomed; even the artists themselves are sharing in the vastly larger pie. As recently as thirty-five years ago, the Budapest Quartet —perhaps the most famous and respected such group of the century —played concerts for a fee of $800; even this fee was often cut in half by a foundation subsidy. Today the Guarneri Quartet gets more than $5,000, and the Juilliard gets about the same. And when top fees go up, the effect is to raise other fees all down the line.

Has the recent prosperity of chamber music produced a golden age of performance? The reviewers certainly seem to think so: every day we read about the "deepest insight" into this, the "greatest performance" of that. But for a sophisticated listener with access to the wealth of chamber-music recordings of the past, the notion that everyone is playing better and better every day in every way can seem hollow indeed.

Just how hollow this notion is may be gauged from a consideration of the recorded legacy of the Hollywood Quartet, perhaps the
best string quartet ever to have been assembled in America. The
Hollywood is now largely forgotten in this country, and does not
even merit its own entry in the *New Grove Dictionary,* the music
world's book of life. Yet from its founding in 1948 to 1961, when
it disbanded, the Hollywood made more than twenty recordings for
Capitol, a Southern California firm later to become the American
subsidiary of the English giant EMI. Now EMI has followed up a
recent reissue in England of the group's performance of works by
Schubert, Brahms, Dvořák, and Smetana[2] with a four-record set of
all the late Beethoven string quartets.[3]

Unpropitious as the name of our old movie capital might be for
a string quartet, in the case of the Hollywood it had the substantial
merit of accuracy. During the group's existence, all its members
were studio musicians, busily and successfully playing soundtracks
written to order by composers gifted at being pleasing rather than
memorable. But it must not be thought that the Hollywood Quartet players were without serious musical credentials. First violinist
Felix Slatkin, for example, was a pupil of Efrem Zimbalist and also
studied conducting with Fritz Reiner at the Curtis Institute. Second
violinist Paul Shure was a leading member of Stokowski's All-
American Youth Orchestra in the early '40s, and is now the concertmaster of the Los Angeles Chamber Orchestra, one of the best
(and most refined) such groups in the United States, if not in the
world, today.

Because of studio commitments, the Hollywood's concert activities were largely confined to the Pacific Coast. Around 1950, however, they began to record. The first of their discs to appear coupled
the Sixth Quartet of the Brazilian composer Heitor Villa-Lobos with
the English William Walton's Quartet in A Minor. It was immediately apparent from this record that the ensemble possessed both
personality and a sense of style. The playing was at once suave and
brilliant, and the vastly different characteristics of the two composers—Villa-Lobos dark-hued and soulful, Walton linear and reserved *à l'anglaise*—were clearly limned.

With their next record, the group engaged (with the addition of
a second cello) the great Schubert Quintet in C Major. Here were

2. EMI HMV RLS 765.
3. EMI HMV RLS 7707.

established the typical outlines of a Hollywood performance: energy along with rock-solid rhythm, melodic sweetness combined with absolute decorum and gravity. Here too was a conception of Schubert that emphasized musical design and structural coherence rather than Viennese charm. The sweetness came from a virtuoso style of string playing perhaps influenced by the ever-reserved musicality and technical brilliance of a fellow resident of Southern California, Jascha Heifetz.

Though the Hollywood Quartet was to play a relatively limited amount of contemporary music, another of their early records demonstrated once again their gifts in this field. To Paul Hindemith's Third Quartet the Hollywood brought every necessary virtue of polyphonic clarity without ever losing the ability to play each melodic line as if it had been written for a beautiful human voice. If the group's performance, on the record's reverse side, of the Prokofiev Second Quartet seemed both softened in outline and somewhat lacking in drive, perhaps the fault lay as much with the work's essential aridity as with the players' execution.

Something of the high seriousness the Hollywood Quartet could achieve at its best is amply conveyed by the group's recording of one of the cornerstones of the repertory, the Schubert Quartet in D Minor, better known as "Death and the Maiden." Here the performing miracle is the perfection of the playing, consisting in secure intonation and rhythmic precision. Comparison with the recorded performances of two historically great quartets, the Busch in 1936 and the Budapest in 1953, places the Hollywood, for all the musical virtues of the others, in a class by itself.

Elsewhere, in the works of Hugo Wolf, Joaquin Turina, the American Paul Creston, and the piano quintets of Brahms and Franck, the Hollywood seems content to play with a kind of dutiful musicality, without the urgency that marks their most vital performances. Sometimes, as in their playing (with an extra viola and cello) of the sextet version of Schoenberg's *Verklärte Nacht,* this attitude of essential noninvolvement emerges as the kind of sentimentality that the underside of Hollywood movie music regularly conveyed.

No such lapses, however, mar the Hollywood recordings of the late Beethoven quartets. Here, playing the greatest music, and arrayed as an ensemble against the phonographic performances of the best groups of the century, the Hollywood emerges at the top.

In order to appreciate the particular achievement of the Holly-wood Quartet, it is first necessary to understand something about the music in which they have so triumphed. These works are extremely difficult to play. To get the notes in tune and at the right time is a virtuoso task for the best players; the *Grosse Fuge* in particular often seems impossible in its demands on force and endurance. But merely to solve these technical problems—and few quartets get even this far—is to leave unsolved the question these works above all others pose: how much "interpretation" does the music need, and even allow?

There has always been a tendency for performers to think that though undistinguished music (and especially trash) plays itself, masterpieces require bounteous contributions direct from the executant's soul. While this attitude is no doubt comforting to celebrity egos, the fact remains that Beethoven's late music is luxuriantly marked with performing directions covering phrasing, dynamics, tempo, rhythmic structure, note lengths, and even affective character. The problem is that these directions come not only close together in the music but even, several of them, at the same time. It thus becomes tempting—sometimes unavoidable—for performers to interfere with the flow by taking extra time to implement the correct degrees of loudness and softness, to obey the indicated tempo changes, to make clear the proper phrase lengths and endings. So adaptable is the human mind that this use of extra time as a crutch is considered "breathing," and therefore in itself an admirable element of the performer's conception.

Contemporary music making is shot through with just such distortions in the performance of great works. Sometimes these and other distortions go by the name of personality; in the case of fairly recondite chamber works, they pass as profundity. Such too is the case in today's playing of the Beethoven quartets. Whether the group in question is the Juilliard, the Guarneri, or the Cleveland, or their numerous satellites, followers, and imitators, the goal of every performance is the same: to inflect each note, to fill each sound with "beauty," "musicality," and "insight." Some groups doubtless play better than others, but the result is the same: manner replaces content, stylistic devices replace the work's own individuality, and the performers replace the composer.

From all this, the Hollywood Quartet is mercifully free. To say that they perform Beethoven without distortion is by no means to imply that they thereby lack commitment to and comprehension of the music. It is the fashion in some quarters to deride the emotional and mental faculties of performers; Igor Stravinsky, for example, cared little for their feelings, and thought that very few had much of a mind. With the Hollywood Quartet we are always confident that they have placed their emotions at the service of Beethoven, and have tried to use their minds to comprehend and perform his instructions.

This is perfectly clear from the first chords of the Hollywood performance of the opus 127, the first of the late Beethoven quartets. So difficult are these chords to play in tune, and properly voiced with the top notes audible, that they can serve as a quick litmus test of a group's abilities. In preparation for this article I listened to fourteen performances of this opening;[4] only from the Hollywood Quartet could the chords be heard with the vital top notes clearly present and in tune. As the first movement unfolds, it becomes evident that the Hollywood is capable of following Beethoven's directions without making things easy for itself. Throughout the changing tempos, the flow is continuous, and the ending is softly graceful without any hesitation. The melodically glorious slow movement is nobly played, with the triplets broadly measured; always there is a long line without any sentimentality. In the third movement the *pizzicati* are marvelously together, and the difficult *Presto* is perfectly executed. The final movement ends as the first had begun, with perfectly played chords.

In opus 130 the *Allegro* is marked by perfect balance of the instruments under trying conditions; the slow passages, as always with the Hollywood in this music, are noble, and again there is no sign of tempo modification as a means of executing extreme dynamic contrasts. Everywhere the delicacy in *pianissimo* playing is remarkable. The *Presto* second movement is truly fast without being rushed; the following *Andante* is always deeply serious, with no outward striving for a "musical" effect. The fourth movement, *Alla danza tedesca* ("in the style of a German dance"), performed without obtrusive gusts of sound, keeps the bar structure correct in the face of the superficial temptations arising from the dynamic and phrase

4. Amadeus, Budapest (1952), Budapest (stereo), Busch, Concord (1980 broadcast), Guarneri, Hollywood, Hungarian, Juilliard (CBS), Juilliard (1979 broadcast), La Salle, Quartetto Italiano, Vienna Konzerthaus, and Yale.

markings. The penultimate *Cavatina* is always grave in expression; even the passage marked *beklemmt* ("anguished," "oppressed") does not break the classical bounds of the movement. And the final *Allegro,* incredibly fast and light, never loses its solid tonal presence.

The seven-movement opus 131 is perhaps the most abstruse (along with the *Grosse Fuge*) of all the late quartets. Wisely, the Hollywood Quartet refrains from an intrusion of performing personality.[5] In the opening *Adagio ma non troppo e molto espressivo,* the tempo, despite its slowness, always seems right; the following *Allegro* is again thrillingly fast and light. After the short *Allegro moderato* third movement, the subsequent *Andante ma non troppo* is delicate and throbbing, with perfectly accurate phrasing from the first violin. At the end of this movement, so simply played, the beauties seem totally straightforward; there is no trace of the impression one often has in listening to this music that the players are undergoing a marvelous public experience. The fifth movement, *Presto,* delicate and light even when loud, is marked by the playing of perfectly in tune octaves between the instruments. The short sixth movement, *Adagio,* is followed with the final *Allegro,* played brusquely but never ripped off; the ending (before the last, loud, chords) is once more a miracle of delicacy.

In opus 132, Beethoven seems more human without being at any time less weighty. In the opening *Assai sostenuto—Allegro,* the Hollywood responds to the music with deeply felt and sonorous playing, again manifesting impeccable intonation and technical ease. The quasi-musette in the subsequent *Allegro ma non tanto* is both sinuous and airy. The slow movement, *Molto adagio,* bears Beethoven's own German title: *Heiliger Dankgesang eines Genesenen an die Gottheit, in der lydischen Tonart*—"Sacred song of thanks of a convalescent to the Godhead, in the Lydian Mode." In the Hollywood

5. What the result of giving in to this temptation sounds like is all too clear from a recording (*Deutsche Grammophon* 2531 077) of Leonard Bernstein conducting the Vienna Philharmonic string section in a transcription of the work; the rendition, dedicated to the memory of Bernstein's wife, comes with the liner note that "Mr. Bernstein feels that this performance is the proudest conducting achievement of his life." A listener with somewhat more distance from the emotions involved might well feel that here the nightmare of musical alchemy has been realized: Beethoven at his greatest has been transformed into bad Mahler.

performance the essential quality of the music is properly an elevated simplicity, with the section marked by Beethoven *Neue Kraft fühlend*—"Feeling new strength"—touchingly gay. The following *Alla marcia* leads into the final *Allegro appassionato,* wherein the Hollywood demonstrates, as it has throughout these works, the rarest ability to be straightforwardly expressive within a disciplined framework. The closing *Presto* section, reached via an *accelerando* the Hollywood manages with stunning neatness, ends with a feverish exaltation few performing groups in any epoch can manage.

So difficult is the *Grosse Fuge*—originally the finale of opus 130 but later detached by Beethoven from the longer work and given its own opus number of 133—that performance lapses are easily (and often) explained away. Indeed, listening to a number of recorded versions of this less-than-twenty-minute work is, for a critic, a worthwhile lesson in charity.[6] But the Hollywood has no need of such indulgence. Precise and strong rhythm, flagging only in some difficult viola syncopations during the first third of the piece, almost flawless intonation, rock-solid bass lines played by the marvelous cellist, Eleanor Aller (first-violinist Slatkin's wife), always clear part-playing,[7] forcefulness without forcing: all these virtues are crowned by a rare feeling for tempo relationships. It is this comprehension of the interlocking nature of Beethoven's many sections that more than anything else distinguishes the Hollywood performances.

Opus 135, the last of the late quartets and the last complete work Beethoven was to write, is a happy and even jocular farewell to music. Far from being the hitherto unknown musical territory the composer explored in other works from opus 127 onward, opus 135 seems almost classical, particularly in its deceptively unassuming first movement.

6. There is, unfortunately, no recording of the *Grosse Fuge* by the much admired Busch Quartet. The earliest performance to which I have listened is by the Budapest Quartet with close to its original personnel. This recording, which dates from before 1930, is an example of how a quartet with a great reputation can be unmanned by this work. I have also listened to recordings, all more or less unsatisfactory, by the following groups: Amadeus, Budapest (1952), Budapest (stereo), Guarneri, Juilliard (CBS), Hungarian, Quartetto Italiano, and Yale.
7. In the *Grosse Fuge,* more than in any other Hollywood recording, one regrets the absence of stereo, valuable as it is for the clarification of dense polyphonic lines. The remastering of the original tape for the present English reissue may provide a decided improvement.

But even here Beethoven's many interpretative directions can, in a mediocre performance, conflict with each other and destroy the momentum of the music. As always, the Hollywood goes ahead without any sacrifice of either expressivity or accuracy. The performance of the opening *Allegretto* manages to be, as written, in two rather than the customary four; the rhythmically difficult *Scherzo* is again distinguished by remarkable cello playing; the *Lento assai, cantante e tranquillo,* so easy for other and lesser groups to ham up by dragging and obtrusive phrasing, is in the Hollywood performance worthy to stand beside the noblest vocal works of Gluck. And the last movement, with Beethoven's questioning musical motto *Muss es sein?*—"Must it be?"—followed by the decisive *Es muss sein!*—"It must be!"—ends with a perfectly played *pizzicato* passage expressing not just honorable resignation after a lifetime's work, but even joyous acceptance.

With this triumph the recording career of the Hollywood Quartet came to an end. But the evidence of its achievement endures, making clear that great artists can survive even when they earn their bread in the environs of mass entertainment, and that great art lives in a world prior to, and way beyond, the welter of fundraising galas, subscription drives, and just plain huckstering we now call the life of culture.

[1983]

IV

WORDS

# George Bernard Shaw as Music Critic

For George Bernard Shaw, in the beginning was the word, and the word was always with him. Indeed, for an admiring public, he was the very word incarnate his whole life long. Whenever and wherever he wrote, a veritable Niagara of rhetoric engulfed friend and foe alike. By turns prophet and diabolist, moralist and cynic, leader and disciple, radical and commonsense liberal, he saw himself as the conscience of literate mankind; all that is certain is that he was a one-man Public Broadcasting Service, telling the educated in a piquant way what they most wanted to know.

Chief among the fields where Shaw cast his glittering pearls was, of course, the theater. Here, of his numerous plays, a large number still hold the stage in productions pleasing both to the box office and to the self-esteem of the participants. *Arms and the Man* (1894), *Candida* (1894), *Caesar and Cleopatra* (1898), *Man and Superman* (1901–03), *Major Barbara* (1905), and *Saint Joan* (1923); all these helped set the intellectual tone of the Anglo-American stage for the better part of the past hundred years. In *Pygmalion* (1912), his greatest long-run success, he provided the framework for what later became, in *My Fair Lady* (1956), a musical fairy tale speaking directly to the new class of social adepts who run—and run down —our society.

And then, just around the corner (in both our past and our present), there are Shaw's politics. His was the silver tongue of Fabian socialism; by mixing advocacy of left-wing programs with a prosperous literary career, he became perhaps our most visible public combiner of high ideals and high income. He spoke in the most deliciously individual way in behalf of social planning. He used the freedoms of an Englishman to plump for the slavery of Russians. Even more, while fighting tooth and claw for every penny of royalties, he campaigned fearlessly for the redistribution of income on a basis of simple equality.

His social positions were no less marked by the kind of contradictions so easily available to the holder of truly simple views. He was a vegetarian and antivivisectionist, whose life was saved from pernicious anemia by liver injections. He spoke enthusiastically for submission to the life-force, while he engaged in an unconsummated marriage lasting close to half a century. He more or less supported Home Rule, but cordially despised his fellow Irish; he campaigned tirelessly for the workingman, but he gladly spent his time with Lady Astor.

The foundations of Shaw's public prominence, oddly enough, were laid neither by his political nor by his social writings. Still less was the beginning of his rise to fame a result of his plays, which were not commercially successful until after the turn of the century. Shaw's early career was instead the fruit of his writing years and yards of criticism, at first of music and then, for a shorter period in the 1890s, of the theater.

Shaw's involvement with music stretched over his whole life. Born in Ireland in 1856 to Protestant parents, he learned music from his mother, a singer. Together with her vocal teacher (one of those mixed genius-charlatans so common even today in that profession) she was responsible, according to Shaw's later testimony, for inspiring his knowledge about musical art. His father, moreover, was a fairly advanced trombone player, though here the evidence seems clouded by the peculiar combination of distaste and flippancy with which Shaw habitually treated the memories of his father and of his own childhood.

In any case—and again, as almost always with the early Shaw, by his own account—at the end of his schooling, still only in his mid-teens, he "could sing and whistle from end to end leading works by Handel, Haydn, Mozart, Beethoven, Rossini, Bellini, Donizetti, and Verdi." But all this was by ear; at the age of fifteen he was not yet able to "play [or] read a note of music." Ever resourceful in self-improvement, he was forced to teach himself the piano "from a book with a diagram of the keyboard."

Now living in London, Shaw began his musical explorations by trying to play, from the notes, a piece that he already knew in sound. This piece was the overture to Mozart's *Don Giovanni*. In Shaw's case, as in countless others, this first musical experience of choice became his preferred sound for a lifetime. Here, in the fumblings of a bright boy thrown on his own by the breakup of his family circle, was determined the basis for the adult Shaw's idolizing of Mozart and his *Don*; that Shaw's only other comparable musical dedication was to the quintessentially un-Mozart-like Richard Wagner only shows how in music, as elsewhere, GBS raised paradox—not to mention antinomy—to the level of a fine art.

Shaw seems to have learned his piano skills well enough to have served as a scratch accompanist for various semiprofessional activities; more to the point, given the economic plight he and his relatives found themselves in, his musical knowledge provided a chance to earn some much needed money by ghosting concert and opera reviews for his mother's old singing teacher. These articles, their authorship undiscovered, were written for almost a year during 1876 and 1877. Aptly enough, considering the sting in Shaw's style, the publication for which he wrote was named the *Hornet*. Unfortunately, we don't seem to know just why the budding journalist ceased his appearances in these pages.

For the next eleven years Shaw wrote intermittently, though not infrequently, about music. He did mostly unsigned pieces for numerous publications, among them the *Saturday Musical Review*, the *Court Journal*, the *Musical Review*, the *Dramatic Review*, *Our Corner*, the *Magazine of Music*, and the *Pall Mall Gazette*.

It was, however, his connection in 1888 with the *Star*, a newly founded London evening newspaper favorable to Gladstone and Home Rule, that finally landed Shaw firmly on the English literary and musical scene. Through the intervention of the radical journalist H. W. Massingham, he had been hired as an editorial writer. But the paper's reformist position hardly extended publicly so far as Shaw's Fabian socialist views, and what he wrote on politics was anathema both to the paper's good-natured editor and also to John Morley, the literary patron saint of late-Victorian liberalism. So Shaw moved over to music, first writing for the *Star* as a second-string critic, and then finally, in February of 1889, under the pawky pseudonym of Corno di Bassetto as the lead critic.

GBS wrote for the *Star* until May of 1890, at the bounteous average of 6,500 words each month. However, he wanted more money for his work than the *Star* was willing to pay. He therefore left daily reviewing for a weekly column in the *World*, a journal in which he had earlier, at the recommendation of the dramatic critic and Ibsenite William Archer, written art reviews. For the *World* Shaw wrote, under his own name, the bulk of his music criticism. This production was indeed sizable; lasting until 1894, it filled three volumes in the Standard Edition of Shaw's works, and amounted to more than 350,000 words.

His leaving the *World,* at least partially because of a negative review that his employers refused to print, marked the end of his regular work as a music critic. Though his major attentions were now to be claimed by the theater—he began a three-year stint as dramatic critic for the *Saturday Review* in 1895, and his eventually successful string of plays had begun in 1894 with *Arms and the Man* and *Candida*—he found time to write *The Perfect Wagnerite* (1898), his famous Marxist-cum-Fabian interpretation of the *Ring des Nibelungen.* This fitting climax to his decade-long concern with Wagner and Bayreuth was followed by a half-century of scattered musical comments and controversies (including an enthusiastic 1910 defense of Strauss's *Elektra,* which Shaw had not yet heard, against the strictures of the then rising critic Ernest Newman). Almost to the end of his life, Shaw continued to play over operas on the piano and to sing along as he played. His last written words on music, published only a few days after his death in 1950, returned to his favorite subject of singing: in a characteristic swipe at the past, his final article was titled "We Sing Better Than Our Grandparents!"

The literary product of Shaw's seventy-five-year involvement with music criticism has now been collected in three small but fat volumes entitled *Shaw's Music: The Complete Musical Criticism.* Most of the material in this new edition has, in fact, appeared previously. Mention has already been made of the three volumes of the standard edition covering the 1890–94 writings in the *World*; this collection, which came out in 1932, was supplemented in 1937 by another volume collecting just about all of Shaw's writings for the *Star* and a small amount of later material as well. *The Perfect Wagnerite,* of course, has from its first publication led an uninterrupted existence; it has appeared in numerous editions, including a large printing for distribution along with a special pressing of the Solti recording of the *Ring.*

A generous selection of the previously uncollected early writings for the *Hornet,* material from the period between Shaw's work for the *Hornet* and the *Star,* along with pieces from his post-music-critic days, appeared in 1961 in boards and in 1967 in paperback; this collection, called *How to Become a Musical Critic,* was edited by Dan H. Laurence, who also edited these newly issued three volumes. The 1961 publication carried an introduction by Laurence, which now appears, in a revised form, in this complete edition. Previously uncollected material, now being republished for the first time, is thus limited to not much more than 160,000 words, something less than one-fifth the contents of this new (and very expensive) set.

Viewed in its entirety, Shaw's music criticism makes clear not only the outlines of his own musical taste and critical approach but also the richness of concert life in London during the last quarter of the nineteenth century. Opera in London then, as in New York today, was king. The earlier works of Verdi were already staples of operatic commerce, and French operas were popular as well. Wagner's work, still called the music of the future, was rapidly becoming the music of the present. Mozart's *Don Giovanni* was drawing full houses. Still to come was Puccini, whose *Manon Lescaut* was not heard by Shaw until 1894.

With opera, it goes without saying, came singers. Though most of those about whom Shaw wrote are now forgotten, he heard enough great vocalists to suggest the kind of golden age about which graybeards babble. The work of several of these singers has been preserved by the phonograph; chief among these are Calvé, Eames, Maurel, Nordica, Patti, Plançon, and Tamagno; the last named, whose singing Shaw described as "magnificent screaming," created the title role in Verdi's *Otello* in 1887, and has left us a 1903 recording of the opening "Esultate," which is at once stentorian and frighteningly heroic.

Among nonoperatic composers widely presented to the London audience during this period, we find Bach, then on the way to his present sainthood; the great choral works, including the *Saint Matthew Passion,* were increasingly being performed by the giant choruses in the large halls dear to Victorian England. The era of Mendelssohn as musician *sans peur et sans reproche* was drawing to an end, though he still was the hero of a large public. Beethoven's reputation was triumphant, produced not only by the symphonies about which George Grove rhapsodized, but also by performances of music as massive as the *Missa Solemnis* and as recondite as the *Drei Equalen* (*WoO* 30) for four trombones. There was a great deal of chamber music being played, from Haydn and Mozart through Beethoven, Schubert, and Schumann. In lighter music, the waltzes of the Strauss family were in vogue; on one occasion, a concert of these works produced such a large crowd that the police had to be called out.

Still new to London audiences—because they were freshly being written—were the later staples of such composers as Brahms, Dvořák, and Tchaikowsky. Some of these works were immediately successful. Such a difficult composition as the *German Requiem* (1868) of Brahms seems to have attracted a following that demanded repeated performances. Tchaikowsky himself conducted his orchestra music in London and Grieg, too, performed here with his singer wife.

Nor was English music being ignored. Handel's *Messiah* was then, as always, a national epic; Purcell, too, was performed. Contemporary native music was given an always respectful hearing. Sir Arthur Sullivan was seen as more than a mere partner of Gilbert, and such now forgotten names as Sir Charles Villiers Stanford and Sir Charles Hubert H. Parry occupied concert programs along with the mightiest of Continental masters.

There were notable performers in this period, too, some of them coming to England to perform their own works or those with which they had been closely associated; others belonged to the then, as always, fashionable breed of virtuosi. Shaw heard Wagner conduct during the composer's 1877 visit to London, and he heard Clara Schumann, as well, in one of her appearances as the musical voice from her husband's grave. Joseph Joachim, performing with Clara Schumann and by himself, personally brought the gospel of Brahms to English shores. The pianists (and composers) Albeniz and Paderewski performed their own music and that of others, as did the mythic violinists Sarasate and Ysaÿe.

The conducting scene in London was not quite so star-studded. Among the English conductors then active, perhaps the only directorial career we might remember today was that of Sir George Henschel, the singer turned maestro. Henschel was the first conductor of the Boston Symphony and conducted that orchestra's premiere performance in 1881; a charming souvenir of his gentle musical approach can still be heard in a 1926 recording of the Beethoven First Symphony with the Royal Philharmonic Orchestra. Not surprisingly, the great luminary of the baton in England at this time was the German Hans Richter. Richter, wrapped in the mantle of Wagner, occupied a position in musical life then perhaps comparable to that of Toscanini in New York during the 1930s and '40s. Given the absence of orchestral recordings before the second decade of the present century, it is difficult to know how well London orchestras played before 1900; the fact that they seem to have been able to prepare difficult new music with a minimum of rehearsal time suggests a high level of competence—if not of inspiration.

English musical education during this period was in a state of rapid expansion. George Grove's founding of the Royal College of Music in 1882 (the college was opened by the Prince of Wales the next year in a ceremony attended by Gladstone), along with his editing of the famous *Dictionary of Music and Musicians,* which now bears his name, and the earlier concerts he managed at the Crystal Palace were to a large extent the necessary groundwork for today's remarkably large and remarkably sophisticated English concert audience.

Into this lively musical world stepped spritely (as Shaw said about Max Beerbohm) the incomparable GBS. His was a new voice, speaking with unbounded authority and equally unbounded audacity. No subjects—the mechanics of singing or the niceties of concert pitch and temperament among them—were too abstruse or too technical for the laws this polycritic was always ready to lay down. But music in detail was hardly Shaw's real strength. He was not, on the most tolerant of assessments, a trained musician. It hardly mattered; there were, after all, established music critics entrenched in English concert life who knew all about music. Shaw knew something much more valuable: he knew what he liked.

In composers this meant primarily, though not totally, Mozart, Beethoven, and Wagner. Mozart, for Shaw, meant *Don Giovanni* and *The Magic Flute.* Beethoven meant the Ninth Symphony, and Wagner the *Ring.* In *Don Giovanni,* Shaw found a compelling formulation of his own view of morality, a view that was later to inform *Man and Superman.* In *The Magic Flute* and the Beethoven Ninth Shaw found his true church. And Wagner's *Ring* was Shaw's politics set to myth, a Marxism for non-Marxists, a Darwinism for music lovers, a jungle story for humanitarians.

It will not have escaped the reader that all these masterpieces were in fact program, rather than absolute, music. Not only did Shaw wage an often vitriolic campaign throughout his career as a music critic against the writing of sonatas and fugues, which he considered the very epitome of old-fashioned irrelevance. Not only did he make clear, furthermore, that program music was what really caught his ear and that of the audience. But he also went so far as a partisan of ideas in tone that one comes away with the impression that what counted for Shaw in program music was not the music, but the program.

Nowhere is this more apparent than in *The Perfect Wagnerite,* the only part of Shaw's writings on music capable of surviving outside the hospitality of a collected edition. Here, amidst the usual Shavian self-reference and self-proclamation, he discusses the characters and the meaning of *Das Rheingold, Die Walküre,* and the first two acts of *Siegfried.* Shaw's treatment is marked not only by length but also by enthusiasm, with full credit given to Wagner for creating a supreme artwork. But when Shaw comes to the last act of *Siegfried* and to the whole of *Götterdämmerung,* he turns sour, making clear that here Wagner has lost his claim to artistic revolution and descended to mere opera. So deep is Shaw's commitment to Wagner's program, rather than to his music, that he seems unable to accept the implications of the fact that the greatest music in the *Ring* comes only when Wagner, from Act III of *Siegfried* on, puts down his program. Wagner's triumph as a composer through surrender to purely musical impulses strikes Shaw as a sellout, something that might be expected of a musician, but is unworthy of an artist.

Despite these strictures (Shaw even came to the conclusion during the 1890s that some of the composer's musical material had become second-rate) Wagner was very much at the apex of GBS's musical pyramid. In this reading of musical history Wagner was the perfection of Beethoven, as Mozart had earlier been of Haydn. Mozart, indeed, as holy as Shaw found him, would have turned out just as well had he used the formal resources of Liszt to clothe his genius.

To his loves, Shaw opposed his hates. Chief among these was Brahms, whose *German Requiem* was to Shaw a special *bête noire.*

Time and again he returned to the attack of a work he found "dreary," "desperately old-fashioned, and empty." He could even be witty at the work's expense:

> Mind, I do not deny that the Requiem is a solid piece of music manufacture. You feel at once that could only have come from the establishment of a first-class undertaker.

It was not only this work of Brahms that aroused Shaw's scorn. Of the Fourth Symphony, for example, Shaw wrote:

> Brahms takes an essentially commonplace theme; gives it a strange air by dressing it in the most elaborate and farfetched harmonies; keeps his countenance severely (which at once convinces an English audience that he must have a great deal in him). . . . Strip off the euphemism from these symphonies, and you will find a string of incomplete dance and ballad tunes, following one another with no more organic coherence than the succession of passing images reflected in a shop window in Piccadilly during any twenty minutes in the day.

What Shaw felt about the *Requiem* and the Fourth Symphony was also the case with the other symphonies, the Handel variations, and at least one of the piano concertos, described as "a desperate hash of bits and scraps, with plenty of thickening in the pianoforte part." With Brahms's chamber music, Shaw relented, finding that here indeed were many lovely, if minor, things.

Mendelssohn, too, was in Shaw's disfavor. Though he admired this composer's "exquisite prettiness" (comparing him to Gounod!), he found the massive oratorio *Elijah* "thoughtless . . . not really religious music at all." After hearing a performance of the Beethoven Ninth, he wrote about how he had to turn down an opportunity to hear the Mendelssohn work: "As to following [the Beethoven Symphony] by going to the Albert Hall on Wednesday to hear *Elijah,* I would rather have died."

The larger works of Schubert also disturbed Shaw, though he granted him a "wonderful . . . musical endowment" as well as "manifold charms and winningnesses." Still, for Shaw, Schubert had only "second-rate brains"; of the great C-Major Symphony, Shaw wrote: "A more exasperatingly brainless composition was never put on paper." Nor did Schumann fare well under Shaw's pen. Of a Schumann symphony (like the Brahms concerto castigated above, otherwise unidentified), Shaw said:

> I cannot understand why we take Schumann and ourselves seriously over a work the last half of which is so forced and bungled as to be almost intolerable. I wish someone would extract all the noble passages from Schumann's symphonies, and combine them into a single instrumental fantasia—Reminiscences of Schumann as the military bandmasters would call it—so that we might enjoy them without the drudgery of listening to their elaboration into heavy separate works in which, during three-quarters of the performance, there is nothing to admire except the composer's devoted perseverance, which you wish he had not exercised. We all have a deep regard for Schumann; but it is really not in human nature to refrain from occasionally making it clear that he was greater as a musical enthusiast than as a constructive musician. If he had only had Rossini's genius, or Rossini his conscience, what a composer we should have had!

He also thought little of Liszt, and he was dismissive of Tchaikowsky—his music as well as his conducting. Of the famous Bruch G-Minor Violin Concerto, Shaw thought that a performance of it could "hardly ever have sounded more hopelessly third-class [it had followed a performance of the overture to *Don Giovanni*], notwithstanding the dignity given to the slow movement by Dr. Joachim's very finest tone." Even Beethoven himself was not totally immune from Shaw's displeasure: early in his critical career, Shaw described the hallowed Thirty-two Variations in C Minor for piano as "a work which presents some technical difficulties . . . but which is by no means a worthy example of the master's resources in the variation form."

Some of Shaw's lesser loves were no less idiosyncratic than his dislikes. He had a youthful good word to say for William Sterndale Bennett, the English clone of Mendelssohn; he liked some of the music of the now forgotten Joseph Rheinberger (1839–1901). Indeed, Shaw was particularly enthusiastic about the works of the very minor German romantic Hermann Goetz (1840–1876). He thought Goetz's *The Taming of the Shrew* (1868–72) "the greatest comic opera of the century, except *Die Meistersinger*," an evaluation that hardly seemed to take into account Rossini's *Barber of Seville* (1816). Of the Goetz Symphony in F Major, Shaw wrote:

> It is the only real symphony that has been composed since Beethoven died. Beside it Mendelssohn's Scotch Symphony is no symphony at all, but only an enchanting *suite de pièces;* Schubert's symphonies seem mere debauches of exquisitely musical thoughtlessness. . . . Brahms, who alone touches him in mere brute musical faculty, is a dolt in comparison to him.

In performance, Shaw went, as all music critics eventually seem to go, for the big guns. He could make distinctions among the famous; he preferred, for example, the playing of the older Sarasate to that of the younger Ysaÿe. He admired English orchestras and German conductors, and he was quick to deride such celebrities as Patti and Paderewski for giving in to their more vulgar and crowd-pleasing instincts. He wrote endlessly, in the best fashion of English critics, about opera productions, showing in this area the true instinct of a stagestruck fan. On the whole, despite his instinct for debunking the mighty, he always had something of a sweet tooth for powerful performing personalities.

Considering all the words he wrote about the stars, it seems unfortunate that he was frequently so offhand in discussing the real immortals who crossed his journalistic path. The greatest of these was, doubtless, Wagner, whose conducting in 1877 Shaw passes by as "unsatisfactory to an orchestra unused to his peculiarities" and "capriciously hurried or retarded" in tempo. And he is brief, too, though complimentary, in his account of Clara Schumann's playing. He was also negative about the conducting of Gustav Mahler and Richard Strauss, two directors whose styles have proven, in quite different ways, to be models for their successors.

Shaw did have an eye for new trends. He was interested in the performance of older music on original instruments. He reviewed a "Viennese Lady Orchestra" playing dances and marches; more seriously, he wrote about the music of women composers—not, it must be said, without an occasional patronizing tone creeping in. He was an early advocate of government support for the arts, and he used arguments that could easily come from our own National Endowment for the Arts; for Shaw, as for our governmental patrons, not only is art a sign of national well-being and individual uplift, but it is also good for trade, tourism, and the tax rolls.

With the onset of age, the coming of the twentieth century, and, above all, the shifting of his interest from music to the theater and his own playwriting, Shaw's musical tastes became a bit less relentlessly up-to-date. Perhaps, scandalous to say, they even backslid. He began to see more than he previously had in the music of Brahms and ventured an apology for his previous condemnation. He began, too, to see virtue in absolute music, predicting a return to it and, with this change, a new vitality for English music, whose early greatness he associated with a purer artistic world than was later the case in the nineteenth century.

Surprisingly, considering his dislike for the heavy English oratorio style and its practitioners, he found good in Edward Elgar and in that composer's weighty *Dream of Gerontius* (1900). In 1932 he went so far as to defend Elgar from neglect with a typical slap at the English audience: Elgar, he wrote, "has given us a land of Hope and Glory; and we have given him back the glory and kept all the hope for ourselves."

Here, then, is the musical content of Shaw's criticism as compiled, it must be admitted, by someone who can hardly be considered a Shavian. Such a rare creature in today's Anglo-American literary and intellectual world might even go on to wonder what there is in Shaw's record to justify the nearly universal assessment of him as the finest music critic in the English language. This strong judgment, which has been widely held for many years, has now been reinforced by the enthusiastic reception given to the present edition both here and in England.

On purely musical grounds, the evidence for this judgment hardly seems sufficient. Hits and misses; sympathies and limitations of taste; excesses of praise and criticism; prejudices negative and positive—Shaw, like other of his successful colleagues, was a manifestation of the *Zeitgeist,* which in his time was full of the end of Victorian musical pieties and the triumph of the shameless Wagner.

But fortunately for Shaw's fame, his criticism rested on far more than his musical virtues. To begin with, his writing was rarely without a lively and sharp personal edge. This quality is not simply a reflection of his own artistic preferences or his willingness to display the workings of his ego. At root, he was personal because he held individual performers (and composers) personally responsible for everything they did or caused to be done on stage. He held them to account not only for how they sang or played, but also for how they behaved and how they looked. Much of the time Shaw's attitude in this respect seems merely catty, as when he returns time after time to remark on how the conductor Richter continued to gain weight after coming to England.

But it is difficult not to feel that this approach went beyond a mere interest in gossip and personalities. In Shaw's writings there was a theoretical underpinning that suggested a philosophy going beyond a mere theory of art to become a scheme of salvation and damnation. He justified his personal orientation to criticism in this way:

> It is the capacity for making good or bad art a personal matter that makes a man a critic. The artist who accounts for my disparagement by alleging personal animosity on my part is quite right: when people do less than their best, and do that less at once badly and self-complacently, I hate them, loathe them, detest them, long to tear them limb from limb and strew them in gobbets about the stage or platform. (At the Opera, the temptation to go out and ask one of the sentinels for the loan of his Martini, with a round or two of ammunition, that I might rid the earth of an incompetent conductor or a conceited and careless artist, has come upon me so strongly that I have been withheld only by my fear that, being no marksman, I might hit the wrong person and incur the guilt of slaying a meritorious singer.)

Mere bluster, one might say, or perhaps a cumbersome try at elfin humor. But there are other passages in Shaw's music criticism that suggest a deeper inability to distinguish art from life, and a corollary difficulty in separating rhetoric from reality. Consider, for example, a stray comment of Shaw's on operatic audiences in Frankfurt as compared to London: "The Jew rules in Frankfurt even more than in London; but he is much less flashy there than here." Later he remarks on the need to do two things to improve the Philharmonic concerts in London: first, restrict the length of the concerts to under two hours; and second, arrange "the compulsory retirement of all directors at the age of ninetyfive, into a lethal chamber if possible."

On another subject, he followed a comment on the inferiority of pianos to the keyboard instruments of Shakespeare's day by sagely observing:

I am aware that the burning of the *châteaux* which preceded the French revolution, and indeed formed the most practical part of it, had its disadvantages, but if anything of the kind ever happens in this country, we shall at least have the satisfaction of knowing that for every country house that perishes, there will be a grand piano the less in the world.

Nor can one ignore in Shaw's music criticism a strong dash of the eugenics movement so beloved by the advocates of social consciousness. This was fashionable stuff during the intellectual reign of Darwinism and of Spencer. And Shaw's idea of improving the breed typically emerged from—and was inspired by—the need to advance past the character of Wagner's youthful Siegfried. It all makes unpleasant reading nearly a century later, in our own age of population control by means fair and foul:

The individual Siegfried has come often enough, only to find himself with the alternative of governing those who are not Siegfrieds or risking destruction at their hands. And this dilemma will persist until Wotan's inspiration comes to our governors, and they see that their business is not the devizing of laws and institutions to prop up the weaknesses of the mobs and secure the survival of the unfittest, but the breeding of men whose wills and intelligences may be depended upon to produce spontaneously the social wellbeing our clumsy laws now aim at and miss. The majority of men at present in Europe have no business to be alive; and no serious progress will be made until we address ourselves earnestly and scientifically to the task of producing trustworthy human material for society.

And shortly thereafter a footnote draws the political implications:

The necessity for breeding the governing class from a selected stock has always been recognized by Aristocrats, however erroneous their methods of selection. We have changed our system from Aristocracy to Democracy without considering that we were at the same time changing, as regards our governing class, from Selection to Promiscuity. Those who have taken a practical part in modern politics best know how farcical the result is.

Here, perhaps, as we move from art to society, may well be found the real interest and the real contemporaneity of Shaw's music criticism. This timely quality, it must be repeated, hardly inheres in the descriptions of assorted pieces and forgotten performers. Nor does it inhere in what is plainly Shaw's questionable and flawed ability to see musical life steadily and to see it whole. In sum, Shaw's music criticism is clearly not a freestanding achievement to be understood in aesthetic terms alone. Indeed, the corpus of Shaw's music criticism is interesting chiefly as a special case of Shaw the playwright, Shaw the progressive social thinker, and Shaw the entertaining scourge of his adoring audience.

Perhaps both Shaw's musical career and its reception until today have something to tell us about music criticism itself. First, from his style we can learn that bluster and even rodomontade is all and that the critic's willingness to attack on a broad front will always make good reading. More important, we can learn that music criticism of bygone days takes its underlying interest not from its comments about the music, which we can hear for ourselves, but rather from its documentation of wider areas and social currents as filtered through the mind of someone who was himself an actor in those cultural movements.

And perhaps we can, in reading all of Shaw's hundreds of thousands of words on music, realize just how brilliant this intellectual freebooter was in summing up advanced thought and passing it off as his own discovery. It is even possible in reading Shaw to understand the extent to which progressive opinion of the 1890s remains progressive today—and even, for some of us, just how ugly much of it all was, and is.

[1982]

# Harold Schonberg and His Times

Though the official announcement remains to be made, the imminent retirement of the senior critic of the *New York Times* is already being widely discussed by the musical community. In the history of a newspaper one man—though he be owner or editor—counts for surprisingly little, and so it might be expected that even a famous critic's departure from full-time activity would be of little interest outside the Byzantine world of journalism and the paper for which he works. Such, however, is hardly the case with Harold Schonberg. The reasons for this writer's particular significance stem not only from his own achievements; in large measure they are a result of the importance of the *Times* and still more the situation of music today.

The preeminent position of the *Times* in musical journalism is a rather new phenomenon. In the past, critical activity, in this country as in other parts of the world, was divided between the daily press and periodicals of weekly, biweekly, or even monthly and quarterly appearance. In the United States, for example, as recently as the early 1960s reviews of importance to musicians as well as to the concertgoing public were carried in *Musical America* and the *Musical Courier;* though of little interest to musicians, magazines of general and wide circulation like *Esquire* and *Good Housekeeping* carried critical columns.

But lately periodical outlets for music criticism have become much fewer. Of the magazines of national circulation, only the *New Yorker* continues its weekly reviews of live performance; *Time* and *Newsweek* seem to run musical material only when "interesting" subjects arise. When the *New Republic* or the *Nation* carries an article on serious music, it is usually a review of recordings, not of live performance. Among local New York periodicals, only the *Village Voice* carries weekly reviews of concerts and operas, while *New York* magazine has in recent months reduced the frequency of its music columns. And of the specialized publications, the *Musical Courier* has long since ceased to publish, while *Musical America* has been reduced to an anomalous existence as an insert, available only on a special subscription basis, in *High Fidelity*.

Thus, for all practical purposes, musical coverage across the country is left to the daily press. Here, in quantity at least, the situation is encouraging. More newspapers, both large and small, carry concert reviews and frequent occasional pieces; increasingly, this material is being written by specially trained personnel. Yet as seriously as all these newspapers take their critics—and as seriously as these critics take their work and themselves—there can be little doubt that reviews outside New York count for less and less as the years go by.

Gone are the days of local critics whose words carried national weight. There have, alas, been few successors to the influence of such local barons of the musical pen as Max de Schauensee in Philadelphia, Claudia Cassidy in Chicago, John Rosenfield in Dallas, and Alfred Frankenstein in San Francisco. Even the still active Paul Hume, who once was taken on by no less a personage than Margaret Truman's father, seems less important both in the Washington, D.C., area and the country at large than he used to be.

The single exception to this story of the diminished influence of daily music criticism is, of course, New York City itself. And even here one critical platform stands out from the rest. It is no exaggeration to say that in today's American musical world only one review is taken seriously—that of the *New York Times*.

It is the fashion in certain circles to rail against New York's premier place in musical life. There is, after all, a great deal of distinguished musical activity outside New York. Several orchestras across the country are at least equal if not superior to the Philharmonic; worthwhile conservatories exist outside of the Juilliard School; opera is done on a grand scale in Chicago and San Francisco. But still the brightest and the best of musical talents are drawn to New York for major periods in their lives as students and performers, and nothing has happened in recent years to affect New York's central role in the dissemination of information and publicity about cultural matters.

While the city's leadership in culture remains intact, however, its once healthy newspaper population is down to three Manhattan dailies: the *Post,* the *News,* and the *Times.* Though the *News* is both sparse and capricious in its coverage, the *Post* does in fact cover all the more important musical events in New York. Nevertheless, neither of these two newspapers is read by a great number of regular concertgoers; as a result, their reviews tend to be ignored or dismissed both by the concertgoing public and the commercial interests who back their opinions with money.

That leaves the *Times,* our—and the world's—only newspaper of record. Covering the news as comprehensively as the *Times* does is expensive, and only a wide, affluent readership, generating a great deal of advertising, can make the costs bearable. To bring in such readers, the *Times* a few years ago added a new section to the paper each weekday (excluding Saturday) dealing with the concerns of the affluent—getting ahead, staying healthy, eating well, and spending money. Career stories, medical opinions, sports, gourmet recipes, decorating advice, all were mixed together with art, antiques, and architecture, as well as drama and dance. Happily, the place of music was not slighted in this hedonistic mélange. Not only did the *Times* continue to cover just about every professional event in Manhattan, making forays even into Brooklyn as the occasion demanded; not only did it continue to cover summer festivals across the United States and even abroad; to all this it now added more human-interest stories, largely written at the instigation and the inspiration of the numerous musical publicists in New York City, about musicians and musical organizations. And, reflecting the *Times*'s drive for young readers, coverage of pop music also increased.

The increase in puff pieces and the pop coverage were a departure for the *Times,* but the paper had always taken serious music seriously. Until 1902 its critic was William Henderson, a recognized authority on singing and singers. From 1902 to 1924 its critic was the eminent Wagnerian Richard Aldrich, whose posthumously published *Concert Life in New York 1902–1923* (1941) remains a unique document of American musical historiography; while Aldrich was away on war duty in 1918–19, his place was taken by the famous publicist of all the arts and fanatic Chopinist James Gibbons Huneker. From 1924 until his death in 1955, the *Times*'s chair was occupied by Olin Downes, one of the pioneers in radio music lectures and the chief and eminently successful advocate in this country of the music of Sibelius. After Downes's death, the

*Times* chose as his successor its longtime staff member Howard Taubman, whose tenure—mostly without incident or very much interest—was a brief five years. Since then, from 1960 to the present, the voice of the *Times* in music has been Harold C. Schonberg (born 1915), already at the time of his selection a veteran of twenty-one years of experience in music reviewing and allied pursuits.

During his years of newspaper reviewing Schonberg has also found the time to produce several books. In 1955 he wrote the volume devoted to chamber and solo instrumental music in the Knopf *Guide to Long Playing Records*; in 1959 he assembled another collection of record reviews, *The Collector's Chopin and Schumann*. He then wrote three less ephemeral books, each devoted to sketches of famous musicians: *The Great Pianists* (1963), *The Great Conductors* (1967), and *The Lives of the Great Composers* (1970). For his music criticism he was awarded the Pulitzer Prize in 1971. (Passionately interested in chess, he has also published a book on famous players, *Grandmasters of Chess*.)

As can be gathered from this ability to turn out all these books while working as a full-time journalist, Schonberg is a fluent and easy writer. He even brags about his fluency; in one *Times* piece denying that short deadlines lowered the quality of reviews, he ended with the cheeky sentences: "Time of writing this article: 72 minutes. Want to make something of it, anybody?" He does more than write quickly. His prose is clear and readable, with simple points simply made. He also has a common touch, speaking familiarly and often using homely colloquial expressions (concerning Beethoven's victory in improvisation over the virtuoso pianist Steibelt, to cite a telling example, he writes that the immortal composer "played him under the table").

Perhaps Schonberg's strongest virtue as a daily reviewer is that he has good ears. What he listens to he hears accurately, picking out the salient aural features of performances in the areas of intonation, rhythm, tone color, and hall acoustics. In the case of pianists in particular, he is quick to notice sloppy playing and to identify its causes, and he is an excellent judge of an audience's reaction to performances and compositions.

The overwhelming personal impression a reader carries from years of perusal of Schonberg's writing is of a passionate love for music and a fan's interest in all its aspects and all its details. An article he wrote describing how much music on the radio meant to him during a 1975 illness touchingly conveys this love; he even enjoyed hearing Chopin played as Muzak during a wait in a Russian airport. Some areas in music naturally interest him more than others. Pianists and composers for the piano are undoubtedly the closest to his heart. About them he writes with the attitude of a baseball nut who knows all the statistics. About nonkeyboard composers and performers he is generally more restrained, in the case of conductors and some symphonic composers reaching a level of cool neutrality.

Of the possibly three million words Schonberg has produced during his tenure as chief critic, something approaching half must have been devoted to daily reviews. These short articles, written within an hour or two of the event and generally appearing the next day, have described and evaluated the most important New York concert and opera performances as well as those lesser occasions that have appealed to the critic's personal taste or sense of longterm significance. As if these events were not sufficiently numerous, Schonberg has also made a point of covering the most important summer festivals, performances of out-of-the-way repertory of the past, of contemporary music that has stirred interest among musicians, and of young soloists who seem destined for fame. The other part of his writing for the *Times* has consisted mainly of Sunday pieces appearing in the Arts and Leisure section of the paper. These weekly pieces, usually running up to 1,500 words, have ranged from composers to performers, from institutions to trends, from previews and retrospects of the New York season to humorous takeoffs on the pompous and the foolish.

A feisty and provocative personality, Schonberg has striven to make his critical presuppositions as clear as his judgments; he rarely pretends to an objectivity he does not possess. In looking at the intellectual and emotional baggage he brings to his work, it is easy to spot one central expectation from and attitude toward what he hears: a pronounced orientation toward personal, emotionally charged music composed or performed by idiosyncratically gifted, demonstrably expressive individuals. For him music is at its least interesting when it is highly cerebral, speaking only to a sophisticated group of like minds. Great music and great performers must, on his view, take their significance from popular passions and concerns.

There can be little doubt that Schonberg, writing on the basis of this conception, has on the whole tended to occupy the broad middle of musical opinion. His book on the great composers is a popular catalogue of the music the large musical public knows and loves, a ratification of the current state of taste. For Schonberg, as for the largest part of the public, music begins with Bach, Handel, and Gluck. It then jumps to Haydn and Mozart and continues with Beethoven and the other giants of the nineteenth century who have made up the bulk of our concert programs for the last hundred years. In the more interesting parts of the book he allows himself digressions from the indisputably first-rank creators to lesser figures like Rossini, Donizetti, Cherubini, and Auber; he also admires Johann Strauss (the younger), Offenbach, and the Sullivan of Gilbert fame. But *The Lives of the Great Composers* ends with a pessimistic appraisal:

> . . . whatever the complex of reasons, it seemed apparent twenty-five years after the end of World War II that there was a hiatus in the mighty line of powerful, individualistic composers that led from Johann Sebastian Bach through Igor Stravinsky and Arnold Schoenberg.

Schonberg's inclusion of Stravinsky and Schoenberg[1] on his list of the elect is, in terms of his own values, misleading. Of the composer of *The Rite of Spring* he wrote in 1970:

> It may be that Stravinsky, "the world's greatest living composer," will end up living more for what he did to music than for what his music did to the majority of his listeners.

His verdict on Schoenberg is even more bleak; in a 1974 centennial appreciation he wrote:

> . . . is it heresy to suggest that Schoenberg may have been an alien growth in the garden of music? History may look upon his music as a biological sport that grew, flourished, reproduced but in its struggle for existence eventually died a Darwinian kind of death for lack of support. For natural selection operates also in music.

1. This is as good a place as any to dispel one unavoidable confusion which, with all its many ironies, continues to cast its spell even on those who know better; Schoenberg the composer is not related to Schonberg the critic.

Despite such feelings, Schonberg has made an attempt to listen to and remain open-minded about the composers of this century. He has a high regard for the supposedly "dry" Hindemith (and for a somewhat similar earlier composer, Max Reger), which is not shared by the public. He likes much of Poulenc, and has some good to say of Shostakovich and Prokofiev; he even seems willing to allow Bartók a place among the few real immortals. He has long been intrigued by the possibilities of electronic means of musical composition, and as late as the beginning of the 1970s he continued to predict a fine future for mixed-media works with an important musical component. He was, furthermore, a booster of Pierre Boulez (as a conductor) at the time of his first appearances with the New York Philharmonic in 1969.

But in the end open-mindedness without affection counts for little; in Schonberg's case it quickly became apparent that the result of his listening to the new was an increasing distaste, resulting finally in a kind of contempt for the reigning schools of avant-garde music—atonality, serialism, and the derivations thereof. He disliked the complexity of this music, what seemed to him its spurious intellectuality, and above all its lack of melody. Though he admired Stockhausen's technological innovations in composition, he disparagingly called him in a headline the "Pied Piper of the Young," at a time when Stockhausen was seen by many musical intellectuals as a combination of Beethoven and the messiah.

About the avant-garde in America he has been particularly harsh. He has not concealed his preference for the unabashedly popular productions of such composers as Sousa and Gottschalk—and Broadway musical comedy—over the serious American composers of our century. He has treated Elliott Carter, whose post–World War II works are so highly regarded by other composers, with a mixture of respect for his tenacity and dislike for his music. Schonberg's constant lament is that American music, and other new music as well, lacks content, that the new trends have hardened into a new academicism. In a typical recent review he describes works by three recognized, living American composers in the same negative terms: one's "musical content is thin," another's "musical idiom is neutral," and the last is "very slick, with more rhetoric than substance."

What Schonberg wants is a return, already noticeable, to melodic writing employing as means rather than ends the experimental electronic and instrumental techniques developed in the last three decades. This eclectic combination of new methods with an older idea of melody he has called neo-romanticism. In an article describing how this kind of music "warms a public chilled by the avant-garde," he praises, as an example, a violin concerto by the American George Rochberg

> that looked back to, believe it or not, Brahms. It was largely tonal, and it had one lyric, haunting movement that still rings in the memory. It was romantic, really romantic, but this was no slavish Romanticism. It was a modern Romanticism, a neo-Romanticism . . . in which Brahmsian post-Romanticism was filtered through a contemporary mind, emerging as something new. Stravinsky had done much the equivalent when he . . . went back to Bach and the Baroque, using old forms that he filtered through his unique vision.

A favorable comparison of a new trend in music to the achievements of Stravinsky is perhaps, for Schonberg, not an unambivalent compliment. What his discussion of neo-romanticism discloses is how much more interested he is in the old than the new brand; he makes this plain later in the same article when he remarks of neo-romanticism that its "Berlioz or Chopin or Wagner" remains to be found.

Indeed, Schonberg's most distinctive contribution to music criticism has precisely been his interest in the original romanticism of the nineteenth century. He has not, save in the case of his favorite piano works, indulged in the endless iterative discussion of slightly varied performances of the top warhorses of the repertory; following the bicentennial of Beethoven's birth in 1970, he even asked for a moratorium on performances of the composer's symphonies. Rather he has enthusiastically assumed the role of cicerone to a lost world of forgotten romantic composers of the nineteenth century, most of them instrumental virtuosos famous in their day but long since rejected by a public interested only in greatness.

Because this music can rarely be heard in New York, Schonberg has traveled as far afield as Butler University in Indiana. To list some of the names he has found there, and occasionally elsewhere, is to enter a musical curiosity shop: Spohr, Raff, Dreyschock, Kalkbrenner, Henselt, and especially Hummel. What is even more curious is the excitement they arouse in him—a kind of unbuttoned enthusiasm he vouchsafes to only the rarest of post–World War I works.

While Schonberg has spent a great deal of time on composers, he has devoted even more time to performers, especially pianists, about whom he has vastly sounder and more stimulating things to say than he does about composers. In general, indeed, he has become today's leading exponent of the cult of star performing personalities—Pavarotti, Sutherland, and most of all Horowitz. It is not simply personality that has attracted Schonberg to such artists. What they possess, in a measure beyond the reach of almost all their contemporaries, is technical virtuosity—to Schonberg the very basis of musical communication. The kind of technique he most values is the kind achieved without noticeable exertion, more as a force of nature than the product of study and, especially, effort. It is perhaps this dislike of palpable effort that has caused Schonberg to devalue the Austrian pianist Alfred Brendel as well as ignore (in his book on pianists) Brendel's teacher, the Swiss Edwin Fischer.

Schonberg, in his own way, is a devotee of the doctrine of authenticity in performance. He wrote testily: ". . . I do not want a modern approach to Bach. I want Bach's approach to Bach. . . ." He is interested in the latest trends in academic musicology, and recently devoted an entire Sunday piece to a new book on eighteenth-century ornamentation. He has been a sympathizer of the modern idea of performing old music on the instruments for which it was written, and in the area of operatic production he bitterly resents both the bringing up-to-date of nineteenth-century operas and the injection of the private visions of stage directors into the original conceptions of composers.

Paradoxically coexisting with this interest in authenticity is a commitment to the freedom of the performer. Schonberg castigates those musicians who make a religion of playing only what is notated in the written text, and calls them by the charged name of "formalists"; he thinks this pernicious doctrine has particularly blighted an entire generation of American musicians.

But one man's freedom is another man's license; Schonberg can no more escape the central problem of freedom in musical performance than it can be escaped in life. To his own musical satisfaction Schonberg answers the question of how freedom is to be exercised by advocating a careful study of past performance practices, to see just how the masters of old went about being free. Because those few whom he regards as the greatest composer-performers of the past—Bach, Mozart, Beethoven, Chopin, and Liszt —made no recordings, and because even the clearest contemporary written descriptions seem unreliable, Schonberg is inexorably driven to recommending the oldest performers he can find who have left records or, better yet, are still alive. To the current lack of excitingly personal young performers he opposes a relatively recent golden age of interpretation as demonstrated by early recordings and an increasingly rare live concert.

A remarkable case in point is his review of the 1979 Carnegie Hall appearance of the ninety-one-year-old Brazilian-born French pianist Magda Tagliaferro. He had heard her some six months before in Paris, and for him, her playing "went back to a vanished age." Though he recognized the pianist's failing strength,[2] he praised her "singing line," "coloristic resource," and "tasteful application of Romantic devices." And it was all urged on piano students:

> To the young pianists who were in the audience, her performance of the Schumann "Carnaval" should have come as a revelation. Not since the days of Rachmaninoff and Friedman has this listener encountered such a basic understanding of, and feeling for, the composer's mercurial moods.

Schonberg's rejection of today in favor of yesterday is by no means restricted to performers on his favorite instrument, the piano. Of the New York recital last year of the then seventy-four-year-old violinist Nathan Milstein, he wrote:

> . . . he is one of the last active Romantics. Certain things are in his blood; he was trained in an old school and he unabashedly represents it. . . .
>
> Mr. Milstein remains the Old Master, and there must have been many in last night's audience who walked out in utter despair. It cannot be easy for aspiring virtuosos to face up to this kind of perfection.

2. What seemed to some in the audience that night a kind of physical decrepitude, which almost totally disfigured the pianist's performances, further impressed at least this listener, in the context of a Carnegie Hall concert before thousands of people, as embarrassing and even frightening.

Now that Schonberg is retiring, the question naturally arises of the effect on music of his two decades as critic of the *Times*. How influential has he been?

On musicians—whether performers or composers—his influence has been slight. Those artists involved in either the composition or the performance of contemporary music have almost universally dismissed him (at least in private, but often in public as well) as a middlebrow, a vulgar philistine read only to be mocked. There has been no rush to follow his advice to write appealing, melodic music; and such efforts as have been made in this direction have hardly excited much interest. Among performers who care about appealing to the audience for which Schonberg speaks, he has been feared as a vast and life-threatening force who must be appeased and enticed by choice of program. But so far as performing styles are concerned, both the general nature of his injunctions and the particular talents and limited flexibility of any individual performer render what he writes most often inapplicable.

It is difficult to know what Schonberg has meant to his readers. No doubt many in the audience have looked to him for guidance in forming their judgments. Yet where Schonberg has, as in his praise of forgotten composers, been original, he has found no response; audiences still want to hear just those pieces of which Schonberg has often said he is tired. Where he has ratified existing taste—as in the case of his enthusiasm for star performers—he is (at least on the evidence of the continuing popularity of his books) read with avidity. It is not, in other words, as a teacher or a leader that Schonberg has been read; he reflects rather than influences the musical orientation of the contemporary audience. And that orientation is to music's past rather than its present or future.

What are we to make of this attachment to the old in music, which Harold Schonberg and his musical readers, in their own different but related ways, share?

It does not seem too much to say that the rejection of the avant-garde by both Schonberg and the public has turned out to be justified. The avant-garde has collapsed; at present neither the serialists of the 1940s and the 1950s nor the mixed-media experimentalists of the '60s and '70s have any friends, even among the musicians who made careers by singing the praises of the new. There has, however, been more in twentieth-century musical composition than the various avant-gardes of the past fifty years. As Schonberg himself has said, and as concert programs demonstrate, much admirable music capable of appealing to the public has been written in our time. Yet it is also true that the accepted new music is successful only by comparison with the despised products of the avant-garde; the audience still mainly demands the three B's.

Why should this be? It cannot merely be a matter of preference for nineteenth-century romantic music, for the audience (if not Schonberg) has taken baroque to its heart, and has refused to accept the musty menu of romantic compositions Schonberg has recommended. It is rather that today's musical public has come to a fundamental decision: it has the music it wants, and it is satisfied with what it has. Just as a Boston dowager is said to have answered an inquiry as to where she bought her hats with the simple "Buy my hats? I *have* my hats," the audience has closed the door to the new, not so much because it dislikes the new as because it is entirely content with the old.

It is possible to view this decision as a just recognition of musical greatness, or as merely another manifestation of the deplorably reactionary behavior of contemporary society. Either way, it seems that the concertgoing public and Harold Schonberg have been very well suited to each other over the past twenty years.

[1980]

# Within a Budding Grove's

*The New Grove Dictionary of Music and Musicians* [1]—the latest manifestation of the renowned English reference work—is here, surpassing in size all its predecessors. Like the battleships built in the twilight of seapower, its mere statistics of displacement and armament seem validation enough in themselves. On kitchen scales, the twenty volumes of this present edition weigh more than seventy pounds; the guns of the enterprise—the contributors—are said to number 2,400, and come from seventy countries. And the heroic vital statistics go on and on. Each volume averages 865 pages; there are altogether, we are told, 22,500 articles, 16,500 biographies, 3,000 musical examples, 4,500 photographs and illustrations, 9,000 cross-references. Again according to the publisher's generous publicity, there are "nearly 1 million words about instruments, nearly 1 million words about musical forms and terms, [and] over 1 million words about non-Western and folk music." Rough calculation suggests a total word count approaching twenty million.

Faced with these riches, an onlooker might well ask: "After such knowledge, what forgiveness?" But the initial problem, of course, is not forgiveness, but evaluation. Any initial judgment of this behemoth of reference works must perforce be based on scattered reading and partial acquaintance.

Moreover, a dictionary—or an encyclopedia, which in fact is what *The New Grove* is—can itself be no more than an account, more or less complete, of the state of knowledge and attitudes about a given area at one particular moment in the unfolding of intellectual, social, and (in this case) aesthetic history. *The New Grove* is, by the publisher's count, the sixth new publication of a work whose first edition appeared just over a century ago. Though another counting of *Grove*'s publishing history would suggest that there are

1. Edited by Stanley Sadie, Macmillan (London) and Grove's Dictionaries of Music (Washington, D.C.), 1980, 20 vols., 17,389 pp., $1,900 (at time of publication).

only five true editions, the point by any reckoning remains the same. *Grove* is not just a set of books but an institution with a history; as with institutions in general, the past tells us not only whence we have come, but where we now are. Any serious consideration of *The New Grove,* then, has to begin with a look at its predecessors.

As was the case with such Victorian phenomena as Isambard Kingdom Brunel's steamship *Great Eastern* and Sir Joseph Paxton's Crystal Palace, Sir George Grove's first *Dictionary* was a wonder of an age that admired size, strength, and ambition. Originally projected to cover music from 1400 on in two volumes, it began with Volume I—"A to Impromptu"—in 1879; by the time Volume II —"Improperia to Plain-song"—appeared the next year, a third volume was envisioned. In the end a fourth, coming out in 1890, was added to the third, which had been published in 1883. Part of Volume IV carried the work's first revision, an appendix edited by J. C. Fuller-Maitland, who then succeeded Grove as editor when the second edition began to appear fourteen years later.

*Grove 1,* as it is called in the standard shorthand, was to a remarkable extent the triumph of its originator. Grove was a professional civil engineer, an amateur biblical archaeologist, and a powerful editor—as well as a music lover of the greatest possible enthusiasm. As an engineer he worked on projects not only in England and Scotland, but also in Bermuda and Jamaica. As a part-time scholar of religion he worked with William Smith on a *Dictionary of the Bible.* In addition, he was a major force in establishing the Palestine Exploration Fund, an organization designed to produce, in the words of a contemporary account, "a series of books which will tell us all we wish to know about the geography, geology, natural history, and antiquities of Palestine." And from 1868 to 1883 he served as editor of *Macmillan's Magazine,* a monthly numbering among its authors Thomas Carlyle and Charles Kingsley (it was Kingsley's attack on Father Newman, appearing in the January 1864 issue of *Macmillan's,* that eventually produced, by way of answer, the future Cardinal Newman's *Apologia Pro Vita Sua*).

Here were assembled the factors that combined to produce the *Dictionary of Music and Musicians.* Engineering had given Grove a taste for great projects. Through the help of eminent professional colleagues he came to work for the Society of Arts, an organization heavily involved with the development of the 1851 Crystal Palace Exhibition. In 1852, when plans were being made to relocate the exhibition buildings at Sydenham, Grove became the Crystal Palace's secretary. Education was to be a dominant function of the Crystal Palace; what better education could a music lover promote than the glorious and uplifting sounds of the masters from Bach to Mendelssohn? Grove now became the organizer of concert life at the Crystal Palace, a role for which, in the best fashion of English amateurs, his enthusiasm was more a qualification than his lack of formal knowledge and training was a handicap.

Though the means were musical, Grove's goals were evangelical. There could be for him little difference between bringing the history of the Holy Land into English homes and bringing great music to English ears. It was, however, Grove's further genius to see that it was not enough to *play* music for the unsophisticated. They must also have it explained to them. This he did by writing attractive and detailed program notes calculated to lead the rising classes from the purgatory of tonal ignorance to the paradise of enlightenment.

But program notes, after all, were at best fragmentary and transient. The Victorian Age was interested in permanence in literature as well as in engineering. There could be nothing more wonderful than bringing everything known about music together in a great compilation, much as Grove had brought the facts of biblical life together in a comparable series of books. Here his business relation with the great publisher Alexander Macmillan smoothed the way to the writing of a musical reference work destined to make Grove's name more enduringly famous than almost any of the army of Victorian engineers, editors, or religious figures of the long summer of British imperial supremacy.

*Grove 1* is doubtless dated. It hardly goes beyond Tchaikowsky, and it contains little awareness of that distant musical past which it has been the task of twentieth-century musicology to substitute for an incomplete compositional present. Nor can it be said that a flood of material on forgotten performers and composers, all alive —and mostly dead—decades before the phonograph, makes for meaningful reading today.

All this having been stipulated, it is still true that the core of *Grove 1* remains as central to musical life as it was a century ago. This core was the consideration, at once lengthy and thorough, of the great composers. Bach, Mozart, Haydn, Beethoven, Schubert, Schumann, Mendelssohn, Wagner: they all bulked large in *Grove 1,* in articles on occasion written, as in the case of those on Beethoven, Schubert, and Mendelssohn, by Grove himself. The entry on Bach was written by A. Maczewski, identified only as a concert director in Kaiserslautern. Mozart and Haydn were covered by Carl Ferdinand Pohl, librarian at the *Gesellschaft der Musikfreunde* in Vienna, and composer, organist, and historian as well. Schumann was done by Philipp Spitta, a music historian in Berlin and a founder of "modern" Bach studies. The Wagner article came from a disciple of the composer, Edward Dannreuther, an English pianist, teacher, and writer of a standard work on musical ornamentation. In a striking example of just how close in time *Grove 1* was to its major subjects, Dannreuther promoted the appearance of Wagner at the London Festival named for him in 1877, and acted as the composer's host during his stay in England; it was at Dannreuther's London house that Wagner first publicly read the entire poem of *Parsifal.*

Some of *Grove 1* reflects an assessment of musical greatness hardly acceptable today. An interesting example of such a lost reputation is the entry on William Sterndale Bennett (1816–1875), an English composer admired by Mendelssohn and Schumann. H. H. Statham (an architect by profession) began his consideration of Sterndale Bennett by calling him "the only English musical composer since Purcell who has attained a distinct style and individuality of his own, and whose work can be reckoned among the models or 'classics' of his art."

But the special character of *Grove 1* lay not in its musical coverage, nor in its sometimes questionable judgments, but in the high ethical intention with which all the writing about great composers was done. Of Bach, for example, Maczewski wrote:

> His art and his family—these were the two poles around which Bach's life moved; outwardly, simple, modest, insignificant; inwardly, great, rich, and luxurious in growth and production. . . . If in a measure he ran counter to the continual encroachments of Italian opera, this may be attributed less to his artistic than to his moral and religious views.

Similarly, for Spitta, Schumann's "soul was too entirely noble and his ideal aims too high to have any purpose in view but the advancement of art." Even in the already clearly dubious case of

Wagner, Dannreuther was at some pains to defend his hero from the charge of anti-Semitism; indeed, he wrote, Wagner's "instinctive irrepressible energy, self-assertion, and incessant productivity went hand in hand with simple kindness, sympathy and extreme sensitiveness. Children liked to be near him."

This insistent message that great music and great human beings went together was conveyed in even larger measure by Grove's own articles. Time and again, when we read Grove today, we can feel the force of Victorian moral sentiments. Nowhere is this more evident than in his treatment of Beethoven:

> One thing is certain, that his attachments to women were all honorable, and that he had no taste for immorality. "Oh God! let me at last find her who is destined to be mine, *and who shall strengthen me in virtue.*" Those were his sentiments as to wedded love.

Beethoven's religion was, for Grove, vastly higher than mere formal observance, and he quoted the composer's own words as proof:

> But that he was really and deeply religious, "striving sacredly to fulfill all the duties imposed on him by humanity, God, and nature," and full of trust in God, love to man, and real humility, is shown by many and many a sentence in his letters.

And for a conclusion Grove quoted an article by Dannreuther in *Macmillan's*:

> A religious passion and elevation are present in the utterances. The mental and moral horizon of the music grows upon us with each renewed hearing. . . . The warmth and depth of his ethical sentiment is now felt all the world over, and it will ere long be universally recognized that he has leavened and widened the sphere of men's emotions in a manner akin to that in which the conceptions of great philosophers and poets have widened the sphere of men's intellectual activity.

While Beethoven was, for Grove, an Olympian, Schubert was of a more human and intimate stature. Grove had heard and read stories of Schubert's vagrant behavior, but he would not accept them:

. . . we must content ourselves . . . with the certainty that, though irregular after the irregularity of his time, Schubert was neither selfish, sensual, nor immoral. What he was in his inner man we have the abundant evidence of his music to assure us. Whatever the music of other composers may do, no one ever rose from hearing a piece by Schubert without being benefited by it. Of his good-nature to those who took the bread out of his mouth we have already spoken. Of his modesty we may be allowed to say that he was one of the very few musicians who ever lived who did not behave as if he thought himself the greatest man in the world. . . . To [his hearers] he is not only a great musician, not only a great enchanter, but a dear personal friend.

In addition to being a passionate advocate of Beethoven and Schubert, Grove was one of the most fervent English propagandists for Mendelssohn, in whose person the particular virtues of Queen Victoria and the Prince Consort were seen to be displayed through art. But Grove was too sophisticated to accept that a full artistic expression could come just from the happy side of life. He therefore neatly reconciled his own aesthetic perceptions with his respect for Mendelssohn as a man:

Now Mendelssohn was never more than temporarily unhappy . . . he was never tried by poverty, or disappointment, or ill health, or a morbid temper, or neglect. . . . Who can wish that he had been? . . . It might have lent a deeper undertone to his Songs, or have enabled his Adagios to draw tears where now they only give a saddened pleasure. But let us take the man as we have him. Surely there is enough of conflict and violence in life and in art . . . it is well in these agitated modern days to be able to point to one perfectly balanced nature, in whose life, whose letters, and whose music alike, all is at once manly and refined, clever and pure, brilliant and solid.

*Grove 2,* in five volumes, was published in stages from 1904 to 1910, its last volume containing, as previously, an appendix. Now edited by Fuller-Maitland, the new edition was solidly based on

*Grove 1.* All the entries discussed above were retained in close to their original form, though additions and corrections were made to take account of more recent developments. The article on Sterndale Bennett, however, was significantly modified by the simple device of cutting out the opening encomium and thus beginning the article merely with an account of the composer's ancestors.

Much, of course, had happened in music between the initial publication of *Grove 1* and the appearance of *Grove 2.* Brahms, for instance, had gone from being one of the most important Austro-German composers (and, in 1879, still very much alive) to something like his present position as one of the immortals. His entry in *Grove 1* had been relatively short, though indeed perceptive and, by today's standards, largely accurate. In *Grove 2,* a long article, calling Brahms at the outset "the last of the great line of German masters," was written by Fuller-Maitland himself, a sure sign of editorial favor. Richard Strauss too received this accolade, though it was awarded with the peculiarly ambivalent attitude that has so often marked this composer's reception into the company of the great.

Among then contemporary composers, Debussy was briefly treated, with cautious respect; he was, however, accused of having "perpetrated things likely to offend musicians' prejudices unnecessarily." Mahler was described (by the editor) "as a composer . . . highly esteemed." Rachmaninoff was called "a pianist of repute, and one of the most talented of the younger Moscow school of composers." Some uncertainty was expressed as to whether Puccini would be seen as a "second Verdi," but his operatic achievement was nonetheless enthusiastically praised.

Of Stravinsky and Schoenberg there was not a word. This was proper in the case of Stravinsky, whose first notable score, *The Firebird,* was not completed until 1910, two years after the volume of *Grove 2* containing "S" was published. And though Schoenberg had by 1908 already written *Verklärte Nacht* (1899), the First String Quartet (1905), and by far the largest part of *Gurrelieder* (1900–01), his music was unknown outside the small circle of his Viennese admirers and the larger, though still hardly numerous, group of his enemies.

During his lifetime George Grove had been aware of the growing American presence in serious music. *Grove 1* had at its inception included four Americans among its fifty-six contributors, including Alexander Thayer, United States consul in Trieste and to this day perhaps the greatest Beethoven biographer. By the end of World War I Grove's successors felt that America deserved a supplementary volume all to itself, and the resulting effort, published in 1920, became the sixth volume of *Grove 2*.

The material in this American supplement, alas, mostly seems to belong to musty newspaper clippings and library archives rather than the historic present. And a further attempt to bring *Grove 2* up-to-date by the addition in this same supplementary volume of selected new non-American names also failed: there was here still no mention of Stravinsky or Schoenberg.

While the years between *Grove 1* and *Grove 2* had witnessed the beginnings of musical modernism, those between *Grove 2* and *Grove 3* (which appeared in five volumes in 1927) saw the final interment of that active creation which had made the nineteenth century the most successful period in musical history. By the mid-1920s all the great composers of the past century were long since dead, and even such relatively marginal and derivative figures as Saint-Saëns and Puccini were gone from the musical scene.

The response of *Grove 3* was to keep its first editor's original articles on Beethoven, Mendelssohn, and Schubert. Though this continued presentation of the words and opinions of the founder could be seen as an act of piety, the retention with only relatively minor editorial changes of major entries on other famous composers (Haydn, Schumann, and Wagner) demonstrated that music itself was well into its twentieth-century process of preferring an unchanging past to an all too altered present.

In at least one area of the accepted repertory, however, revision was definitely under way. From being an only recently rediscovered old master in 1879, Bach had by 1927 become a vivid and timeless contemporary presence. *Grove 3*'s response to this reassessment was to replace Maczewski's old entry with a new one, double the length, by Charles Sanford Terry, the English authority not only on Bach but on his whole talented family. Whereas in *Grove 1* Bach's works had a "magical attraction which they exert on those who make them their earnest study," for *Grove 3* he was unfairly disfavored by "the standards of the generation that followed his death, to which his sons conformed. Hence the neglect which obscured his grandeur for nearly a century. . . . He awaited the advent of a generation better equipped to fathom him."

But the more interesting contribution of *Grove 3* hardly lay in its treatment of the already historic, but in its documentation of the contemporary. Among the many composers it treated whom we today might call "modern," several stand out. Bartók and Prokofiev now finally made their appearance, both in discerning evaluations by Eric Blom, an English critic later to write *Everyman's Dictionary of Music* and, at the end of his life, to edit *Grove 5*.

The three composers who are now seen to comprise the Second Viennese School also made their debut in *Grove 3*. Schoenberg received a long and even reverent treatment from the English critic and specialist in contemporary music Edwin Evans. As a whole the entry betrayed little acquaintance with the actual sound of Schoenberg's music, and seemed content merely to list some of the composer's more novel formal procedures and to describe the subjects and plots of Schoenberg's rather lurid vocal works. Berg's and Webern's entries contained little more than biographical information, though the article on Berg (by another English critic, Scott Goddard) downplayed the lyrical side of his music, and that on Webern (again by Evans) did mention his distinctiveness as a miniaturist.

Alphabetization making, as it often does, strange bedfellows, the entry on Strauss, the apostate from modernism, was followed by one on Stravinsky, the hero of the avant-garde. Here—in contrast to the general verdict of succeeding decades—the honors went clearly to the German.

A revised edition of the 1920 American supplement was published in 1928 to go with *Grove 3*. In large measure it was in fact unaltered from its first appearance eight years earlier. The only new material was an appendix giving minor factual additions and death dates for 100 of the figures listed in 1920. Strangely, this edition was kept in print until as late as 1957, even though it failed to account for an entire generation of American composers ranging from Samuel Barber to Virgil Thomson, a generation that finally brought American music onto the world scene.

*Grove 4*, a supposedly new edition published in 1940, was actually nothing more than the five volumes of *Grove 3*, with yet another new supplement bringing matters more or less up-to-date.

But there was in the new supplement still no entry for Virgil Thomson, even though *Four Saints in Three Acts* had been something of a long-running success on Broadway in 1934. Even more surprising, considering *Grove's* later editorial policy, there was no entry for George Gershwin, who by the time of publication was already dead and a canonized figure in American music. But at least the supplementary volume did come to grips with the mechanical reproduction of music; it contained an excellent (for its time) piece by the famous physicist and astronomer Sir James Jeans on "Electric Transmission of Sound."

So the status of *Grove's Dictionary of Music and Musicians* at the end of World War II was that of a palpably Victorian document, strong on appreciation of the greats, and cautious in recognition of their successors. Up to this point, though many musicians and critics had been involved in its production, *Grove's* had remained essentially a music lover's companion. It had taken little account of the great expansion in academic studies of musical forms and styles produced by the movement of music into the universities both in England and in America.

A new edition was clearly necessary, this time to contain a significant amount of current coverage of both composers and knowledge about music. The need was supplied by *Grove 5,* which was published in 1954 in nine volumes. Not only was *Grove 5* half new, with newness defined as material written specifically for this edition; and not only had the whole enterprise increased vastly in size, with the nine volumes averaging 928 pages compared to the third edition's five volumes averaging just under 800 pages each; a supplement to *Grove 5,* containing amplifications and corrections and rounding out the 1950s, appeared in 1961 as well. In a concession both to new methods of book distribution and the expansion of the musical audience, the whole set was made available in paperback at a modest price (under $100).

Even at first glance, *Grove 5* seemed very different from its predecessors. The pages now looked more modern, with a more legible typeface and clearer headings. The editing too seemed more precise, and on occasion even pedantic; numerous cross-references made finding items easier than it had been in the past. Extensive and detailed listings of major composers' works provided invaluable reference material; increased coverage of contemporary composers provided a guide, no matter how sketchy, to the state of musical practice—if not to the state of musical taste.

In spirit also *Grove* 5 differed from its predecessors. New writers, musicologically trained, were beginning to replace the older school of enthusiasts who, under George Grove's leadership, had given such an amateur tone to the endeavor. Folk music was now seen as vastly more important, and a new sense of what one of *Grove* 5's critics called "Buy British" as a criterion of musical choice was suggested in both coverage and description. America remained a slighted colony, an attitude all the more difficult to accept after the expansion of our musical life in both composition and performance in the 1930s and '40s.

Now finally gone was the heart of George Grove's personal contribution to the work—his set pieces on Beethoven, Mendelssohn, and Schubert. In place of their high Victorian tone was a more sober analysis, reflecting the approach of the scholar-critic rather than that of the devotee. Gone too was the spirit of the uplifting moralist. Of the many examples of this change, the article on Beethoven is perhaps the most significant. Here Grove's moral tributes were toned down, where they were not either qualified out of existence or ignored altogether. For William McNaught, the English critic and editor, Beethoven

> was beyond a doubt a dominating, overwhelming person who wielded the power over men that we ascribe to force of will and role of intellect. . . . In this field it is not easy to make out a case for Beethoven as a man of mental parts. . . .
>
> A difficult question is presented by Beethoven's lack of rectitude in business dealings. The facts are stubborn and would prompt a harsher description.

As to the moral content of Beethoven's music, McNaught was clearly undecided:

> In work after work Beethoven carries the hearer to a plane of feeling where something is happening beyond the composition of music. What it is, what it can be, is the elusive question; and because it is unanswerable it has gathered a motley of answers that are the natural prey of skeptics.

Despite all the efforts made in *Grove 5* to adjust to a more modern temper, the new edition hardly satisfied all the critics. What bothered many observers—among them the American musicologist, historian, and critic Paul Henry Lang—was the still insufficient attention paid, or so they felt, to academically trained writers on music capable of seeing the art as an intellectual discipline requiring historically oriented study. For Lang as for others, what was wrong in *Grove 5* was not what was really new about it but rather what was old. Despite the throwing overboard of much of the work of Grove and his original associates, Lang found the whole process inadequate:

> . . . many of the hoary old entries have been retained, others exchanged for new ones of questionable, even lesser value, still others reworked with "additions" that did not remove the old Victorian high collar but only added a new necktie.

The stage was thus now set for *Grove 6,* a publication that might reflect the twentieth century in music as *Grove 1* did the nineteenth. The requirements were several: completeness, detail, scholarship, and objectivity. Completeness meant, in contemporary terms, not just a full coverage of "serious" music. It meant still more a properly encyclopedic treatment of folk music (now a fully sanctified form of artistic, not merely indigenous, expression) and a thoroughgoing attempt to describe, even if not fully, the entire range of contemporary popular music. Detail meant exhaustive lists of the works of all the major composers, and extended lists for minor figures; it also meant articles on both composers and formal subjects, in some cases long enough to constitute small books in themselves. Scholarship meant that *Grove 6* must in the main be written by musicologically, in addition or even opposed to, musically trained critics. Objectivity seems to have had two meanings: if a composer was worthy of inclusion, he was deserving of favorable comment; as a trade-off for this generally positive attitude, all enthusiasms must be avoided—especially those which went beyond music to the wider significance of art and life.

Viewed in these terms, *Grove 6,* as edited by the London *Times* music critic Stanley Sadie, is an undeniable success. More than almost anyone will ever want to know about music is here. Indeed, any serious reading of all that these volumes contain would occupy many years, if not a lifetime.

Even with the attempts to give some coverage to pop music, and despite all the words (which seem to this reader at once dull and unenlightening) on folk music, it is clear that the fate of *Grove* 6 will be determined by its coverage of serious and would-be serious music. Here everything is the state of the (academic) art, both in the treatment of composers and in the discussion of what is called at the Juilliard School the "literature and materials of music."

There are, it strikes me, few basic critical reassessments in *Grove* 6. Perhaps the most noteworthy information capable of striking readers as new to be found in these volumes concerns the true cause of Tchaikowsky's death—suicide in the face of a threat of exposure as a homosexual. In formal subjects, *Grove 6,* with its extensive and quite current bibliographies, will doubtless provide suitable introductory material for many students. The articles on composers, moreover, will surely serve journalists and program-note writers as an inexhaustible source of material.

When one leaves the main entries, there are, as might be expected, many criticisms possible; many of these criticisms will inevitably involve omissions. Given *Grove* 6's evident mission to be both self-explaining and self-referring, it seems regrettable that there is no article on the English critic C. L. Graves, author of the *Life and Letters of Sir George Grove.* In a more important area, it is surprising to find no entries for the significant American music critics Carl Van Vechten and B. H. Haggin. Though the writings of these two men are quite different in their taste and manner— Van Vechten loved the provocative and even the camp, and Haggin brings to the discussion of music and musicians something of the seriousness associated in literature with F. R. Leavis—they were both, one suspects, disqualified for inclusion in *Grove* 6 by the fact that neither had been suitably trained as a scholar.

Other omissions here often seem to be related to some vestigial English bias in coverage. There are, for instance, no entries for Franz Rupp and Paul Ulanowsky, two of the most active and respected accompanists living and playing in America in the years around World War II; this is so despite Rupp's association with Fritz Kreisler and Marian Anderson and Ulanowsky's work with

Lotte Lehmann. By contrast, the English accompanist Ivor Newton, who played for the soprano Conchita Supervia, is given his own, laudatory, article.

Also left out are several important American instrumental teachers, including Isabelle Vengerova (the teacher of Leonard Bernstein, Lukas Foss, and Gary Graffman), Olga Samaroff (the teacher of William Kapell and herself a successful touring concert artist), and Adele Marcus (the teacher of Horacio Gutiérrez and Byron Janis). Significantly, the piano teacher Ilona Kabos, Hungarian-born and resident in England for much of her life, though hardly more distinguished than her American counterparts, does receive the honor of an entry. And perhaps even more important, there is no entry in *Grove 6* for Dorothy DeLay, a mentor of both Itzhak Perlman and Pinchas Zukerman, and arguably the most successful violin teacher in the world today. Also inexcusable is the omission of Rosario Scalero, the composition teacher at the Curtis Institute in Philadelphia of Samuel Barber, Gian Carlo Menotti, Mark Blitzstein, Hugo Weisgall, and Lukas Foss.

Perhaps another example of relative slighting can be seen in the area of the phonograph (called by *Grove 6*, in accordance with English usage, the gramophone). There is here an admiring article on the English record producer Walter Legge of EMI, and one on John Culshaw, his colleague at Decca. But there is no entry for Goddard Lieberson, the brilliant producer and executive at American Columbia responsible for recording many of Igor Stravinsky's works in the composer's own, last performances, for the (almost) complete recordings of the works of Arnold Schoenberg, for the preserving of great chunks of the conductorial repertory of Bruno Walter, and for the daring Modern American Music Series, which remains the most important original recording project undertaken in the United States.[2]

In light of the present concern in England as well as in this country with the problems of funding music, it is surprising how

2. Plans are, it seems, afoot to correct these defects in coverage by publishing within the next three years an American supplement to *Grove 6*, under the joint editorship of Sadie and his "principal adviser on American music," H. Wiley Hitchcock. But however complete the coverage in the new volume, the damage done to an assessment of American musical life will remain through the clear message that colonial production has been, and is to this day, on a different level from that of the mother country.

few entries there are on recent individual patrons of the art. Henry Lee Higginson, the Maecenas of the Boston Symphony Orchestra from its founding until World War I, is only mentioned in the context of an article on Boston musical life; there are no entries for the Guggenheim Foundation or the Martha Baird Rockefeller Fund for Music. Furthermore, one of the twentieth century's most important patronesses, the Princesse Edmond de Polignac, is missing (nor is she mentioned in the article on music in Paris), even though her commissions included works by Stravinsky, Prokofiev, Falla, and Poulenc.

In *Grove 6,* despite the intention expressed by the editor in his preface to cover "people concerned in the business of music," the category is so defined as to exclude the commercial organization of musical presentation. As a result, there is little in it about how music is marketed, and how those involved in such marketing influence musical taste. Though there is a warm entry on Sol Hurok, there is no article on such a historical figure in music management as the late Arthur Judson or on such a present power as Ronald Wilford. Also lacking is an entry for Columbia Artists Management, the booking colossus that Judson founded and Wilford now heads. To leave out these men and their corporate creation while including such a merely publicity-conscious promoter as Hurok is to ignore the reality of commercial musical life in favor of the now waning glitter of New York's Russian Tea Room.

Consistent with the acceptance in *Grove 6* not only of all schools of serious music but also of all music anywhere, is a tendency to downplay the political context in which twentieth-century musicians have found themselves working. This effort to concentrate attention on more refined matters than mere politics can be seen in the coverage given to both Right and Left, to those musicians involved with either Nazi Germany or Soviet Russia. Thus the English critic Martin Cooper's entry on Germaine Lubin, a soprano at the Paris Opera before and during World War II, treats her collaboration with the Nazis as "a sympathy with Germany unusual among the French," produced by her "musical experiences at Bayreuth, her friendship with the Wagner family, and her general musical orientation." Similarly, Cooper describes the pianist and Vichy collaborator Alfred Cortot as possessing "a knowledge and love of German culture [which] predisposed him favorably toward the German occupiers of France in 1940–44."[3] About the Austrian conductor Clemens Krauss, Ronald Crichton soothingly writes:

> The flair he showed in his operatic career deserted him in politics. He made no bones about his Nazi sympathies: he was ready to take over the premiere of Strauss's *Arabella* (1933) when Fritz Busch, for whom the opera had been intended, was hounded out of Dresden; his immediate predecessors in Berlin (Kleiber) and Munich (Knappertsbusch) had both resigned for political reasons. Against these acts of public indiscretion must be weighed private deeds of kindness to Jewish artists in trouble.

In the case of the Soviet Union, *Grove* 6's coverage is rather more complicated. Boris Schwarz, a specialist on Soviet music at Queens College, is generally tough-minded in his contributions, and particularly so in his extended article on Shostakovich. In the case of lesser figures, the entries all too often are given over to the keeping of resident Soviet nationals. Thus the entry on Alexander Goldenweiser, the piano teacher of Dimitri Kabalevsky and Lazar Berman and also a turn-of-the-century associate of Rachmaninoff, Scriabin, and even Tolstoy, makes no mention of his supporting role in the 1948 Stalin-Zhdanov attack on Soviet composers (a role amply documented in the West by no less pro-Soviet an observer than Alexander Werth). Though the article on Mstislav Rostropovich (by an English writer) mentions the conductor-cellist's political courage and departure from the USSR, the one on Rostropovich's wife, singer Galina Vishnevskaya (by I. M. Yampolsky, the author of the Goldenweiser entry), makes no mention of the artist's politics or of her leaving her homeland.

But the most important omission of all is the absence here of any really serious consideration of the great questions of music today. As one example, the entry on the avant-garde (there is none on modernism), less than a column in length, avoids both serious observation and any side-taking. The last words of this article are little but a confession of default: ". . . the term 'avant-garde' remains more a slogan than a definition."

3. Vivid proof of Cortot's attitude, if such be needed, may be found in a photograph included in Albert Speer's memoirs, *Inside the Third Reich*. It shows the pianist gazing, in a way at once worshipful and leering, at Frau Speer.

Not only is the question of the permanent value of twentieth-century music thus undiscussed; other basic questions are either ignored or taken for granted. Chief among these are: the worth of the past in terms of the present; the role of music as an art in the living of life. While these questions have no ready answer—and perhaps no contemporary answer at all—they are inescapably posed by what we know as the crisis of musical repertory, composition, and performance.

In spite of these omissions, it is clear that everything about *Grove* 6 recommends it for reference collections. It is large; it is expensive; it is the work of a collective rather than of an individual; it is scholarly rather than enthusiastic; it is professional rather than amateur. Here, in these twenty volumes, is evidence not just of the rise of musicology. Here is something more: a conception of music as institutional rather than individual, as the proper domain of students rather than music lovers, of librarians rather than readers. Here, indeed, is an encyclopedia that by its very format and existence symbolizes music as we are increasingly seeing it in America and the world: the ward of the state and of great institutions, a massive, moderately diverting academic circus to go along with the bread the state and institutions increasingly also promise to supply.

In the final analysis *Grove* 6—unlike those of its predecessors fully stemming from *Grove 1*—seems another, albeit impressive, document of modern intellectual life. There is so much in its pages of human ambition and human activity—but in the end the persistent failure to consider a wider meaning for music makes it all seem like a massive necrology. It is not that those connected with *Grove* 6 do not value music highly; of course they do, and the completion of this huge project is proof enough of their dedication. But the refusal to discuss ultimate values raises the issue Shakespeare treated in Hamlet's words about the Polish campaign:

Two thousand souls and twenty
   thousand ducats
Will not debate the question of
   this straw:
This is the imposthume of much
   wealth and peace,

That inward breaks, and shows
    no cause without
Why the man dies.

Perhaps the problem of *Grove 6* is precisely that severing from *Grove 1* the critics of *Grove 5* demanded. For in giving up the passé musical judgments and intellectual apparatus of an earlier age, something else was lost as well: the high Victorian seriousness displayed by George Grove and many of his important contributors. In line with the spirit of the great Victorians, of whom Grove himself clearly was one, the function of music was taken to be the making of better men, charitable to their fellows, dedicated to freedom under conditions of righteous order. For *Grove 1* the greatest music clearly did this in the greatest degree, and the rest was but filler.

No one can deny that the twentieth century has been unkind to this notion of human betterment resulting from the experience of art. Hitler's mobilization of a political and social world that self-consciously based itself on the German *Kultur* of Beethoven and Goethe is surely enough to suggest a deeper and more troubling relation between art and life. Wagner's (fortunately) unique combination of musical greatness and moral depravity has had horrid consequences for civilized society since his cultural ascendancy began over a century ago.

Yet what is important for us now is not any proven connection between art and morality. The beneficent result of music on man which Grove and his colleagues celebrated did not depend for its efficacy on the music's being moral, but rather on the desire of men for moral guidance. This desire lay at the heart of the Victorian use of art and learning. The great ideas of that now vanished age, from abolition and the extension of suffrage to education and beauty, were moral ideas, justified less for themselves than for their uses. That music was seen as one of the most important tools for moral progress was of vital importance for the propagation of the art;[4]

---

4. It is clear from *Grove 6* that an unintended result of this prevailing ethical withdrawal is a lessened ability to make even specifically musical judgments *sub specie aeternitatis*. Thus in a long article on Beethoven, musicologists Joseph Kerman and Alan Tyson—sympathetic as they both are to Beethoven's music and personality—seem compelled to retreat from full endorsement of what they no doubt see as sublime music: "The five late string quartets," they write,

that music was used in the implementation of such a benign vision now seems to us a rare grace.

Hardly less important in *Grove 1* was the idea, dear to its founder, of an artistic hierarchy based not only on the professional criteria of good and bad but also on the cultural idea of high and low. *Grove 1* did not accept what was in the world of music; it chose. It was primarily concerned with the greats rather than with the masses, with art music rather than demotic musics. Put another way, *Grove 1* was concerned, both in music and in life, not with what is, but with what can be.

For *Grove 6* everything is music, but music is—music. In what may stand both as epitome of *Grove 6* and epitaph for *Grove 1*, the new edition characterizes the founder in strangely deflating terms:

> Grove was in nearly every way a typical "great Victorian," with a zest for self-education, a conviction that the achievements of the nineteenth century could hardly be surpassed, a belief that most objectives were attainable through hard work, a high sense of morality that caused him great personal problems, and a desire for respectability.

After such knowledge, indeed, what forgiveness?

[1982]

---

"contain Beethoven's greatest music, or so at least many listeners in the twentieth century have come to feel."

# The Real Vladimir Horowitz?

It cannot be easy to write the biography of a living person. The first problem is that of authorization: asking the cooperation of the subject inevitably raises the possibility of a veto over the whole work, while going it alone deprives the biographer of both private documents and the testimony of the one individual who knows the biographical material better than anyone else. Without the subject's cooperation, the contributions from friends and associates, too, are more difficult to obtain, except for the occasional and suspect expressions of bitterness and rejection. Hanging over everything is the threat of a suit for libel, restricted, at least until a recent court decision, to the complaints of living plaintiffs. When to all these hindrances is opposed the advantage of treating a whole life as a completed field of study, there can be no surprise that the best biographies are written after the subject's death.

But to put the matter this way is to argue on behalf of scholarship. Viewed another way, there is considerable reason for telling the story of a worthy subject while that person still lives and breathes, whatever the obstacles. Relevance and even notoriety attach to the celebrity of the living, which is why publishers are always interested in writings on the famous: the public is always there.

In the world of classical music today only one figure can attract this kind of interest. Vladimir Horowitz is an historically great pianist. Despite his fame, he has made efforts for more than half a century to keep his private life free from public scrutiny. He has spoken to the press only under controlled conditions, and even then he has always taken refuge in a carefully articulated display of whimsical eccentricity. Completely alien to him has been the kind of candor that Arthur Rubinstein displayed in his innumerable media encounters and two autobiographical volumes. Because Horowitz has been so successful at confining the descriptions of his life to superficial generalities, what has been published about him has mostly discussed his piano playing and its effects on audiences.

Despite a restricted amount of personal material on Horowitz, his life has been the subject of unbounded speculation, especially within the musical community. Two much-noted retirements from concert life—a short one in the 1930s and another lasting from 1953 to 1965—were the cause of many rumors about the state of Horowitz's physical and mental health. His much publicized marriage in 1933 to Arturo Toscanini's daughter Wanda seemed on at least one occasion on the brink of dissolution. A daughter born to that marriage in 1934 was widely known to be unhappy and a persistent burden to her parents; a bad motorscooter accident in 1957, causing serious injury, and her death under unexplained circumstances in 1975, only fueled further gossip.

Added to the discussion of these subjects have been rumors about a still more embarrassing problem, that of the pianist's possibly other than purely heterosexual orientation and behavior. It was widely known in the music world that Horowitz had frequently traveled on his concert rounds with a male companion. It was known that he had limited his teaching almost entirely to young male students. His style of dressing—favoring extraordinarily elegant clothes in striking colors and combinations—seemed hardly typical of revered classical musicians, and his behavior to the press often seemed fey. It was said, too, among pianists, that Horowitz's style of playing, although astonishingly forceful in loud and heroic passages, seemed at times almost artificially refined in delicate and quiet music.

Binding all of this interest and speculation together has of course been that which stimulated it in the first place: Horowitz's extraordinary success as a pianist, both with his real and would-be colleagues and at the box office. Rarely within living memory have earning power and professional respect in classical music so gone together as in the case of Horowitz. From each retirement, whatever its cause, he has emerged more successful than before; his return to the concert stage in 1965, and his first concerto appearance in twenty-five years in 1978, were the major American musical events of their decades. Throughout his seventies he continued to learn and program large new works, and achieved with them a level of performance in no way inferior to that which he had achieved with compositions he had known since his student days. And the public kept coming. Lines at box-office windows, scandals over ticket availability and allocation, high prices—all of these contributed to Horowitz's being the highest paid (per event) classical instrumental attraction of the last decade: his take-home pay from each concert in this period averaged around thirty-five thousand dollars. For the moment, the culmination of Horowitz's career took place last May in London. At the invitation of Prince Charles, Horowitz returned to Europe for the first time in thirty-one years. He played two concerts in London's Royal Festival Hall, the first televised live to the United States. Beginning the concert with "God Save the Queen," Horowitz took London and much of the world as well by storm—again.

Now we have the first biography of Horowitz,[1] written by Glenn Plaskin, a free-lance writer. This lengthy (more than two hundred thousand words) book follows a chronological course through the pianist's long life. The book's text is followed by numerous references to interviews granted to the press by Horowitz and his wife. Included, too, is material from newspaper reviews and biographical articles. Plaskin, by his own account, has talked to some six hundred and fifty people in connection with this book. Some of these interviews have borne fruit; he quotes several of Horowitz's colleagues, including Rudolf Serkin and Nathan Milstein; all of Horowitz's major students, including Gary Graffman and Byron Janis; one of the pianist's traveling companions during the 1940s, Lowell Benedict; a friend during the 1970s, the composer Phillip Ramey (now a program editor of the New York Philharmonic); a close friend during the early 1930s, Alexander Steinert, a composer and member of the Boston music-store family; and Natasha Saitzoff, Horowitz's first cousin and only relative now living in the United States. To all these sources is added a classification described in the notes only as "anonymous source."

The result of all this effort is a book that makes its points by length and repetition rather than by insight and argument. There are here, too, many anomalies. Plaskin introduces a hostile review from a German newspaper by saying that the review gave Horowitz and his manager "particular reason to pause," although he names

1. *Horowitz: A Biography of Vladimir Horowitz*, William Morrow, 1983.

no source for this assertion. Horowitz is described, on his own evidence, as having played during the 1922–23 season "twenty-three concerts of eleven different programs containing more than one hundred different works, and never [having] performed the same composition twice." Plaskin doesn't explain how this is possible. He also seems insecure about the repertoire Horowitz was playing at this time: he has Horowitz playing the Poulenc *Toccata* and *Presto,* for instance, but they did not appear before 1928 and 1934.

The sloppinesses mount up. Horowitz is described on one page as having failed to practice the Beethoven "Emperor" Concerto properly and sufficiently before a lesson; later Horowitz's own story (told to a "friend") that in 1932, when he was preparing for his debut with Toscanini, he still had never even heard the "Emperor" is repeated by Plaskin without comment. Other strange things happen in Plaskin's sources. Dealing with events around 1926, he writes that "Occasionally he [Horowitz] gave mildly indiscreet interviews to the press." He then goes on to quote Horowitz's own words about a visit to a bordello where he practiced the piano while a friend occupied himself with a girl. The footnote at the end of the quotation refers to a 1978 interview with Hubert Saal in *Newsweek.*

Other uneasy formulations betray Plaskin's uncertainty in dealing with factual material. The English record label HMV is described correctly in one place as being (in 1929) RCA Victor's "London affiliate"; some pages later it is described, wrongly, as "RCA Victor's English subsidiary." Plaskin accepts without comment Horowitz's statement that his recording of the Liszt Sonata took up eight 78 RPM sides, when in fact (as properly shown in the book's excellent discography) it takes up only six.

Despite their tendency to undermine our faith in the author's grasp of his subject, such carelessnesses would be of little significance were the book to supply original and compelling insight into Horowitz's art and life. But this it does not do. Plaskin has especially little of interest to contribute to our understanding of that area of Horowitz's life that would seem to be of greatest importance: his piano playing.

Here, Plaskin is content to echo, often at great length, received opinion. According to that opinion, Horowitz is a paragon of speed,

control, sonority, excitement, and showmanship. Even so, his playing lacks emotional penetration, even in the music—Chopin and
Liszt preeminently—he admittedly plays supremely well. Almost
without fail Horowitz has been found to lack sympathy with and
commitment to the music of the great composers, including Bach,
Mozart, Beethoven, and Schubert. Indeed, much of the musical
portion of Plaskin's book consists of quotations from newspaper
reviews, which he presents uncritically.

Plaskin clearly agrees with the conventional diagnosis of Horowitz's shortcomings, and he has no trouble finding the reasons for
them. Put simply, they are greed and ambition, which are everywhere in evidence—even when they don't seem to be. Thus Plaskin
begins a paragraph describing a 1935 Carnegie Hall recital with a
review praising Horowitz for showing a "deeply serious commu-
nion" with the Chopin B-flat Minor Sonata rather than "personal
exhibitionism." He then goes on to another review of the same
concert, which finds the pianist's attempts to be more than a virtuoso dashed by the audience's enthusiasm for his technical prowess
in the program's display pieces. For Plaskin the point is made:
Horowitz was "inevitably attracted to such demonstration because
of his vanity and his ever present desire for more success and
money."

But there is abundant evidence—in his words, in his playing,
and in his business decisions—that there is rather more to Vladimir
Horowitz than greed and ambition. He did not always succumb to
the pressure to play showy music. A year after the Carnegie Hall
concert, for example, he played, as he had before, the Brahms
D-Minor Concerto (certainly one of the few piano concertos to rank,
for musicians, with the greatest classical and early romantic symphonies). The orchestra for this performance was the Amsterdam
Concertgebouw under the very serious Bruno Walter, whom even
Plaskin describes as Horowitz's "all-around favorite conductor."
Plaskin does not describe the Brahms performance; he doesn't even
quote from the press notices. Instead he proceeds to make mention
of a subsequent recording session and the pianist's unhappy emotional state. Fortunately, a private-label recording of this performance exists; it is in fact widely available today. It contains an
extraordinary performance on the part of Horowitz no less than of
Walter—profound, weighty, and altogether glorious. Surely a

reader is entitled to know Plaskin's opinion on this historical document, relevant as it is both to a description of Horowitz's playing
in the 1930s and to his musical achievement in general.

There is a discussion of Horowitz's 1940 recording of the Brahms
B-flat Major Concerto with Toscanini. But here again Plaskin
clearly suggests that his objection to Horowitz is not just that he
has played too much music unworthy of him, but also that he has
never managed to penetrate great music at all. Again Plaskin begins
his description of the performance (which preceded the recording
by three days) with a musically favorable review, this time from
Olin Downes in the *New York Times*. The review talks of the pianist's "growth as interpreter"—but immediately Plaskin takes
it all away, now giving the credit to Horowitz's father-in-law,
Toscanini, and even quoting Horowitz as a witness against himself:

> When I played the Brahms [Second] Concerto with Bruno
> Walter it was completely different. . . . Toscanini had his
> own conception and I followed, even if it was sometimes
> against my own wishes.

And Plaskin goes on:

> At the rehearsals, there had been little discussion between
> Toscanini and Horowitz, for the interpretation had already
> been carefully planned in Riverdale [Toscanini's home].
> "There was no dialogue," recalled orchestral violinist Edwin
> Bachmann. "The undercurrent was one of fear—Horowitz's
> fear of Toscanini."

As it is with Brahms, so it is with other great works. Of the
pianist's now classic 1932 discs of the monumental Haydn Sonata
in E-flat Major he only remarks that they were part of a series of
"his most brilliant recordings." Of the phenomenal 1934 discs of
the immensely tricky Beethoven Thirty-two Variations in C Minor
Plaskin says not a word. He is content to describe Horowitz's
(unrecorded) 1968 performance of the Haydn C-Major Sonata by
quoting Harold Schonberg's dismissive remarks; there is no mention at all (except in the discography) of Horowitz's—fortunately

recorded—great live performance of the Haydn F-Major Sonata in 1966, with its touchingly inflected ornamentation in the slow movement.

Plaskin does have a great deal to say about the business aspects of Horowitz's career. Those who care for such matters can learn all they want to know about the artist's fees. They can learn too about Alexander Merovitch, the personal manager who was responsible for launching Horowitz's career (along with those of Gregor Piatigorsky and Nathan Milstein) in Germany and elsewhere during the 1920s. There is much material here too on Horowitz's relations during the 1930s with Arthur Judson, the closest approach to a dictator the American music business has ever known. One can also read in this book about Horowitz's attempts to use smaller managers who might provide personalized service without charging the standard and large commissions of the giants.

Musicians who have often wanted to keep all the fees for themselves by doing without a manager will enjoy reading about Horowitz's short-lived efforts in this line. In one of the few witty moments in the book, Plaskin quotes F. C. Schang, one of the longtime powers of Columbia Artists Management, writing in *Variety*:

> My company managed Horowitz in the early 1930s, but he left for financial reasons. It killed him to pay commissions. . . . We all wish him success even if he wants to lone-wolf it in his old age. For by managing his own affairs, Horowitz will have a manager who pleases him and one that he can afford.

Sadly, there is little doubt that for many readers—musicians and laymen alike—the most interesting parts of this book will be the many sections that deal with Horowitz's personal life. Plaskin strongly suggests that the pianist was from his youth a homosexual; that he married Wanda Toscanini because of the musical power and influence of her father; that Toscanini and Wanda alike destroyed Horowitz's will, thereby producing his retirements and emotional difficulties; that Horowitz was not cut out to be either a husband or a father; that he neglected his daughter and was unaffected by her death; that his wife, despite being a good caretaker, has been callous about his problems and remains so today.

Plainly this constitutes a formidable indictment of Vladimir Horowitz, and of his wife. Insofar as their behavior affected their daughter's tragedy, Plaskin's accusations—some straightforward and some only implied—have an even darker side.

To be taken seriously, charges such as these must be made to seem something more than plausible; they must be convincing. While a biographer often begins his work on the basis of the old adage "Where there is smoke there is fire," he cannot end there. It is indeed true that the standards of proof applicable to a biography are hardly so rigorous as those required in a court of law. But even in a literary work an author must show that he has done something more than assemble all the available gossip, serving up the result in a sauce of association and suggestion.

Numerous as Plaskin's interviews and contacts are, evidently he has not been able to get those closest to Horowitz in the past and present to talk, at least for the record. The lips of his physicians are sealed. His lawyers and accountants, too, are unavailable for comment. Many friends—including the pianist Ania Dorfmann and the teacher Olga Strumillo—are absent from the references. So are the personnel of Steinway & Sons, those specialists in both pianos and artists who have been in a position to observe Horowitz closely for many years.

At the center of Plaskin's problems of demonstration, of course, is the fact that his book is unauthorized. It bears repeating that this lack of cooperation from Horowitz and his immediate family (a classification that includes not only his wife but other members of the Toscanini family) has meant almost no direct personal information from these sources. And from the private material written by those most concerned, Plaskin quotes nothing but a few letters, all dating from 1951 and before.

As a result Plaskin is forced to make the spicier parts of his book in the manner of Alice B. Toklas's shortage-ridden "Restricted Veal Loaf." There are a limited number of remarks about Horowitz's liking for homosexual company that are attributable; for the rest Plaskin relies on assertion without reference. Thus his first intimation bears no source:

> Moves to extend sexual freedom were then [in post-revolutionary Russia] considered an integral part of the revolution, and

the large cities became a haven for groups of sophisticated musicians and artists who enjoyed the bohemian atmosphere. Responding to the freedom of the times, Vladimir would occasionally make something of a spectacle of himself by walking the streets of Moscow in an enormous fur coat, his face apparently shimmering with makeup. It was rumored that he had had a liaison with an older actor in Leningrad and that he spent time with a group of effete poets and artists who took drugs. It was also said that on more than one occasion the family of his friend Simon Barere had to pull him from sailor bars in Odessa.

Then there is Plaskin's use of anonymous sources. Thus, material about the pianist's homosexuality must be taken on trust. Nowhere is this more true than in the discussion of the Horowitz-Toscanini marriage. Plaskin appropriates friend Nathan Milstein for his argument in the following way:

Nathan Milstein appears to have regarded Horowitz's predilection good-humoredly. Said one intimate: "Milstein and I met in Prague. He was not going to be able to see Horowitz on October 1 [no year is given by Plaskin], his birthday, and wanted to give Volodya a present, so he gave me some money and asked me to take Volodya out to a homosexual club when I saw him in Copenhagen. He knew Volodya would appreciate it."

The above is in a footnote; the subsequent text sentence runs (again without a source): "Nevertheless, Horowitz sometimes spoke excitedly about his wedding plans."

Plaskin's next paragraph is essential to his understanding of the marriage. He uses several quotations to show Horowitz's thoughts about getting married: "Wanda knows I am a little perverse"; "I am not in love. I can't love anymore. I love the piano"; "Toscanini is like an icon to me and Wanda is part of the icon." "Still, I like her as a woman," he admitted, "and when we kiss I feel like a man." All these quotations are credited to anonymous sources.

A reader might feel only slightly more confident of Plaskin's use of named sources. Thus, in one of the most up-to-date references to

Horowitz's tastes, Plaskin quotes the pianist Charles Rosen, testifying at secondhand:

> Tom [Shepard] told me about the impossible photographs Horowitz wanted for the [record] covers. He kept choosing pictures of himself leaning against the piano, with a very, very long cigarette holder, looking out at the camera like sort of a drag version of Marlene Dietrich. They would then have to persuade him that that was not a very good likeness.

Perhaps the strongest piece of evidence of Horowitz's orientation Plaskin adduces is the following story, told to him by the Broadway conductor Lehman Engel:

> Wanda and Volodya were not having a glamorous time in Chicago [in 1943], and there was no apparent closeness between them. Wanda was motherly in a cool sort of way but seemed bored and wanted to have some fun, so we played gin rummy in the hotel room after the concert. No one was paying any attention to Horowitz and Wanda didn't seem to care. He seemed to be passive and childlike in her presence. Yet on another occasion he asked me to take him to some male bars, and there he was completely animated, over-eager—anything but timid.

At last, one feels, this is solid material. But even here checking is difficult; Engel, alas, is now dead.

Whatever the exact nature of Horowitz's sexuality, it is clear that in an important way Horowitz functioned as a heterosexual. For Plaskin this is itself a subject for attack. He tells us, without citing his sources, that Horowitz had been, from 1940, a patient of the esteemed psychoanalyst Lawrence Kubie, "a strict Freudian who was attempting to exorcise the homosexual element from Horowitz." Plaskin goes on:

> Kubie believed that homosexuality was an aberration that could be "cured." Horowitz, controlled by his wife and psychiatrist and bound in by the repressive social climate of that time, found little validation of his genuine feelings. Kubie's unenlightened treatment only made him feel increasingly depressed . . . Dr. Kubie's treatment seemed, in fact, to be

counterproductive, amplifying Horowitz's anguish. "We did a lot of jawboning on our train trips," said Benedict [Horowitz's traveling companion in the early 1940s], "and he told me that his breakdown in Europe was hardly voluntary. It became clear that his attempt to deny his homosexuality, to mitigate it or extirpate it, had been a prime factor in that breakdown."[2]

From here it is not very far to Arthur Rubinstein's remark, from a 1980 interview with Plaskin, that "Wanda was a very hard woman —hard as stone. They really never had a happy marriage and the weight of this fact certainly contributed to Horowitz's nervous collapse." And even Rubinstein's words, harsh as they are, seem cautious compared with the quotation that immediately follows them—from yet another anonymous source, though admittedly a source "not sympathetic" to Wanda or her family:

> . . . after his marriage, Horowitz forfeited a chance for personal happiness. Toscanini and Wanda slowly broke his back, and he simply did not have the resources to combat such pressure.

Not only does Plaskin blame Horowitz's troubles on the efforts of those around him to interfere with his sexuality, he also blames the fate of the pianist's daughter on a lack of attention:

> Largely neglected by a self-absorbed father and a mother whose self-defined purpose was to minister to her genius husband, Sonia began to behave in an aggressive and unpredictable manner . . . Horowitz's attitude ranged from indifference to feeling burdened by Sonia, while Wanda seemed to be more concerned with the child and to feel some guilt over her condition.

Plaskin later attempts to show that Horowitz was even willing to deny his daughter's paternity. He quotes Philip Ramey on Horowitz's explanation for his wife's refusing, at the last minute, to attend a party:

2. Plaskin does give the source, an interview with Lowell Benedict, for this quotation.

In the taxi, Volodya grinned and said "don't worry. Now we'll have more fun! She is depressed and neurotic and very difficult. You know, her daughter died." I was a little startled by that, and shot back, "*Her* daughter?" "Yeah," he replied, suddenly looking glum.

Even when attributed, all this is dreadful stuff, but it is even more dreadful when it is based, in its most damaging part, not on hard evidence but on either the testimony of anonymous sources or the recollections of onetime associates and acquaintances. Yet, hard as it might be for a fastidious reader to admit, there could indeed be a reason for dragging all this dirty linen out in public. That reason consists in using an artist's personal life to explain his art.

Given his desire to downgrade Horowitz's musical accomplishment, Plaskin might have laid Horowitz's concentration on the small works of a less profound nature to his sexual orientation. He might have tried to make the case that a man of Horowitz's psychology could not understand late Beethoven. He might have asserted that supposedly brittle Scarlatti sonatas and delicate Chopin mazurkas are more suitable to an essentially feminine temperament than are Bach fugues. Along the same lines, he might have attempted to cast some light on the particular magic by which Horowitz was able to realize so completely the Sonata (1949) of Samuel Barber, a composer who, unlike Horowitz, never married and who moved in a largely homosexual musical world.

Unfortunately, Plaskin is content to leave the connections between Horowitz's art and life unexplored, except for the crassest considerations of self-interest and career. To say that he might have tried to explore them is not to say that he would have been successful. The ties binding sexuality and artistic expression are both subtle and complex and it may well be that any definitive account of their relationship is impossible. At any rate, he might have tried, and he did not.

Certainly Vladimir Horowitz has a right to be remembered in some other way than by this scrofulous book. That other way is by his playing, as it exists in the memories of his audiences and in the many phonograph records he has made. In toto his records achieve a higher standard than that achieved by any other pianist of this century. It will be remembered too that Horowitz left RCA Victor —and Plaskin himself tells the story—because the company wanted him to boost his falling record sales by recording Gershwin's *Rhapsody in Blue.* Horowitz refused, because he took his art seriously. There are worse epitaphs.

[1983]

# V

# PROVIDERS

# Music, Education, and Music Education

Every time is crisis time for those who live in a world of annually revised budgets. This is, in a special way, the lot of the large group of people who teach music in our schools and universities and who make up the faculties of instruction in our professional colleges of music. Yet the present anxiety felt in the world of music education is something special, tied only in part to the current controversy over government funding levels in education and culture. What is going on in the working lives of music educators is nothing less than a calling into question, by the spirit of the age, of their justification for existence as artists and teachers.

We may begin with the crisis in music itself, at the heart of which is the lack of widely accepted contemporary compositions. This is a new situation in our musical history. Bach wrote music for weekly use; what his audiences heard from his pen was as a rule what he had just written. Mozart, despite ill health, economic privation, and often self-inflicted personal difficulties, was a famous and admired figure of his time. Beethoven's patrons possessed a complete awareness of their protégé's standing among the immortals, and this despite his personal touchiness; his compositions were eagerly awaited, for the most part enthusiastically received, and widely circulated in both authorized and pirated editions.

The situation of new music in the high romantic era, from Schumann and Chopin to Brahms and Wagner, and even for some time after, was also one of vibrant health. The most advanced composers were heroes of the age, international celebrities, darlings of the aristocracies of taste and money. Verdi was a national symbol of Italian unification. Even Mahler, less successful as a composer than he might have hoped, was the subject of newspaper bulletins as he lay dying in Vienna. As late as the 1920s, the first performances of the operas of Richard Strauss were the occasion for trainloads of opera lovers to come from all over Europe to pay their homage to the master.

In our time, things are different. Our greatest orchestras, our largest opera companies, our most distinguished music schools are elegant and capacious museums, preserving musical antiquities as if they had come freshly off the compositional press. Our most exciting performers, intellectually, are those who go back to original texts, original instruments, and original conventions. A performance of a "new" old *bel canto* opera causes all the excitement of an original discovery; the completion of a hitherto unfinished Mahler symphony or Berg opera dwarfs in importance the premiere of any conceivable new composition.

Exceptions to this rule of ancestor worship are few, marginal, and distinguished more by laudable motives than by any long-term musical influence. Concerts of contemporary music are ill-attended, except if they offer works that can be plugged into the drug-oriented popular culture. When, from time to time, famous soloists perform new or newish works, they do so with the air of Jack Horner discovering his virtue. For musicians older or younger, audiences sophisticated or new, administrators of series large or small, critics and teachers, the desirable repertory is just about the same. Give us the famous names of the past, they all cry; let us hear the great music from Bach to Mahler, the music that sounds as music should. What is new is disqualified even before it is heard, and once it is heard the invariable reaction is: never-more.

Side by side with the fixation on the past there has been in recent years a redefinition of what the word music itself means to serious people. To our forebears, the word conjured up a refined, elite art, a product of man's intelligence at its most highly civilized and most highly disciplined. In the past, too, music was seen as the opposite of everything ugly, everything primitive, everything merely temporal. It was rather an expression of the sublime, the beautiful, and the eternal. If it made use of folk elements, and it did, these were transmuted into universal and timeless forms.

Now this conception of music has been challenged as limited, insular, arrogant, and irrelevant. In formerly polite musical society, an unlimited amount of folk music stands on an equal footing alongside the once carefully delimited greats; this folk music is the product of myriad cultures and societies, usually non-Western and in most cases in either early or blocked processes of growth. Deriving inspiration from this mass of material is a constantly expanding body of overwhelmingly commercial popular music that speaks to and for a broad and unsophisticated audience.

Thus, in the world at large, serious music has been swamped by demotic musics, to the extent that it has taken on the character of a *recherché* amusement for the few. Moreover, this "amusement" has lost much of its legitimacy as a higher or more refined or more intellectually demanding and rewarding enterprise. So thoroughly have the boundaries of taste been crossed that even the new, gigantic *Grove Dictionary of Music and Musicians,* the ultimate arbiter of what belongs to the musical family, treats folk and pop music as no less deserving of our respectful consideration than the products of the so-called classical tradition.

If there is a crisis in serious music, there is also a crisis, at once similar and different, in education. The similarity lies in the widespread loss of faith in our educational present; the difference lies in the fact that education, because it serves so many needs and busies so many bodies, is now as always the recipient of numerous well-funded and well-intentioned schemes for improvement.

The last happy period in American education seems to have been the halcyon decades between 1945 and 1965. Expansion was then the order of the day, in both secondary and college programs and facilities. The postwar baby boom and the flood of returning soldiers from World War II and Korea guaranteed a long-term academic constituency. The peacetime expansion of the domestic economy promised jobs for graduates. America's new standing in the world provided an atmosphere of confidence and optimism for our various educational endeavors.

But even during this era of good feelings, the issues that were later to rack the entire system were already making themselves felt. In 1954 the decision in *Brown* v. *Board of Education,* that racial separation in education was unequal and illegal, served to insure that all public schools (and especially those in and around the big cities) would be drawn into the unsolved race problem in American society. In 1957 and 1958 our initial failures in the space competition with the Soviet Union brought demands, soon accepted, for concentration on scientific, mathematical, and technical curricula across the entire education board. The rise of college-student disaffection, first publicly marked in the 1962 activities of Students for a Democratic Society, then exploding in the Berkeley riots of 1964, suggested that the population of our schools could no longer be considered malleable clay in the academic potter's hand.

These developments, hardly inclusive of all that was going on at this time, may nonetheless stand for the changes that overtook our educational system and produced our present condition. To say this is not to disparage the civil-rights drive for equal treatment under law, or to deny the need for scientific education in a world increasingly formed by technology, or to deprecate the complaints of students cast adrift on a sea of professional indifference. But however we may sympathize with these causes and those who put them forward, candor requires that we acknowledge some of their effects on the realities of present-day education.

The broadest effect here has been in the humanities and the study of the humanities. No matter how the precise content of the humanities is defined, *study* of the humanities presupposes a certain level of cultural literacy; yet it became increasingly apparent in the years of educational expansion that new school populations, the children of parents badly served by schools in the past, did not possess the requisite literacy and could not be efficiently accommodated by traditional curricula drawn from an elite culture. Moreover, given the fixed number of school hours in a day, the increased attention given to scientific and technical education had to mean a diminution in the time devoted to other, presumably "softer" subjects: i.e., the humanities. Finally, when large numbers of bright students, alienated from the polity and the society, took to primitivism and irrationality, the study of a body of material based on the norms of Western civilization and the quiet pursuit of reason could not help degenerating.

The resulting state of affairs has been almost universally recognized as dismal. Unfortunately, the remedies prescribed have been so many nostrums, patent medicine for the anxious and the gullible. Open classrooms; the new math; programmed instruction; the trimester system; student participation in academic governance; alternate schools; pass-fail grading—the best that can be said of these quack products is that many of them have already been mercifully forgotten. For where these remedies were tried, they often made a bad situation worse. By further weakening an already precarious academic discipline and administrative routine, in many cases they brought learning almost to a halt. Indeed, much of the college cohort of the decade between 1965 and 1975 now resembles something of a lost academic generation.

In the humanities, the traditional understanding of what is meant by a liberal-arts education has been eviscerated, but no new definition has achieved any kind of consensual support. The classical definition of humanistic education sees it as more than a procedure, based on words, for amassing knowledge and gaining analytic skills. The humanities are not just an approach or a method, a way of establishing critical distance. The humanities are based first and foremost on content, and that content is the great works of Western tradition, what T. S. Eliot in *Notes towards the Definition of Culture* so nicely calls "the legacy of Greece, Rome, and Israel." The skills needed for the study of the humanities are not special but general; the humanities demand literacy, rationality, orderly thought, hard work, memory—and love. The rewards of the humanities are, however, rather more special. For what they teach is value, or rather the set of values that has built and integrates our otherwise pluralistic societies.

It was to instill these values that the humanities *used* to be studied; now, the situation is quite different. To see just how different, we may look briefly at three recent events in the field of education.

The first of these events was the 1980 publication of *The Humanities in American Life,* the report of the Rockefeller Commission on the Humanities.[1] Here a collection of notables, giving short shrift to questions of content, addresses instead the condition of the job market for humanists. The report finds this market in poor shape, and recommends a spate of measures to improve school enrollments and hence academic employment. Most of the proposed measures, though misguided, seem fairly benign. But underneath the tone of sweet persuasion is a deeper suggestion: that programs in the humanities be *mandated,* that curricula be prescribed, that government, educators, and large business enterprises get together to keep these programs funded and rolling along. As for the reasons all this is to take place, here the report falls back on dreary invocations to the benefits of a critical habit of mind and the need to learn about

1. See my review in *Commentary,* April 1981.

other cultures. Of positive content, besides a nod to Shakespeare and a pious summoning up of Melville, there is nothing.

The Rockefeller report at least wears the trappings of high-mindedness. By contrast, an article that appeared last March in the *New York Times* reveals just what the humanities look like at the level of daily educational activity. The article begins with a bow to Harvard's then two-year-old program in general education. It quotes Dean Henry Rosovsky, who diagnosed the problem for which this program was intended to provide a cure as the "breakdown of common discourse" among educated men and women. The *Times* notes that what is put into question here is the very definition of an educated person. At Florida A&M, for instance, the new general-education program includes:

> . . . courses in nutrition and the benefits of lifelong participation in sports.
>
> "We give students an opportunity to succeed and get them into the mainstream," said Eva C. Wanton, the director of general education. "That's our definition of an educated person."

And the *Times* goes on:

> Some schools are using required course lists to expand their students' understanding of other cultures. At Mount Holyoke College . . . the faculty has voted to require each student to take a course in "some aspect of Africa, Asia, Latin America, the Middle East, or the nonwhite peoples of North America."

And still more:

> . . . under the guidance of Herbert Simon, a Nobel Laureate in economics, Carnegie-Mellon University in Pittsburgh has adopted a new core curriculum designed to give students a sampling of high-level skills rather than expertise in one field.

Finally the article describes one basic reaction to the very notion of general education today:

> At Indiana University, distribution and other requirements were recently tightened, but the faculty committee that proposed the changes rejected a core curriculum, saying that that

"elitist idea dominated education throughout the '50s and ignored the Far East, blacks, Latinos, and other cultures."

Thus by easy stages we are led back, in the name of general education, to that very "breakdown of common discourse" which general education is supposed to combat.

The third recent event in the continuing debate over the humanities was the release last September of a policy statement from the Alfred P. Sloan Foundation, entitled *The New Liberal Arts.* The policy advocated by the Sloan Foundation is that liberal-arts students be required to devote greatly increased attention to applied mathematics, computers, and technology, disciplines the report finds to be the cornerstones of late twentieth-century life. After the policy itself has been described, the document goes on to offer responses to it by prominent figures in American education; with the exception of a troubled rejection by Jacques Barzun, the responses are favorable. Indeed, the final contribution by Richard Warch, President of Lawrence University, is positively enthusiastic, and amounts to an embrace of the prospective technocratic takeover of American education. For President Warch, ". . . we must create and offer courses that help students to develop habits of thought that will permit them to think ultimately in computerizable ways."

Before passing from the subject of education proper, let me cite a brief passage from an article in the Summer 1981 *Daedalus,* an issue devoted to "American Schools: Public and Private." One particularly interesting article in this issue discusses explicitly the competence and dedication of those who will be teaching in the years to come. Here J. Myron Atkin, dean of the Stanford School of Education, makes some disturbing observations:

> Today's college freshman is less likely to aim toward a career in teaching than his counterpart at any time during the last thirty years. Furthermore, the intellectual ability of those who intend to teach, as measured by standardized tests, is markedly lower than that of college majors in every other field except ethnic studies.

Although Dean Atkin's remarks are directed specifically at high-school teaching, one feels that they are of significance for education across the board.

Given the crisis in music and given the crisis of values and content in education, what, then, is the present status of music education? To be blunt, it is that of a musical generation coming out of school half-educated, unsure of any future course, and all too inclined to substitute career advancement and security for musical satisfaction and commitment.

Wherever one looks one sees graduates narrowly trained in professional skills, ignorant of music as a whole and of the wider body of learning and culture of which music is but a constituent part. There has been a decline in the morale of college music faculties, combined with an excessive preoccupation with intra-departmental rivalries. Students tend to have a low regard for the teaching of music as a worthwhile goal, and an excessive regard for careers in performance. There is also a disturbing tendency to de-value the study of music as a serious enterprise, and to promote instead a notion of music as ego therapy for the socially disadvantaged, or as a tool for democratizing elite values.

Before considering these charges further, let us concede that there may well have been, over the last generation, something of a rise in the *average* technical proficiency of young music students. In the area of the piano, for instance, more students are playing more difficult pieces more or less accurately than they could ever have done before. Yet however fast the fingers fly, what is lacking is musical involvement; to ask students about what they have played, or about music other than what they have practiced, or have heard stars perform, is to be met with stares of resentful bewilderment.

On a more general level than that of the most talented, the level of potential elementary- and secondary-school teachers of music, and of the musical audience in general, one wonders how much blame for the present low state of musical literacy should be laid at the door of those blessings of technology and automation that go by the name of programmed instruction and, in music, group study. It is certainly hard to believe that the apathetic young faces staring into television monitors or listening through earphones to a master's voice are engaged in anything having to do with the humanities or with art; in particular, it is doubtful that learning a musical instrument as if one were doing calisthenics in a stadium can produce more for the student than a brute facility (unless one counts a heightened sense of personal alienation as an educational

gain). Indeed, wherever there have been attempts to utilize technology and so-called modern teaching methods in music, the result has been of value mostly to the firms selling the necessary hardware and software.

Not only new music but all music not written for their own personal instruments is for today's students *terra incognita*. It is not just students in small towns who have never seen a major opera performance or heard a great symphony orchestra in adequate acoustical surroundings. Students who have come to New York at great cost for the express purpose of studying music seem rarely to go to concerts, and when they do go it is generally for the purpose of checking out real or fancied competition.

The low level of general culture among music students is alarming. At the Aspen Music Festival, where I give lectures and master classes every summer, I find little or no comprehension of literary or generally nonmusical references. Last summer, for example, an audience of 100 students and auditors at a lecture on Liszt's *Mephisto Waltz* seemed to include no one who knew the vague outlines of the Faust legend, not to mention Lenau's or Goethe's or Thomas Mann's treatment of it. Piano teachers are familiar with the unpleasant experience of trying to teach Debussy and Ravel to students who have no mental image of French painting to help inspire their musical understanding.

As for the junior faculty who teach music in our colleges, they are badly underpaid and beset by the paucity of opportunities for advancement and the oversupply of applicants for the few positions available. For young white males entering the job market, Max Weber's advice in 1918, offered to Jewish students wishing to become scientists, seems particularly apt: the words Weber quoted were Dante's, *Lasciate ogni speranza,* abandon all hope. Naturally, with the conditions of promotion so gloomy, the academic pecking order assumes a greater importance than the hierarchy of musical angels in heaven, and mere survival, achieved at the cost of no matter how much intrigue, becomes a triumph in itself.

For talented students and graduates, teaching is now a distant second choice. The most meager performing opportunities are seen as vastly more meaningful than the prospect of teaching any but the most brilliant and gifted pupils. Not even the inherent greatness of the subject matter—once a point of special pride—serves any longer as a justification for the teaching of music. For that greatness has been systematically devalued by the same processes that have reduced the study of the humanities to the lowest common denominator of self-expression and self-diversion.

Just as the humanities have their Rockefeller report, so arts education has its own. Quaintly titled *Coming To Our Senses,* it is the work of a panel chaired by David Rockefeller, Jr., and sponsored by the American Council for the Arts in Education. In broad outline, this report states a familiar message: art is everything and everything is art. The arts are "ideal vehicles for training our senses, for enriching our emotional selves, and for organizing our environment." Arts education is

> making art, knowing artists, and using art as a general tool of learning. . . . Direct creative and recreative experience— learning *in* the arts—is of unique educational value . . . learning *about* the arts is learning about the rich world of sensation, emotion, and personal expression surrounding us each day . . . learning *through* the arts has the potential to enhance one's general motivation to learn and develop one's respect for a disciplined approach to learning.

What *kind* of art, one is tempted to ask, can have a place in this rich catalogue of fashionable goals? One of the report's recommendations, headed "Beyond 'Music and Art,' " asks for an end to "rigid definitions of the medium, time of creation, or culture from which the art emerges." With what, then, are we left? In music, the report's melody is clear. Out of 334 pages, exactly three clauses —not even sentences—are concerned with the great composers. The report's approval is directed, rather, toward such "innovative" programs as "early-morning jazz, rock, and soul sessions; and after-school piano and guitar classes." One assumes the piano classes will be properly "innovative" too, indiscriminately including everything from Bach to the Beatles, from Beethoven to Bacharach.

This report is only a symptom of a strong tendency in music education today: the treatment of all subject matters as equal, and nonelite subject matters as more equal than others. The emphasis on self-expression, for which read arbitrary, unsophisticated, mock-artistic creation, renders impossible either the maintenance of standards or the imparting of objective information. Finally, the attempt to use art to achieve extra-artistic goals ("organizing our environment") represents merely one more effort, like those of the 1960s and '70s, to bring about social change by other means.

What is to be done? The era of expansion in both music and education is over. Music cannot long expand unless there are successful creations of permanent value, accepted as such by sophisticated taste. In serious music few such works are currently to be heard (in popular music, what is successful is also meretricious and transient). In education generally, the great need of the day is for basic verbal and computational skills, to be mastered not by means of advanced technology but simply with books, pencils, and paper. Yet funds for education are tight, and in constant dollars actually declining. In addition, lower birth rates mean lower student populations and hence still lower levels of funding.

Where expansion seems impossible, contraction is just around the corner. It is contraction that music educators will have to accept, and turn into an opportunity to raise standards, sharpen their concentration on quality and content, and redefine their purpose. That purpose is teaching music not as a form of self-expression or as leisure-time activity, but as part of the great tradition of learning and culture. The goal is training audiences, not just—and perhaps not even primarily—musicians; training and honoring music lovers and teachers of music, not just—and definitely not primarily—performers.

The arts are necessary to our lives as citizens. But without an educated citizenry the arts will never prosper. Here is where the Rockefeller reports, with their vacuous celebrations of the unique educational value of the arts (and the humanities), have things precisely backward. Educational fads and quack remedies, the neglect or denigration of the values of elite civilization, the breaking down of intellectual standards—all these cut off the limbs on which artists and educators sit. Before there can be any significant reform of music education, there must first be a readiness to take serious music seriously and to relearn the proper ends of education.

[1982]

# Broadcast Music

Ours is the age of the electronic transmission and reproduction of music. Where once the musical experience of the listener was formed by face-to-face contact between musicians and audience, today one artist can perform for the whole world, and one solitary listener can have an almost unlimited choice of program material, some in live performance, most in the form of private or commercial recordings.

It all began with Edison's infant phonograph of a century ago. Its first years were creaky, squawky, and exclusively vulgar. But by the early 1900s—most brilliantly through the first efforts of Enrico Caruso—the acoustic reproducer became a worthy kind of musical instrument. It could be "played" by anyone able to wind the motor and place the pickup on the record.

Yet no matter how many acoustic records were sold, no matter how many young people found their first experience of musical art through these pieces of shellac compound, in fact the phonograph collapsed in mass consciousness when the radio became commercially viable after World War I. Even the inefficient radios of the mid-1920s sounded better than the old phonograph records. Moreover, listening to the radio was at first even more satisfactory than hearing the then newly introduced electrical discs. And radio programming was always changing, always up-to-date; best of all, after a single original investment, radio programs were free.

Since it had usually been thought that popular culture was a mass phenomenon and high culture a matter of elite taste, it was only to be expected that the airwaves would be filled with dance and show music appealing to the widest audience. Surprisingly, however, serious music was also present at the creation of broadcasting. Not only was the best in music quickly perceived as a means of earning respectability for radio and its entrepreneurs, but performing organizations across the country eagerly embraced radio for the twin purposes of music education and of bringing the organizations themselves to public notice.

No musical institution was more perceptive in this regard than the New York Philharmonic. As early as 1922, some concerts of the Philharmonic, at first originating from the Great Hall of the City College of New York, had been broadcast on station WEAF. Soon these concerts found sponsors, among them the American Telephone and Telegraph Company and later the Radio Corporation of America. As time passed, more concerts were broadcast each year; finally, in 1930, the Philharmonic inaugurated a series of regular weekly broadcasts of full-length concerts, transmitted from Carnegie Hall under the auspices of the Columbia Broadcasting System.[1]

Other established orchestras, including those in Philadelphia and Boston, had been eager to follow the Philharmonic's lead. In addition, individual radio stations employed staff musicians to present programs of classical music featuring soloists, chamber ensembles, and even full orchestras. What single stations could do, the quickly expanding networks could do better. Network orchestras played for an increasing number of variety shows containing the classics. In 1937, with the founding of the NBC Symphony Orchestra for Arturo Toscanini, commercial support of serious music on radio reached its climax. For seventeen years this orchestra, bearing in every way the stamp of Toscanini's dominating musical personality, remained in the forefront of American musical life, bringing art to millions and glory to NBC.

Thus, throughout most of the age of radio, orchestral music, performed by the leading artists of the day, was available nationally on two weekly broadcasts and locally on frequent though scattered presentations of equally important concerts. Opera was nearly as fortunate. Back in the technological dark age of 1910, the Metropolitan Opera had been the scene of an experiment by radio pioneer Lee De Forest in which a performance of *Cavalleria rusticana* (then only twenty years old) starring Caruso was broadcast to a small

1. It is significant (and perhaps even startling to an observer of today's world of serious music) that the prime mover in the relationship between the Philharmonic and CBS—which continues in reduced circumstances to this day (1980) —was the legendary impresario Arthur Judson, at the same time manager of the orchestra and a founder and major stockholder of CBS.

audience comprised of radio amateurs, ships in the harbor, and a few invited engineers and journalists. Real broadcasting did not begin until Christmas Day of 1931, when *Hansel and Gretel* (in the original German) was transmitted, underwritten by NBC. The first sponsored broadcast of the Met was presented at the end of 1933, and in 1940 Texaco began its historic assumption of responsibility for the Met Saturday matinees, a responsibility it has borne without interruption to the present.

In general this reasonably satisfactory state of affairs continued without change until the war-delayed coming of television in the 1940s. At first gradually, and then with frightening speed, both the excitement and the audience left radio. Before many years had passed, radio became merely an outlet for brief news summaries and endless circulation and recirculation of records, mostly pop and mostly ephemeral. Staff musicians were let go, first at the local level and then by the networks.

The final sign that the great days of music on radio were over came in 1954, when corporate management decided not to retain the NBC Symphony after Toscanini's withdrawal that year on account of the debilities of age. Something of NBC's attitude toward its artistic responsibilities may be gathered from the story told in *Agitato,* Jerome Toobin's entertaining memoir (1975) of his years in music administration. As he describes what happened, a committee of the orchestra, in order to get NBC to change its decision, met with Samuel Chotzinoff, an NBC executive (and former pianist and music critic) who had responsibility for music programs. The committee members poured out their hearts to Chotzinoff, explaining the importance of the orchestra to music, to NBC's parent RCA, and as a living tribute to their revered Maestro Toscanini. Toobin goes on:

> Chotzinoff listened and, when they were through, said, "Do you really want to honor Toscanini? Then die." A pause. "Your orchestra, I mean," he concluded, lamely.

The orchestra, of course, died. Though the players tried to keep the orchestra going under a new name, Symphony of the Air, the glorious ensemble soon petered out. Although it would be nice to report that CBS behaved better with the radio broadcasts of the Philharmonic, the unfortunate truth is that nine years later, in

1963, the corporate axe fell on these concerts as well; the broadcasts stopped altogether by 1967.

What was now unavailable on radio was hardly to be found on television. At first glance this might seem something of a puzzle: why should serious music have been unable to make the transition from radio to television in the same way as soap operas, variety shows, sports, and live news coverage? There are in fact two fundamental reasons, the first relating to the nature of music, and the second relating to the inherent attributes of television as a medium of communication. These reasons are well worth examination, for they remain as valid today as they were in the time of radio's decline and television's growth.

The musical reason for the failed transition to television is quite obvious and indeed almost a truism. Music, after all, is sound; it is meant to be heard, and when it is clearly heard, it is, in principle, fully experienced. The visual aspect, welcome and even vital as it is to many, is often felt by the most experienced and trained listeners to be a distraction and sometimes even an adulteration. It is basically this fact that accounts for the spectacular long-term success of phonograph records and audio tape, and that accounted originally for the wide following of art music broadcasts on the radio. Such was the case when the radio (and the phonograph) had not reached the present state of high-fidelity reproduction, and it is even more the case today, when the sound available on radio far surpasses anything that can be heard from currently mass-marketed home television sets.

From television's side, music seemed for many years both irrelevant and unrewarding. Because the number of channels in any one locality was originally limited to little more than half of the twelve places on the dial,[2] and also because in television, equipment and production are more expensive than in radio, the audience served by each channel must be many times larger than that served by any radio station in a given area. Thus, television had to aim from the first at the broadest possible audience at every moment.

So television found little room in its schedules for great music. Still, attempts were made: some programs that had found large audiences on radio by presenting tuneful classics in star perfor-

2. And so it remains today, despite the opening up of the UHF channels, more numerous but also more difficult to receive and tune.

mances—most notably the "Bell Telephone Hour"—did have several years of television life. Opening nights at the Met were televised in 1948, 1949, 1950, and 1954. How unseriously these presentations were regarded is clear from the unhappy fact that no copies exist today. NBC made a valiant effort in the early 1950s to establish a continuing opera theater, and one of the fruits of that effort was the commissioning and presentation of Gian Carlo Menotti's Christmas staple, *Amahl and the Night Visitors,* in 1951. CBS, too, tried. Building on the success of Leonard Bernstein in handling musical subjects for the "Omnibus" series in the mid-1950s, the network began in the 1957–58 season to present the conductor with the New York Philharmonic, at first in children's concerts and then in regular programs. The regular programs were eventually discontinued, but the children's concerts, hugely successful, continue on CBS, on a limited basis, today.

But despite these isolated flashes, the generalization holds: there has been no room in the normal operation of television for serious musical art. However, television has not had to remain restricted to normal operation. The 1950s saw the rise of educational broadcasting, and, as has happened before in American history, the idea of education came to justify elite taste and its satisfaction. Music was to be one of the major beneficiaries of this new development, for here was a way to do something for culture and at the same time have the bill paid by the government, either directly, through legislative appropriations, or indirectly, through tax deductions for charitable contributions.

National Educational Television, a forerunner of the present Public Broadcasting Service, began with a series presenting the Boston Symphony Orchestra; by the 1962–63 season NET was sporadically televising the concerts of many orchestras, mostly American but occasionally foreign. In addition to these national transmissions, local educational stations showed admirable initiative in producing programs of soloists and ensembles at minimal cost (and with minimal remuneration to the artists). These often touching simple productions were frequently exchanged with other local public stations for widespread but haphazard broadcast.

Lacking, however, was the kind of money needed for luxurious presentations. And lacking too was central organization and sponsorship to guarantee integrated efforts in production, publicity, and fundraising. These two desiderata were provided by the political and social developments of the past two decades.

After the assassination of John Kennedy in 1963, the putative association of the late president and his wife with high culture—or at least with the celebrities of high culture—made arts centers and support for the arts seem a fitting memorial. The Great Society of Lyndon Johnson, though hardly so aesthetically presumptuous as Camelot, did just as much to create a climate favorable to public spending on art and music; aid to artists and performers came to be seen as a most desirable kind of unemployment relief.

The result of all this has been the rise of public culture, expressed institutionally by the phenomenal growth of the Public Broadcasting Service and the National Endowment for the Arts. The NEA has by now become the major factor in determining the level of support and the direction of musical life in America. PBS has in effect become a competitive fourth network, spending large sums of money on both production and the publicity it feels necessary to insure that its programs are watched by a large and ever-growing audience. While NEA and PBS policy decisions are no doubt made independently, their actions are closely related. The NEA supports many PBS programs, and PBS presents the work of the major recipients of NEA patronage. The result of this common effort in music is the offering on PBS this season of the most ambitious, well-thought-out, and well-financed opera and orchestral programs in American television history.

The evidence of the first half of the current season is stunning. During this period PBS has shown six operas in live performance, including Verdi's *Otello* and Kurt Weill's *The Rise and Fall of the City of Mahagonny* from the Metropolitan Opera; from the New York City Opera came another Weill opera, *Street Scene;* Gounod's *Faust* was performed by the Chicago Lyric Opera, Ponchielli's *La Gioconda* by the San Francisco Opera, and Bizet's *Carmen* by the Vienna Opera. Also from Vienna came a concert of operatic excerpts entitled "A Night at the Vienna Opera," a Bernstein performance of the Mahler Ninth Symphony, and a performance under Herbert von Karajan of the Bruckner Ninth. The Dresden State Orchestra was shown in a concert at the United Nations in New York. Among American orchestras, the New York Philharmonic appeared three times, featuring such famous soloists as Joan Sutherland, Marilyn

Horne, Emil Gilels, and Luciano Pavarotti. The Philadelphia Orchestra appeared in a tribute to its retiring music director, called "Ormandy at 80," and the Boston Symphony presented weekly concerts previously taped and edited to one-hour length. Two additional operas were shown, though not in live productions: Poulenc's *La Voix humaine* and Menotti's *Amahl.*

Many of these events were intended to be shown more than once. They were usually rerun almost immediately on the stations where they were first shown, and then circulated to noncommercial outlets on the UHF band, where they will continue to appear for some time to come. Because of the recent proliferation of home video-recording equipment, innumerable copies, some of quite remarkable fidelity, now exist in the hands of music lovers everywhere; their existence has been legitimated by a federal court decision. Equally legitimate, and vastly superior in sound quality, are audio tapes made on home cassette machines from the FM simulcast broadcasts that often accompany major PBS television music transmissions.

Given opera's use of visual as well as aural elements, it is plain that of all musical forms it stands to gain the most from television. Indeed, the same selling point might be made for opera on TV as is made for sports: one sees it better at home than from even a good seat in the stadium.

At least so it seemed in the Metropolitan Opera *Otello,* a telecast of the current season's opening night in September. The star of the performance, aside from the brilliant singing of Placido Domingo in the title role, was the picture. Seen in the opera house, the Met production is impressive in its opulence; when translated to the screen, the richness of color and the clarity of the action are striking. Rarely can members of a chorus have seemed so convincing under the clinical eye of the television camera as they did in the opening crowd scenes. The camera work was smooth and varied, a tribute to the experience the Met has gained through its increasingly frequent television presentations. Best of all was the ability of the production to sustain, throughout the opera, the illusion that the television picture was a representation of physical reality rather than of more or less adequate sets.

The San Francisco *Gioconda,* broadcast some days earlier, did not quite come up to the Met's standards. One was always conscious of watching a staged performance; despite the provision of a real fire on board ship at the end of Act II, the sets seemed all too often the product of the carpenter's and painter's craft rather than solid wood and stone. While the cast did include the internationally renowned Pavarotti and Renata Scotto, their efforts seemed inadequately supported by the orchestra and the conductor. Still, despite the flaws, the performance came across as worthy and enjoyable.

By contrast, the Vienna *Carmen* was extraordinary in several ways. From the first notes of the prelude, one's attention was seized by the powerful conducting of Carlos Kleiber and the brilliant playing of the Vienna Philharmonic. Domingo was Don José, and he sang just as beautifully as he had in the *Otello*. Dramatically and musically the only major flaw was the Slavic sound and mood of Elena Obraztsova; her Carmen seemed no more related to the atmosphere of the opera than her Amneris at the Met several years ago had seemed to fit into Verdi's *Aida*. But dwarfing all other considerations was the physical quality of the video image itself. Razor-sharp and delicately colored, the image seemed to reflect a higher level of technical achievement than can regularly be seen in this country.

The Chicago *Faust* was disappointing. Inferior orchestral playing, and tacky sets attempting to convey a kind of delicate, allusive atmosphere ill-suited to the limitations of television, combined with fussy and often pointless stage direction to produce the total effect of a provincial performance, despite the presence of an international cast, including Mirella Freni, Nicolai Ghiaurov, and Alfredo Kraus.

The two Weill operas, *Street Scene* and *Mahagonny,* made strikingly different impressions. Though *Street Scene* has been a box-office success in New York, its presentation on television seemed much of a piece with the general run of City Opera efforts in recent years —earnest, ambitious, and withal still lacking. In the past the City Opera has made its mark by bringing something of the virtues of the American musical theater to opera; with *Street Scene* it has attempted to present as an opera a work that started life as a musical. Whatever the value of such an experiment in general, here, where Weill's music and Elmer Rice's story both seem dated, the result was stiff and affected.

Much attention was naturally centered on the Metropolitan *Mahagonny*. Though the opera was written in 1930, its choice for production by the Met represents the culmination of much effort to find viable contemporary works. While *Mahagonny* is indeed more up-to-date than almost everything else the Met does, it is surely ironic that in its quest for contemporaneity the Met should have come up with a work so bitterly and mockingly hostile to the economic system and social ethos that built and supports the opera company.

These considerations aside, of all the operas seen on television this season, *Mahagonny* seemed by far the most appropriate to the screen. Bertolt Brecht's libretto is gripping and incisive in its cynicism; mainly because Weill's mostly thin music nowhere gets in the way, the English words, well and clearly enunciated by the singers, were almost always easily distinguishable. The acting, too, was excellent, and the characters came across forcefully. Teresa Stratas scored a memorable success in the role of Jenny. Though she may have lacked the offhand decadence Lotte Lenya might have brought to the role, Stratas nevertheless sang magnificently, looked touchingly beautiful, and projected a waiflike and deeply moving personality. The production was simple but suggestive, and visually striking with its hints of between-the-wars poster style. Finally, because the production was in English, the television screen was not disfigured by the ubiquitous subtitles, which marred the Italian and French operas discussed here.

Little need be said about the presentations of *Amahl* and *La Voix humaine*. Whatever charm Menotti's score may have possessed at its first appearance has long since faded, and in its latest production the work seemed sentimental and even mawkish. Poulenc's quintessentially French work, dependent as it is on the exact sounds of the French words written by Jean Cocteau, seemed in English hysterical without being affecting. What was fatally lacking in this performance was style and manner; the work's back-to-back billing in one evening with a rendition of the words without music acted by Liv Ullmann in Scandinavian-English only made too much of a poor thing.

Despite the criticisms that can be made of specific productions, it must be concluded that so far this season television has gone a long way toward justifying its employment for opera. The medium's present limitations—principally the near-universality of small-screen sets producing wretched sound, but also the more basic lack of three-dimensional visual representation—seem less significant than the possibility television offers of bringing operas in high-level productions to those who have little or no other opportunity to experience them. For those who do, television must in the foreseeable future remain a distant second-best to live performance.

Because orchestra concerts are so much less dependent than operas on the visual element, they also seem decidedly less interesting on television. The instruments of one orchestra look, after all, very much like those of another, and they are all played in much the same way; oddly enough, one emoting, gesticulating, coiffured conductor also begins to look like all the others. Not only is the resultant effect one of boredom; paradoxically the repetitive screen images serve to concentrate attention not on the music but on the activity of music making, and on the peculiar and funny-looking ways that some people behave. Even the merest hint of such a reaction on the part of a viewer can distract attention from the music and eventually come to discredit the entire musical enterprise.

The most absorbing of the recent televised concerts were those that offered something other than interchangeable performances of the music. Star singers, for example, are not interchangeable; their fame rests not only on vocal excellence but on the specific persona each one communicates visually and aurally to an audience. So it was to be expected that orchestra concerts starring singers would prove the most interesting.

The first of these star events produced domestically during the past season was the Joan Sutherland–Marilyn Horne concert in October, with Miss Sutherland's husband, Richard Bonynge, leading the New York Philharmonic in the accompaniments. The singing was self-assured and brilliant, and the combination of great vocalism with the backing of a major orchestra proved as irresistible on television as it had during a dress rehearsal in the hall.

The second vocal concert was less distinguished musically and also rather more controversial. Tenor Luciano Pavarotti is the most reliable, accurate, sweetly strong-voiced Italian tenor before the public today; his personality is compellingly charming and altogether winning. The concert, again with the Philharmonic, was conducted by Zubin Mehta, whose long suit is also vibrant public charm. Whereas Pavarotti's singing on this occasion impressed some observers as less fresh than it had been in the past, Mehta's conducting seemed, at least to me, some of his best work in New York to date. It was vivid and colorful (a careful performance of the Beethoven *Egmont* Overture excepted), and nicely calculated to draw forth the last ingratiating drops of tuneful passion from the famous works Pavarotti had chosen.

Perhaps the mood of the entire concert was best caught in one of the closing selections, the beginning of Act III of *Tosca* from the short orchestral introduction through Cavaradossi's familiar aria *"E lucevan le stelle."* Mehta and Pavarotti were joined by a boy soprano (as an unseen shepherd's voice) and the violinist Itzhak Perlman to sing the few lines of the Jailer. It was Perlman's vocal debut and possibly, as a New York critic hinted, his farewell too. He really did not do badly, but one could only wonder on what musical grounds he had been chosen. The effect on the total performance was predictably again one of charm—Perlman's personal aura combining with the palpable air of friendship among the participants on the stage. The suitability of all this charm to the tragedy of *Tosca* remains debatable.

Still another concert of the Philharmonic, along with Mehta, featured Soviet pianist Emil Gilels. Here the fare was undeniably substantial. The program began with the Third "Leonore" Overture of Beethoven, continued with the Bartók Concerto for Orchestra, and ended with the famous Tchaikowsky Piano Concerto. After a dutiful and sometimes rough rendition of the Beethoven and a persuasive account of the Bartók, the Tchaikowsky closed the concert with a resounding thud. The once perfect technical mastery of Gilels is now in lamentable condition, a fact ignored only by those who hear what is in their memories rather than what is being played. Close camera work made only too obvious the pianist's present plight. Here television was—perhaps inadvertently—revealing, and none of Mehta's motions on the podium or the hyperbolic comment with which these programs are liberally supplied could conceal the pathos.

Two programs presented something rather different from the reproduction of a concert. The Eugene Ormandy commemoration by the Philadelphia Orchestra included the familiar Second Symphony of Rachmaninoff, a work much performed by the conductor. Viewers were also given a sizeable portion of Ormandy's recollections of Rachmaninoff, as well as his own thoughts on what he had accomplished during his Philadelphia tenure. Even more solid as verbal material were the musical comments and rehearsal excerpts of Leonard Bernstein that accompanied his performance of the Mahler Ninth Symphony with the Vienna Philharmonic. On this occasion, as always, Bernstein proved himself our cherished master of the *haute vulgarisation* of music; in addition, the performance itself was movingly conducted, and most beautifully played by the orchestra.

Indeed, it is sad to report that throughout all the events I have seen recently, performance honors were captured by European rather than American orchestras. The broadcast of the Dresden State Orchestra under Herbert Blomstedt from the imperfect acoustical ambience of the General Assembly Hall of the United Nations, for example, was a revelation of orchestral ensemble and musical penetration by the players; the performance of the *Meistersinger* prelude alone seemed on a level rarely approached in this country.

As if to prove how little television has to offer the straight performance of music, the most satisfying television orchestra concert this season, the performance of the Bruckner Ninth with the Vienna Philharmonic, had little need of visual manifestation at all. The hour-long program was almost completely filled by the symphony; there was thus time for little more than a minute of the spoken word. The customary shots of orchestra and conductor were tasteful and restrained; Karajan's ample movements and grimaces were seemingly meant for the orchestra rather than for the viewers. Incredibly refined orchestral playing of the most affecting warmth, led by a conductor whose analytical skill is no less acute than his ear for timbre and melody, produced a mood of total absorption in the music.

It would be kinder not to spend too much time on the one major adult presentation of serious music on commercial television so far this season. This was the highly touted NBC production "Live From Studio 8H." Once again, the stars (with the addition of soprano Leontyne Price) were familiar from PBS: Mehta, Perlman, and the New York Philharmonic. The program was tied to the mythic name of Toscanini. Not only was the concert broadcast from the studio whose name was a byword for the poor sound of many Toscanini records, but the music played on this occasion included works by composers "identified," in the words of the NBC press release, "with performances by Toscanini and the NBC." The point was further driven home by an intermission feature, with Mehta as host, showing kinescopes of Toscanini conducting (in 1948 and 1949) breathtaking actual performances of the orchestra.

Faced with such competition, Mehta and his forces did not come close to a draw. Leontyne Price, in excerpts from Verdi's *Aida* and *La Forza del destino,* was vocally variable, alternating beautifully produced notes with hollow chest tones and strident tops. The orchestral performances of the overture to *Forza* and Wagner's "Ride of the Valkyries" seemed both ragged and booming. While Perlman may well have been made uncomfortable by being restricted to the last movement of the Beethoven Violin Concerto, his facial expressions while playing betrayed nothing but amused satisfaction. Only the Ravel *Daphnis et Chloé* Suite no. 2 sounded on a high level, an achievement for which credit must be given not merely to Mehta but also to Pierre Boulez, whose immaculately prepared performance of the complete score was one of the glories of recent Philharmonic history.

A further comment must be made. The NBC program was interrupted and blemished by the intrusion of commercials, no less vulgar for all their pretentiousness. But the PBS programs were similarly blemished by commercials. On public television these are not, of course, called commercials, but in their effort to sell a product they are commercials in everything but name. The product they sell is, in theory, music and culture; in practice it is the performing institution and the careers of the stars the institution has engaged. Everyone appearing on these programs speaks in honeyed tones of the wonder of it all. Phrases like "the really great superstars" and "star-studded" abound; during the Joan Sutherland–Marilyn Horne program the announcer described what he saw as "marvelous reflections of joint admiration and satisfaction on the faces of [the artists]." Almost everywhere souvenir booklets are hawked, and sometimes free gifts and premiums are offered. It is all dismayingly like TV sports—but lacking the occasional objectivity and even skepticism of sportscasters.

The reasons underlying this hucksterism are all too plain. For the artists the goal is what it always has been—fame and money. For the institutions, the goal is, simply put, survival. In a time of rising budgets, reduced participation by big contributors, and loss of contemporary intellectual relevance, the only hope lies in an expansion of the uneducated audience. A massive new audience can hardly be expected to enter concert halls and opera houses; its natural habitat can only be television land.

The participants in this quest are quite open about their intentions. The morning after the Met *Otello* (which indeed may have reached as many as ten million viewers), the *New York Times* quoted the company's executive director as saying:

> We average 25,000 letters from people who haven't been on our lists with each new telecast. . . . The wider we reach, the more access we have to both federal funding and private contributions.

And the Met's president added:

> We hope to get considerable revenue from electronics of all sorts—cable TV, video discs, cassettes and tapes. . . . We've got to play to the widest possible audience. And with satellite television, the world is there.

Meanwhile, far from the klieg lights and PR agents of television, serious music on radio has taken a new lease on life. For now, more than thirty years into the age of video, the real music lover's home is still radio. The once despised radio now offers an unequaled variety of great music, in concert performances from all over the world. So much, indeed, is available that one's experience of it is limited only by the time one has for listening—and by the number of FM tuners and tape recorders one has available to record simultaneous programs.

In the New York metropolitan area, for example, in addition to the Metropolitan broadcasts of the entire season, there are available during the year the Salzburg Festival and the performances of the San Francisco Opera, along with weekly concerts by the New York Philharmonic, the Boston Symphony, and the Philadelphia, Cleveland, and Chicago orchestras. Chamber music is broadcast from the Library of Congress, and solo recitals from Carnegie and Tully halls as well as the 92nd Street Y. The Chamber Music Society of Lincoln Center, the series at the Frick Museum, the Amsterdam Concertgebouw, the Berlin and Vienna philharmonics, the Budapest Festival, the Aspen Festival, even festivals of Women's Music. . . . The list is endless, and the result is a cornucopia of today's musical life.

From the standpoint of the performers whose work is now being widely circulated and the music lovers whose every taste is now being supplied, this plenty on the airwaves can only be welcomed. For these producers and consumers more must always seem better. Yet the very success of the electronic transmission of music poses several disturbing questions. Is all this activity, on radio and television alike, good for the continued existence of live concerts? What is the effect of all this easy access to acknowledged masterpieces on the writing and the writers of new music? Has all this easy listening thinned the ranks of those most vital members of the audience, the cultivated amateurs who experience music by playing it themselves?

Perhaps all these questions are no more than polite ways of getting at the most troublesome problem of all: is there a limit to the desirable size of the audience for high musical culture? Individual programs and performers will come and go but this problem will remain, and it will increasingly be the task of an independent music criticism to address it.

[1980]

# PBS *Flogs the Arts*

A disturbing trend is increasingly evident in the presentation of the arts on public television. There is, to start with, a concentration on blockbuster productions and series, ranging from histories of art (often indistinguishable from sumptuously produced travelogues) to imported stagings of Shakespeare. In music this approach has meant relying for the most part on the Metropolitan Opera and the New York Philharmonic, the two still viable music-performing components of Lincoln Center; it has also meant highlighting star turns by famous singers and instrumentalists performing a repertory notable for high tune content, if for little else.

If this were all that were going on, matters would be dreary enough, especially considering the hopes once entertained for the elevation of taste through public broadcasting. But there is more, and worse. The Public Broadcasting Service has discovered that there is gold in the arts. Now that PBS is seen to be in a financial crisis—caused by escalating costs and declining government support—the watchword is *fundraising*. For this, the arts provide a medium both glamorous and persuasive.

In the visual arts, the emphasis here is on auctions, in which second-rate art goes to the highest bidder. With the possible exception of the buyer, everybody benefits in this process; the local station takes in donations while the donor of the art—often a commercial gallery—receives copious mention, credit, and tax deductions. But all this is relatively small time, because the art involved is so run-of-the-mill and the general atmosphere so determinedly loving hands and local. It is otherwise, however, with the musical fundraising promotions. These involve celebrity talent displayed in an atmosphere alternating between pretentious high-mindedness and the hard sell of a cerebral-palsy telethon.

Just how music is currently being used to raise money was demonstrated by the "Gala of Stars" broadcast in March to climax PBS's latest campaign for memberships and donations from the viewing audience. The three-hour show had been taped earlier at the New York State Theater in Lincoln Center. There were two masters of ceremonies for the program: Schuyler Chapin, formerly general manager of the Metropolitan Opera and now dean of the School of the Arts at Columbia University, was the suitably refined wrap-around host, serving in the higher cause of public television; Beverly Sills warmed up the audience in the hall, with her special combination of opera-star glamour and folksiness. New York-area viewers were offered, as well, extended glimpses of the WNET boiler room, its banks of telephones presided over by some of the most determined-looking grandmother types available from central casting. The ringmasters for these fundraising volunteers were two of the station's announcers, young women who together managed to convey an impression of show-business insouciance combined with fear of the malign consequences for the life of the mind if the fundraising goal was not fully met. It wasn't, by the way, and both the life of the mind and PBS, seemingly unchanged, are still with us.

Although the appeals for money seemed to go on nonstop, there indeed was a good deal of music on the PBS "Gala." James Levine, identified incessantly as "Maestro James Levine, music director of the Metropolitan Opera," conducted the American Symphony Orchestra. It must be said that this busy conductor's ability to direct a wide range of music from memory, as he did during the "Gala," testifies to an impressive musical facility. Unfortunately, as so often happens at his Metropolitan Opera performances, that facility is uncomplemented by a feeling for style, for structural coherence, or for musical detail. The American Symphony Orchestra, perhaps the only self-governing full-sized orchestra in this country, also confirmed an unhappy judgment on its artistic accomplishment: self-government, no matter how laudable in other venues, does not produce a reliable intonation, rhythmic precision, and easy responsiveness.

The musical evening began with a troubled and rushed performance of Mozart's overture to *The Marriage of Figaro*. Next, two highly regarded members of George Balanchine's New York City Ballet, Suzanne Farrell and Sean Lavery, danced a work choreographed by Balanchine to the music of Gluck. Their performance lacked the polish and discipline one might have expected. The next event, the last before the "Act I" intermission, featured American pianist Garrick Ohlsson playing the last movement of Tchaikow-sky's First Piano Concerto. This movement inevitably sounds tawdry in isolation from the first two movements of the work. Ohlsson's performance, helped along not a bit by Levine's workaday rigidity, was marked by a kind of reserve and lack of involvement better suited to washing out someone else's laundry.

The intermission featured a kaleidoscope of images of backstage and rehearsal activity, along with a montage of artists bowing to the audience at the 1981 "Gala." The music returned with Elisa-beth's great display aria from the opening of Act II of Wagner's *Tannhäuser*. As sung—or rather, shouted—by the American so-prano Grace Bumbry, dressed in a wildly inappropriate orange gown with orange feathers at the sleeves, the aria made a convincing argument for Tannhäuser's tendency to prefer the seductive Venus to the chaste Elisabeth. The *"Là ci darem la mano"* duet from *Don Giovanni,* performed by Mirella Freni and Nicolai Ghiaurov, at least had the advantage of their authentic, if not quite first-rate, vocal-ism. Much the same could be said of the aria from *Macbeth* sung by tenor Carlo Bergonzi. When Sherrill Milnes sang (and acted out) Iago's *"Credo"* from *Otello,* the penalty that richly talented singers pay today for their stardom was abundantly clear. At the outset, Sills told the audience that Milnes's appearance at the "Gala" was lucky, since he had only the previous night been singing *Henry VIII* (by Saint-Saëns) in San Diego. Not surprisingly, considering the rigors of his schedule, Milnes's voice was uncharacteristically thin and wan.

Next followed what turned out to be the musical highlight of the evening. An extended excerpt from Act III of Offenbach's *Tales of Hoffmann* featured three lesser-known American singers, James Morris, Catherine Malfitano, and Jean Kraft. (Their names were not mentioned in John O'Connor's dutiful review of the event in the *New York Times*.) Here was impressive work: conviction, drive, creative absorption. Even Levine seemed fully involved in the music. Interestingly, Offenbach's music—the cream of light French music near the end of the nineteenth century—proved to be perfect for television and for its purpose here: the transmission of high culture to an American mass audience.

After another long intermission, filled with fundraising pep talks and exhortations, the stage performances resumed with an excerpt from George Balanchine's setting of English music-hall tunes,

*Union Jack,* performed by Patricia McBride and Bart Cook. Lynn Harrell then played the opening movement of the Dvořák Cello Concerto. Following the lighthearted dancing, this long immersion in romantic sentiment felt strange indeed. It seemed mocked and trivialized by what had gone before.

After time out for yet another noncommercial commercial break, Carlo Bergonzi returned to sing a popular Italian folk song, introduced by the following pointless words of Sills:

> I know that most people think that any time they hear an Italian song it's a Neapolitan song. Well, it's not. But tonight you're going to hear a real Neapolitan song.

Real or unreal, Italian or Neapolitan, the song (Levine played the piano accompaniment) lacked in performance the essential atmosphere of garlic and tomato sauce, and Bergonzi's concluding high note failed utterly. Grace Bumbry then sang "Bless This House" and Nicolai Ghiaurov "The Drunkard Song," a Russian creation. All three efforts demonstrated just how much personality is needed to perform nonclassical music effectively, and how painfully trite such music can be without it.

The climax of the evening for the audience came next, in the "person" of Miss Piggy, the puppet prima donna familiar to afficionados of "The Muppet Show." In the *Times,* O'Connor referred to her appearance this way:

> . . . very nearly stealing the show, Miss Piggy shows up to do one of her inimitable routines with Miss Sills and the conductor James Levine, both of whom are gracious and understandably amused.

Considering that Miss Piggy's routine included her attempting to show how a pig would behave if she became an opera singer and her characterizing the conductor as "big-mouth Levine," the artists' graciousness and capacity for easy amusement seem remarkable indeed. Following Miss Piggy were the pop singer Cleo Laine and her husband, saxophonist John Dankworth. (The transition was managed by Miss Laine's singing the Bessie Smith song "Gimme a Pig-foot and a Bottle of Beer.") Laine's cabaret singing is doubtless enticing, but there was something incongruous about her being accompanied by no less than the music director of the Metropolitan Opera. Such an incongruity will doubtless be applauded by those levelers of art who speak in the name of "the people," but for others such an attempt at mixing genres can only be seen as a bad job done by all.

After one more hype-filled intermission (featuring Miss Piggy herself), Mirella Freni returned, this time with an excerpt from *Don Carlos*. Then a "surprise" occurred, one that must have been rehearsed with the orchestra the morning of the taping: as if by magic, Placido Domingo materialized just as Sills was apologizing for his not being able to perform at the "Gala" due to his commitments across the plaza at Lincoln Center. Fully costumed, he proceeded to sing the aria—from *Adriana Lecouvreur*—he had just finished a few hundred feet away at the Metropolitan Opera House. His performance only renewed one's fears that, having attempted to emulate Luciano Pavarotti in becoming a pop vocal hero, he will soon follow Pavarotti in losing that vocal finish which distinguishes a big voice from a tight shout.

The musical extravaganza ended with a portion of Leonard Bernstein's *Candide,* taken from the current New York City Opera production. It seemed attractive enough on television, though hardly in the league of *Tales of Hoffmann.* Perhaps the tawdriness of the setting swamped the art itself. Certainly this has happened with many of PBS's musical offerings, on this and other occasions.

It need hardly be said that this particular PBS offering was not the first such extravaganza in the history of musical show business. It is not because their artistic level was so disappointing, however, that the performances on this particular program deserve serious attention. It is rather because the artistic content of public television is exemplified in this "Gala." Moreover, that content is offered to us as a justification for support of the entire enterprise, which, as even its staunchest supporters will readily acknowledge, consists of a great many programs that have little or nothing to do with the arts. The arts are certainly the moral foundation for the many, many appeals and exhortations that define the purpose and set the tone for an event like the "Gala."

The tasteless and offensive words that accompanied the artistic performances provided a further key to the present state of the arts on PBS. They expressed a sovereign contempt for the audience whose dollars and good will were being so avidly solicited and a contempt too for the very idea of art itself.

Schuyler Chapin began the festivities on a false note by talking of an "equal" partnership between the people who present these programs and the audience that pays for them:

> I'm Schuyler Chapin. Just moments from now you will witness this grand house of the New York State Theater filled with the appreciative audience of this year's Gala of Stars, but more importantly these seats represent just a fraction of the Gala viewers across the country. So let me ask you to take your seat, with pride. After all, tonight's Gala is the essential partnership of the arts with you. [*He points at the camera.*]

Stripped of the fashionable rhetoric, a rather clearer idea of what this partnership consists of emerged from a later piece of hectoring, spoken by the more impassioned of the two local announcers:

> Mid-Fairfield friends of Thirteen [Channel 13] donated $2,500 to the cause, and that's the kind of partnership we really need.

In short: Yours to pay, ours to reason why.

Another constant theme of the evening was the idea that art was something for everyone, and that works of art were everyday adornments to life. Beverly Sills spoke about the success of public television in bringing opera to the masses:

> Samuel Johnson once wrote a dictionary, and he defined opera as that "exotic and irrational entertainment." Well, thanks to PBS, we ain't exotic no more. Mad scenes may be in but exotic is definitely out.

Here is a fashionable—although indefensible—attitude toward opera as an art form: it's all one melodious sitcom holding up a mirror to daily life. Try telling that to Aida, or to Elektra.

Miss Piggy's appearance, too, represented a theme of the "Gala." What she brought to the event was a hard-edged satire on the very idea of art (not to mention public television). No more need be quoted than Miss Piggy's testimonial to public television: "I love PBS because it shows all the things that are important to a pig." Chapin's response (in a throaty voice) seemed perfectly in character with the evening: "Couldn't have said it better, and I couldn't have said it better." Then, consummate fundraiser to the end, he kissed her. Doubtless this is humorous to some, but there is something both cheap and mean-spirited about it also—unless, of course, one thinks that pigs too are art lovers.

Perhaps the most disturbing aspect of the evening's commentary demonstrated how far public television has gone in its search for successful marketing methods, regardless of the effect they have in destroying the very enterprise its supporters are trying to help. There was a constant attempt—throughout the evening—to arouse feelings of guilt in noncontributing viewers. On one occasion the WNET announcer pulled out all the stops:

> What about those of you who haven't responded? What about those of you who are sitting watching that program tonight, enjoying it and not calling? I don't know how you can stand it. I really don't. What happens when you go to work tomorrow? You talk about the programs you've seen this weekend, and they ask you if you are a member.

Such psychological attack—a moralistic hard sell—makes commercial television seem by comparison gentle and respectful toward its audience.

PBS is not just the victim of rising costs and declining subsidies. The self-regarding concerns of its executives and backers and their ambitions to rival the commercial networks at public expense are threatening the educational purpose that is supposed to underlie what was once naïvely thought of as educational television. If PBS now seems to be fighting for survival, the question arises whether there is anything worth preserving. The PBS "Gala of Stars" went far to suggest that there is not.

[*1983*]

# The NEA: Funding the Piper

Though in the United States all the arts are now publicly subsidized on a broad front, music has received a lion's share of the official cultural dollar. This support has come to music, it would seem, for two reasons: music is at once more "pure" than other art forms and at the same time has a history of commercial viability. Music's purity lies in the fact that, unlike painting and sculpture, it provides little of material value to the collector; it is thus spared the costly and contentious apparatus of dealers and museums. And unlike repertory theater and dance, music managed for at least one century—from roughly the middle of the nineteenth century to at least the end of World War II—to pay much of its own way in this country, helped along by the devotion of individual music lovers and assorted social and ethnic groups. So music, of all the arts, must have seemed a deserving and not too demanding candidate for the helping hand of government.

To speak of music's commercial viability is of course not to forget that this possibility of financial success for musicians—soloists, supporting players, and teachers alike—could only arise when orchestras, opera companies, and schools existed to provide the necessary institutional structure. But these institutions have always had the kind of aspirations to distinction, comprehensiveness, and permanence that have made them sure money losers; as a result, their deficit had to be made up outside the normal play of market forces.

Historically, this task was performed by America's rich, and the institutional history of musical America from the turn of this century until quite recently is a story of their attentions. Our two most famous music schools were named for their patrons: the Juilliard School was founded after a bequest in 1919 by cotton merchant Augustus Juilliard, and the Curtis Institute was begun and endowed in 1924 by Mary Louise Curtis Bok of the Curtis publishing fortune. Among orchestras, the Boston Symphony was founded in

1881 by Henry Lee Higginson, who remained the major financial support of the orchestra almost until the day of his death in 1919. In New York, the name of Otto Kahn was long associated both with the financing and management of the Metropolitan Opera, and the same is true of the relationship of Clarence Mackay and Mrs. Lytle Hull to the New York Philharmonic. Though the names elsewhere were not often as famous, this story of private contributions to music was repeated across the country, and constitutes a noble chapter in the history of capitalist philanthropy.

But as increasingly the mere accumulation of money no longer served to legitimize its possession—and as income and inheritance taxes began to take a bite out of great fortunes—foundations established by the rich came to share in the exercise of patronage. In music, for example, the Guggenheim Foundation as early as the 1920s awarded fellowships to many American composers, including Aaron Copland, Roy Harris, and Roger Sessions. More recently, the Martha Baird Rockefeller Fund for Music specialized in grants to individual musicians for specific projects. Nor has foundation help been limited to composers and soloists; countless grants have over the years been made in every field of American musical life.

Important as the activities of individuals and foundations have been, they pale in significance when compared with the scope and influence of the enormous Ford Foundation grants to music, which began in 1966. This giant among American philanthropies found itself in the early 1960s swelled by an enormous rise in the value of its holdings of Ford stock, and under an activist administration decided to support the arts in a big way. Within that general area it searched, in the words of the head of its art program, W. McNeil Lowry, for a field in which its funds would have the "greatest . . . national impact." That field was the orchestra, and the Ford intervention by sheer size alone changed the economic situation of American music.

On strictly musical grounds it is difficult to understand the compelling need for this massive subsidy. There was no large number of new or ignored masterpieces awaiting first and repeated performances by major orchestras; there were no unserved audiences clamoring loudly for concerts; there were no vastly original styles of interpretation requiring the founding of new groups to do them justice. Nor had the level of orchestra performance declined; indeed, the pinnacle of American orchestral playing—in the quality of our major orchestras and the interest of their repertory—had already been reached by the early 1960s.

There were, however, other than purely musical reasons involved. Rather than arising out of considerations of artistic need, the grants first came out of a desire for economic and social equity. The condition of the orchestral musician was seen as depressed. Not only did he on the average earn less than a mere schoolteacher, but his work in the orchestra was, except for players in the few largest groups, most often less than full time; few American orchestras were then engaged on a fifty-two-week basis. A financial situation that was tolerable for members of great orchestras (with their longer seasons and greater opportunities for teaching and outside performance) seemed intolerable in the case of lesser organizations in the smaller cities and towns. Here musicians were forced to support themselves outside music as best they could, frequently working as schoolteachers but often in fields totally unrelated to the arts.

All this the Ford Foundation was determined to correct. It did so in a complicated but decisive manner, contributing money in the form of endowment funds (which required matching by local sources) and yearly subsidies for current expenses. Its goals were clearly stated: to raise the level of performance by enabling musicians to concentrate on orchestral playing, to make it possible for orchestras to expand their audiences, and to make the musical profession more attractive by increasing the income of its members.

Through the Ford grants sixty-one orchestras in the major and metropolitan categories received a total of $80 million ($165 million including matching funds). The response to this largesse was quick and predictable. Whereas in 1957 the average annual budget of the most important American orchestras had been no more than $600,000, by 1971 (the year when most Ford grants were being wound up) the average budget, after correction for inflation, had reached $2,800,000. Expenses had risen to meet income. Triggered by an often preexisting union militancy, most of this rise had taken place in musicians' salaries, thus fulfilling the purposes of the Ford grants. Not only were fees per rehearsal and performance increased, but managements found it necessary to increase the number of concerts given so that it might be possible to compensate musicians for more services as well.

But regardless of the real gains made by musicians in the Ford-grant period—and it must be stressed that for their higher salaries they were now working harder than ever before—the enduring result of the Ford program was heightened expectations on the part of the musicians. Past gains were seen as meaningful only when they could be continued and extended. Musicians were quite understandably unwilling to be left behind by the increased affluence of other skilled professionals. Postponement and denial of the musicians' demands resulted in strikes, generally lowered morale, and a pervasive climate of friction between players and management. The Ford Foundation could not satisfy permanently the demands its money had made possible; indeed, it had explicitly warned the orchestras that it bore no further obligation after the expiration of the grants.

But here as elsewhere in American life, where foundations have led, government has carried on. The necessary ideological and statistical basis of such an assumption by government of a hitherto private responsibility had been prepared by the publication in the 1960s of two lengthy foundation-supported studies of the financial prospects for the arts. The first of these, the Rockefeller Brothers Fund panel report (1965), attempted to survey the state of the performing arts and their actual and potential sources of support. Today, after more than a decade of the growing socialization of culture and communication, the Rockefeller report, in its painstaking attempt to preserve the private aspect of patronage, makes nostalgic reading. The real weight of this report, however, may be gathered from the fact that of its eleven chapters only one, that dealing with the state of orchestras, choral groups, chamber music, opera, theater, and dance, is longer than the section demonstrating the desirability of government aid—and it is longer by only one page.

It was left to the 1966 econometric study, *Performing Arts—The Economic Dilemma,* by William J. Baumol and William G. Bowen, paid for by the Twentieth Century Fund, to provide an argument particularly attractive to friends of official planning and subsidy. These two Princeton professors explained that government support was not only necessary to make the arts better; it was necessary in order to keep them alive at all. The reason was simple. In other areas of our automating society, technological progress, by saving labor costs, allows prices to decline relative to purchasing power. In the labor-intensive arts, on the other hand, both the inability to automate and the rising wages demanded across the society as a whole will soon price the arts out of the consumer market. Not only was government seen as the patron of last resort for the arts; once it had been agreed that the arts confer general benefits on the community, such patronage was for Baumol and Bowen a necessary response to the needs of the society.

It can hardly be overlooked that the critical years for both large-scale foundation activity and the beginnings of government involvement coincided with the palmy period of Lyndon Johnson's Great Society, before the escalation of the war in Vietnam. The transvaluation of private expenditures by government determinations was the regnant political principle of the day, so it is not surprising that board members and trustees, in whose hands the making of business and financial decisions in the arts had lain for so many years, were as quick as were artists to give up fears of political intervention and control.

The entering wedge of federal arts policy—if one exempts the controversial WPA experiments of the 1930s as belonging to the area of unemployment relief—was the Eisenhower Administration's use in the 1950s of appearances abroad by American artists as an extension of foreign policy. After several attempts in the early 1960s, Congress in 1965 passed a bill, signed by President Johnson, establishing a National Foundation on the Arts and Humanities, made up of three institutions: the National Endowment for the Arts (NEA), the National Endowment for the Humanities, and the Federal Council on the Arts and Humanities (a body coordinating the endowments' activities with other federal programs). This structure, in broad outline, remains unchanged today.

In the beginning, federal funding was small in absolute terms. In its first year (fiscal 1966) arts appropriations barely exceeded $2,500,000, and the next year they reached $8 million, a level they were approximately to maintain through fiscal 1970. But from this point on the rise was steady and large; in fiscal 1971 the appropriation doubled, as it did the following year. Increase followed increase, and total appropriations for the arts in fiscal 1978 are at a level of $115 million.[1] And in many states, the same story can be told. Not only are all the state arts councils funded by the federal government through the diversion of twenty percent of endowment funds through bloc grants, but some states—most notably New York—have themselves become powerful movers in financing the arts, working in general conformity with Washington's leadership.

Music was, as might have been expected, one of the prime gainers from the increase in federal funding at the beginning of the 1970s. In the orchestral area, for example, orchestras, which had received $3,761,000 in 1971 (the year of the ending of the Ford grants), were by 1974 receiving $7,172,000; the 1977 funding level had risen to $12,250,000, of which $6,335,000 was for normal support and $5,915,000 was in the form of challenge grants requiring high rates of matching from new private sources. Much the same has happened in opera. Opera companies, which in 1971 were the recipients of only $598,000 in federal funds, were given $5,840,000 in 1977, of which $2,750,000 was in challenge grants.

Though these large institutional grants take up by far the greatest part of the NEA music funds (amounting in all to $12,750,000 for normal support purposes in fiscal 1977), other and smaller projects were supported as well. In 1977, for example, $1,450,000 went to groups offering help to artists in career development; $845,000 was given to the jazz/folk/ethnic category; $470,000 was allotted to composer/libretto fellowships; $220,000 was provided for contemporary music performance; $130,000 went to grants outside regular NEA programs; $45,000 was given to the smallest program of all, a pilot project in choral music; and, finally, closing out 1977 NEA activities, $230,000 was earmarked for central musical service organizations such as the American Symphony Orchestra League, and $300,000 was allocated for audience development.

The evidence of how this money has been spent is all around us. As with all government programs, at the center stands a large and powerful bureaucracy publicly proclaiming its vital role in the currently improving state of things. Though in theory artistic decisions are made by panels of outside notables drawn from the fields in which grants are to be made, it is plain that residual as well as day-to-day power lies with the large permanent staff, often picked on a

---

1. A similar sum goes to the humanities.

revolving-door basis from the flourishing and comfortably paid arts-administration establishment. This power not only resides in the staff function of preparing agendas for the panel meetings and providing reports and recommendations for panel actions, but also in the large role of the staff in picking the panelists themselves.

Outside the Washington offices of the NEA at Columbia Plaza the telltale signs of public subsidies may be found in concert and opera programs across the country. It is a rare musical event presented by a nonprofit organization that does not prominently feature on the printed program, just below the listing of works, composers, and performers, the legend "This event is made possible by a grant from the National Endowment for the Arts"—or an individual state council, or a combination of the two. Similarly, arts institutions make a practice of giving leading space in their publications to publicity releases of the NEA announcing new and continuing grants described in glowing terms by the current chairman of the Endowment.

Beyond the requirement all these mentions prominently fulfill—of giving credit to government for distributing taxpayers' money—the fruit of all this spending is evident in vastly increased musical activity. In itself this increase did not begin with government help, for as the 1965 Rockefeller report regretfully noted, the rise of the previous two decades had occurred in amateur participation, with symphonies and opera companies (except for the largest and best) frequently staffed by part-time professionals and even music lovers. But since the mid-1960s the expansion has involved the professionalization of music, with ever smaller presenting groups engaging full-time performers and specialized administrators.

For the increased pay that has made this professionalization possible, more musical events are being performed than ever before in American history. With the rise in amateur activity, this increase in the number of performances had already begun to take place in the 1960s. The total of orchestra concerts given yearly went from 2,903 in the 1961–62 season to 6,758 in 1969–70, and the total of orchestras giving them went from 271 to 620 in the same period. But, significantly, the increase in orchestras did not occur evenly during these years; the great jump—stimulated even if not directly supported at first by new funds—occurred in the season immediately following the development of the Ford plan and the passage

of the first federal arts-support legislation in 1965. And a set of statistics on the period from 1965–66 to 1973–74 presents a similar picture; during this time, the number of performances increased by eighty percent.

Perhaps least affected by these changes, save in their increased access to publicly funded electronic media, has been the elite category of orchestras like the New York Philharmonic and the Boston Symphony. Such orchestras have for years been so busy as to make expansion of their seasons and enlarging of their regular concert audiences difficult. But on the level of the less prestigious institutions the change has been enormous. Seasons have become year-round, and musicians have been able—and in many cases have found it necessary—to devote themselves more or less entirely to their orchestral duties.

Another example of the rise in musical activity made possible in some part by public funds is the present ubiquity of summer festivals, formerly few and, save for such exceptions as the summer season of the Boston Symphony at Tanglewood, small and short. Now the summer, always in the past a dead time for music, has become perhaps more active than the winter. So great is this activity that experienced orchestral players are in short supply for those festivals unaffiliated with all-year orchestras because of the contractual demands made on the musicians by their full-time employers.

In opera, traditionally the most expensive of musical formats, the story is largely the same. The number of performances has increased significantly, new companies have been established, and untold new operas have been commissioned. Perhaps most important, live opera has become a staple on public television, allowing the presentation of frequent productions not only from the Metropolitan Opera, but also from the New York City Opera, and such summer festivals as Wolf Trap.

As might have been expected, more has come from government than simply the money to pay for what musically qualified people want to do. The money itself has often been transferred with the requirement that it be matched by private contributions. Frequently the matching rate has exceeded a one-for-one formula, and has gone as high as three private dollars for each governmental dollar. While this requirement has often had only a purely formal significance, in that the private funds used for matching purposes in many cases would have been contributed anyway, the general effect of matching has been to spur arts institutions to seek out new sources of nongovernmental support. Though the result of the recent increase in private contributions has been to quash the fear that government support would drive out individual and corporate philanthropy, the very prestige of government participation has made official commitment to a particular organization or program the necessary imprimatur for attracting help from an increasingly skittish, fearful, and guilt-ridden private sector in search of moral justification and public acceptance. Furthermore, the effect of this stamp of approval has not only been the facilitation of nongovernmental support; the weight thus put on official policy has enabled government programs and officials to exert an influence on arts activities out of all proportion to the still small percentage contribution of public funds to overall budgets.

Nor have the arts avoided the need to practice grantsmanship. Getting the grants is the name of the game, and the principle applies from the most prestigious down to the newest and smallest applicant. Thinking up projects that will make successful grant applications has become an art itself worthy of public support. At a recent meeting of a young arts group and the regional representative of the NEA, advice was tendered that the first grant the institution requested should be for funds to bring a specialist to recommend what grants to apply for. Further advice was also forthcoming: the specialist asked for should be an individual (who was named) renowned for his success in obtaining federal subsidies— more than twenty grants in one year, or so the story went. To one listener's quizzical comment that such success must take a lot of time and effort, the dry rejoinder was that the specialist had two people at work in this area full time.

Reassuringly, fears of political censorship have proven unfounded, though plainly music does not provide as much occasion for direct control as the theater or realistic painting. And music itself has recently seemed to be in retreat from the kind of social engagement popular a decade ago. A cynic might remark that in any case so little of revolutionary importance is going on in music today that even the blindest obscurantist would be hard put to find anything provocative enough to occasion suppression.

More controversial has been the use of political appointees to fill the highest-level endowment positions. President Carter's choice of

Joseph Duffey, a political supporter, to head the National Endowment for the Humanities was skeptically received in the scholarly community; his appointment of Livingston Biddle as chairman of the NEA was widely taken as an all too plain acknowledgment that the choice was a perquisite of Democratic Senator Claiborne Pell, the head of the Senate subcommittee dealing with endowment matters—and Mr. Biddle's previous employer.

Furthermore, both the NEA and the state councils are susceptible to the ideological winds of change blowing in Washington and the country at large. Only this past fall the NEA announced the creation of a new post, that of arts-endowment representative for minority concerns; more publicly significant has been the pressure in the media recently brought to bear on the New York State Council on the Arts to allocate a designated and high percentage of its large funds to black and Puerto Rican culture. In general, it is increasingly obvious that arts funding is seen by political and social activist groups as providing the means of increased visibility for their causes as well as prestige employment for their leaders and committed supporters.

One could only become more conscious of this connection between politics and support for the arts as the travels of Joan Mondale, America's Artistic First Lady, unfolded last summer. On her trip to the Rocky Mountains, for instance, the vice president's wife —who seems to enjoy being called and calling herself "Joan of Art" —combined appearances at money-raising affairs for Democratic congressional candidates with a speech on government aid to the arts at the Aspen Institute for Humanistic Studies, where, joined by Livingston Biddle, she also participated in a seminar on funding the arts. Local news broadcasts made no attempt to separate the political and nonpolitical aspects of her viceregal visit, lumping them together seriatim under the rubric "woman makes good."

Clearly the arts have become good political business. The publicity is free, the cause beyond criticism, and the opportunity thus provided to bring together politicians and rich potential contributors who are used to giving is unparalleled. But beyond all these particular aspects of public arts policy, what have been the direct *artistic* consequences of the spending of so much money? The immediate, crude answer is that they have been nil. Music itself has changed remarkably little due to government subsidy. In order to understand why, one must remember that government support in this country began as the support of artists rather than art, and that this support has been channeled largely through traditional institutions able, at least in principle, to prove their worth in the marketplace.

The result is that artists have been paid to do what they have been trained to do and what their predecessors were doing before public help came on the scene. Orchestras have played much the same pieces, and opera companies have produced the same operas as they have for most of the years of this century. There has, it is true, been some circulation in the constituents of the standard repertory, most notably in opera, but one's impression is that the pace of even this normal circulation is rather less than it has routinely been in the past. New works have been put on, but they have merely replaced yesterday's new music in whatever program niche performers have always felt they must allow the current creative crop. And the same iteration of the past is seen in the help that has found its way into professional music education; almost all of the curricula of our best music schools would hardly have been out of place in the Austria, Germany, or Russia of seventy-five years ago.

What has changed is that the musician's tasks are being performed for many more people than ever before. As far as opera is concerned, a high NEA official was recently heard to remark happily that now, after the last decade of expansion and government support, more people are attending opera in the United States than the games of the National Football League. The exact figure for 1977–78, according to an article in *Opera News,* the publication of the Metropolitan Opera Guild (which has a membership of 110,000), is 9,760,000, a one-year gain of six percent; an estimated corresponding figure for 1963–64 was 1,700,000. The same story can be told about orchestral audiences. Material required to be submitted in support of 1976–77 NEA orchestra grant applications disclosed such prodigies of annual attendance as 1,564,049 for the Los Angeles Philharmonic, 887,400 for the New York Philharmonic, 690,420 for the Cincinnati Symphony, and even 85,800 for the small Winston-Salem Symphony.

These statistics are truly overwhelming, and to quote them is to comprehend that the arts are no more immune from our national fascination with body counts than was our military effort in Vietnam. The error is the same: the confusion of quantity with success.

But whereas in Vietnam bodies were counted even when they were alive, in music today it is difficult to escape the feeling that the audience is counted even if many of its members are, for all artistic purposes, dead.

Public support, having begun as support for music through aid to musicians, now turns out to have been all along support of the audience as well. These two neatly interlocking goals have become a vicious circle in which support of the one requires support of the other. Indeed, at present, it is possible to see that expansion has been the real goal of public support from the beginning. This goal provides the justification for the proliferation of government funds, and the extent to which it has been accomplished is by now the chief criterion of the success of the entire program.

In the days of Richard Nixon, the NEA talked about "outreach" of the arts; now, under Jimmy Carter, Livingston Biddle talks about "access" to them. It would be a mistake to allow the differing rhetorical associations of these two words—*outreach* suggests doing good from above and *access* suggests entitlement from below—to obscure the fact that in our society only those public expenditures that serve the greatest number in a fairly equal fashion can receive moral validation and survive the scrutiny of opposition, press, and citizenry.

So, as part of obtaining that portion of their daily bread necessary to getting the rest, musical institutions, no less than art museums, have been chasing after the audience—both in the usual places and in newer ones like inner cities and barren wastes, youth centers and homes for the aged, schools and prisons. And those whose bodies have not been available in person have been reached through public television, which has been used to bring both the most intimate chamber music and the grandest opera into the home.

An example of this search for an audience is the remarkable story of the services provided to the community by an orchestra as small as the Albuquerque Symphony. From 1970–71 to 1971–72, these services increased from 14 to 100; by 1974–75 they reached 199. It is not clear, however, that this boom reflected a golden age of the concert audience in New Mexico. For almost the entire increase is represented by the publicly funded category called in the early 1970s "ensembles in schools" but later (reflecting the inflated language of the bureaucracy) "Workshops, Lecture/Demonstrations,

Educational or Community Programs." In 1970–71, there were none of these events; in 1971–72, there were suddenly 84; and by 1974–75, there were 161. The growth in concerts was quite a bit less dramatic. From 14 in 1970–71 they rose to 16 the next year, and reached 38 in 1974–75—but the 1974–75 figures include 16 "Performances for Children/Youth." In fact, the regular concerts in this period increased from 9 the first year to 10 the next, and three years later went to 22.

A large percentage of the audiences described above can be loosely called "contracted"—a euphemistic way of saying that the listeners do not themselves pay via the box office for what they are given. But "ticketed" audiences—those who do pay individually and presumably make personal decisions to attend—have not been ignored either. All the techniques of direct-mail advertising, so noxious when they are used to sell a commercial product, are being brought to bear on the consumer. Governments and foundations alike sponsor experts who travel around the country advising local groups how to move their artistic product.

What kind of audience can be found through this undignified, vulgar, and half-crazed search? Is there any reason to agree with the prevailing assumption of the arts merchandisers that serious culture —the "best," as Livingston Biddle likes to call it—is now or will in the future be attractive and meaningful to millions without intellectual training, background, or even any clear idea of what they are being either forced or gulled into attending?

An answer to this question can hardly come easily to anyone who is either a reasonably convinced democrat or a professional active in the world of culture and ideas. Democratic societies—in the past and perhaps even today ours more than any other—are founded upon two assumptions: *Vox populi, vox dei* remains the ultimate political sanction, and our ultimate cultural article of faith is that the "common man" is capable, given an opportunity, of learning, mastering, and liking every achievement of civilization from the most recherché to the most complex. In America this faith has underlain our huge education industry, and it is plain that our current attempts to dragoon an audience for music are merely another facet of our cultural *levée en masse*.

However, it is not clear that democratic hopes in politics and education can so easily be extended to high culture. Perhaps the strongest evidence that such optimism in the field of music is unwarranted is precisely the subtle and not-so-subtle changes presently being made in musical programs designed to attract and please these new hordes of virgin concertgoers. Something of the spirit of this attempt to find a kind of repertory attractive enough to bring in an audience may be gathered from two items, the second immediately following the first, here quoted in their entirety from the October 1978 issue of *Symphony News,* the publication of the American Symphony Orchestra League:

"Mozart, I Love You Madly"—a series of three pairs of weekend concerts conducted by Maurice Peress, highlighted the *Kansas City Philharmonic*'s September activity at the Grace and Trinity Cathedral.

EXPANSION/DEVELOPMENT
An expanded 1978–79 season opened October 3, for the *Oakland Symphony Orchestra,* with the addition of a new five-concert Friday night pops series. Titled TGIF (thank God it's Friday), the new series will allow the orchestra to reach new audiences and increase the association's earned income.

No one would want to be caught saying that there is too much Mozart being played, but one can hardly go wrong pointing out the questionable nature of forays outside the body of classical music as a means of drawing the masses into culture. Such pops concerts, employing serious musicians, proliferate, with a repertory drawn from the smash successes of Broadway, pop music, and the movies. Last season, for instance, found the Los Angeles Philharmonic Orchestra under its then music director Zubin Mehta playing a concert at the Hollywood Bowl for 17,500 screaming pop-music fans featuring music from *Star Wars.* On a level less vulgar but more quixotic, the NEA has just sponsored a meeting in New York City of figures from opera and Broadway to begin its program of grants to develop a new hybrid form of musical theater. The *New York Times* headlined its report of this meeting "Figaro Meets 'Fiddler,' " and quoted soprano Beverly Sills as saying, in deploring opera's insistence on voices large enough to do without microphones, "If amplification conveys more emotion to the public, what's the big deal?"

It is here that the new policy of public involvement, and the atmosphere in which it is being carried out, will in the long run have artistic consequences. To speak of audiences dragging down his art is a humiliating admission for an artist to make, for it reflects on his art as well as his ideology. Every artist needs an audience before whom to do his work; the audience is the sounding board against which his productions can be tested, and its approval is the criterion of his success. Once these facts are admitted, it is an easy jump from wanting some audience to wanting an ever and infinitely larger one.

Unfortunately, it is the artist's search for support and verification that allows the inevitable lowering of quality attendant upon rapid expansion of the audience to affect his work. We have seen how tempting it is to do what an audience wants in order to get it to come in the first place. Equally tempting, though less easy to pinpoint, is the playing to the gallery felt to be necessary to get the audience to return. Two examples of this cheapening come immediately to mind. It is likely that such an overriding concern for audience approval has produced the current vogue in orchestral playing for forced orchestral tone in general and blaring brass in particular. It seems even more likely that the present ossification of American operatic production in the "grand" style of monumental surrealism reflects a fear on the part of opera administrators that the mass audience to which they are appealing will tolerate neither experiment nor refinement.

While we can hardly be surprised at the desire of all the parties to the bargain of public funding—artists, administrators, and government alike—to agree about the search for the largest possible audience, what finally makes our present official support of music and the other arts such a new departure is the separation it reflects of patronage and consumption. In continental Europe a long tradition of what might be called participant support marked the flowering of eighteenth- and nineteenth-century music; from the Esterházys with Haydn and the Archduke Rudolph with Beethoven, through the aristocratic piano students of Chopin, and to Ludwig of Bavaria and Wagner, patrons of music savored what they supported. Vestiges of this tradition still remain, in the musical sophistication of the European educated classes. Even in England, the erstwhile *Land ohne Musik,* the former prime minister Edward

Heath has devoted much of his life to amateur performance of great music.

But for the United States, having lacked for so many years an autochthonous high musical culture, the situation remains different. Here our numerous governing cadres have neither historical nor present attachments to such high culture. For reasons of political convenience our leaders are willing to arrange for the transfer of public monies for artistic purposes. That they have up to this point done so with a surprising amount of disinterest is perhaps no more than a sign of their basic uninterest. It is this uninterest that makes them so eclectic in their practical decisions. Thus freed from any burden of their own tastes, they are able to preside smilingly over the gradual vulgarization of what was once a civilized glory.

[1979]

# EPILOGUE

## *The Audience for Music*

The prologue of this book ended with a defense against a likely charge of negativism. Indeed, even before the prologue, I had begun matters with an epigraph suggesting (on the authority of no less than Schlegel and Schumann) that the artist works for an audience of one—and that one experiences the art only in secret. In a world where the voice of mass society is the voice of God, where the greatest happiness of the greatest number has become merely a happiness with numbers, to speak of art as properly addressed to so limited an audience is nothing if not negative.

Is this a fair way to talk about music? This book is, after all, about music; music has always enjoyed something of a large audience, and current attempts to sell music as if it were breakfast cereal can be seen as only trying to keep matters as they always have been. Not only do the well-known financial pressures on music presentation about which we read so much today suggest the need to find economies of scale, but most composers (and almost all performers) have measured their success by the number of their listeners. Whatever their worldly politics might be, musicians have always been imperialists when it comes to their own careers.

It would seem, then, that the triumph of institutions in our musical life, which I have tried to describe in this book, is not only inevitable, but desirable. Who can bring in these great numbers, if not great institutions, operating as quasi-public bodies? What else can guarantee musicians security of employment and proper reward for their labors, if not the governmental mobilization of support? Who should arrange the encounter between musicians and their listeners, if not an administrative class trained in such complex and necessary tasks? Why, in other words, should we take a stand against history?

To pose the questions in this way is, of course, to predetermine the answers. It is, moreover, to ignore what seems to me the most significant problem I have tried to identify: the triumph of musical institutions has been a triumph not of music, but of institutions. Wherever we look today, as institutions predominate, music languishes. Not only is this true in composition, where creators have always suffered at the hands of their backers; it is true as well even in performance, and even in the case of the spectacular musical decline of that creature par excellence of public television, Luciano Pavarotti.

I suppose the problem is, at heart, metaphysical: Are we to make history, or is history to make us? I, for one, prefer to take my stand with the individual. "Nice customs," Shakespeare wrote at the end of *Henry V*, "courtesy to great kings"; artists are royalty, and, as royalty must, determine the conditions of their own reception. And an ideal audience, too, is royalty; as I have written elsewhere,[1] "The enduring audience for art is largely self-selecting, a relatively small public marked by the willingness to make sacrifices of other pleasures for the sake of artistic experience"; this observation seems to me not only true to the history of art but also to the experience of the artist.

For the need of the artist—and this is true whether the artist in question is musician or painter, playwright or poet—is not so much to be loved and admired as it is to be *understood*. Here, finally, is the limit on the size of the audience, and here is the basic reason our present attempts to insure the survival of art by expanding the audience have come to naught.

Understanding is not a public process; it is a phenomenon much better comprehended by Schlegel than by sociologists. It is private, it is individual, and it is restricted, if I may borrow a phrase, to consenting adults. The marketing of art fails because it treats adults as children who will go wherever they are glamorously led. To do this is not only to underestimate adults, but also (as in today's arts education) to underestimate children.

Here, it seems to me, is a way we can approach the question of the true size of the audience for music and the other arts. The

1. *Mandate for Leadership,* Washington, D.C.: The Heritage Foundation, 1981.

audience is composed of those who deeply want to come; the artist's work is its own best—and only—advertisement. Beyond a minimum of arrangements and notification, everything rests on the quality of the relationship between the artist and those who singly witness the art.

So, in the end, the size of the audience for art ought not to be our concern. Our concern must be for the art and for the nature of our commitment to it. We live altogether too much in an age when (to appropriate Engels for my own purposes) the advocates of culture have transformed quality into quantity rather than quantity into quality. The time has come to put a stop to the selling of music. It is now plain that art is too beautiful to be left to its boosters.

# ACKNOWLEDGMENTS

Many good friends have helped me in innumerable ways on this book. My editor at David R. Godine, Publisher, William B. Goodman, has worked with me over many months with insight, patience, and on occasion, necessary force. In what may be best about it, this book is his as well as mine. I have received much assistance from the publications where all save one of these essays first appeared. At *Commentary,* I want to thank Neal Kozodoy, Brenda Brown, and Marion Magid, and at *The New Criterion* Erich Eichman, Jeanne Wacker, Eva Szent-Miklosy, and Robert Richman. Four associates in particular have been close friends, trusted colleagues, and influences I deeply value: my debts of gratitude to Norman Podhoretz, Hilton Kramer, Hugo Weisgall, and Michael S. Joyce will be appreciated by all who know my work. To my wife, my mother, and my son, I give not just thanks but love. And I want to dedicate this book to the cherished memory of my father, Max Lipman. He was a man who always set great store by a lonely position.

# INDEX

# *About the Author*

A pianist and critic, Samuel Lipman is a member of the National Council on the Arts and of the artist faculties of the Aspen Music Festival and the Waterloo Music Festival. He is the music critic at *Commentary,* the Publisher of *The New Criterion,* and the author of *Music After Modernism* (New York, 1979). His writing has appeared in *The New York Times Book Review* and *The Times Literary Supplement* (London), and has earned him the ASCAP-Deems Taylor Award for critical journalism in music three times. Mr. Lipman lives in New York City with his wife, the pianist Jeaneane Dowis, and their son.

## The House of Music

has been set in Intertype Garamond No. 3, a modern rendering of the type first cut by Claude Garamond (1510–1561). Garamond was a pupil of Geoffroy Tory and is believed to have based his letters on the Venetian models, although he introduced a number of important differences, and it is to him we owe the letter which we know as old-style. He gave to his letters a certain elegance and a feeling of movement that won for their creator an immediate reputation and the patronage of Francis I of France.

*Composed by Dix Type, Inc.,*
*Syracuse, New York*
*Printed and bound by The Book Press,*
*Brattleboro, Vermont*
*Typography design by Tim Hanrahan*